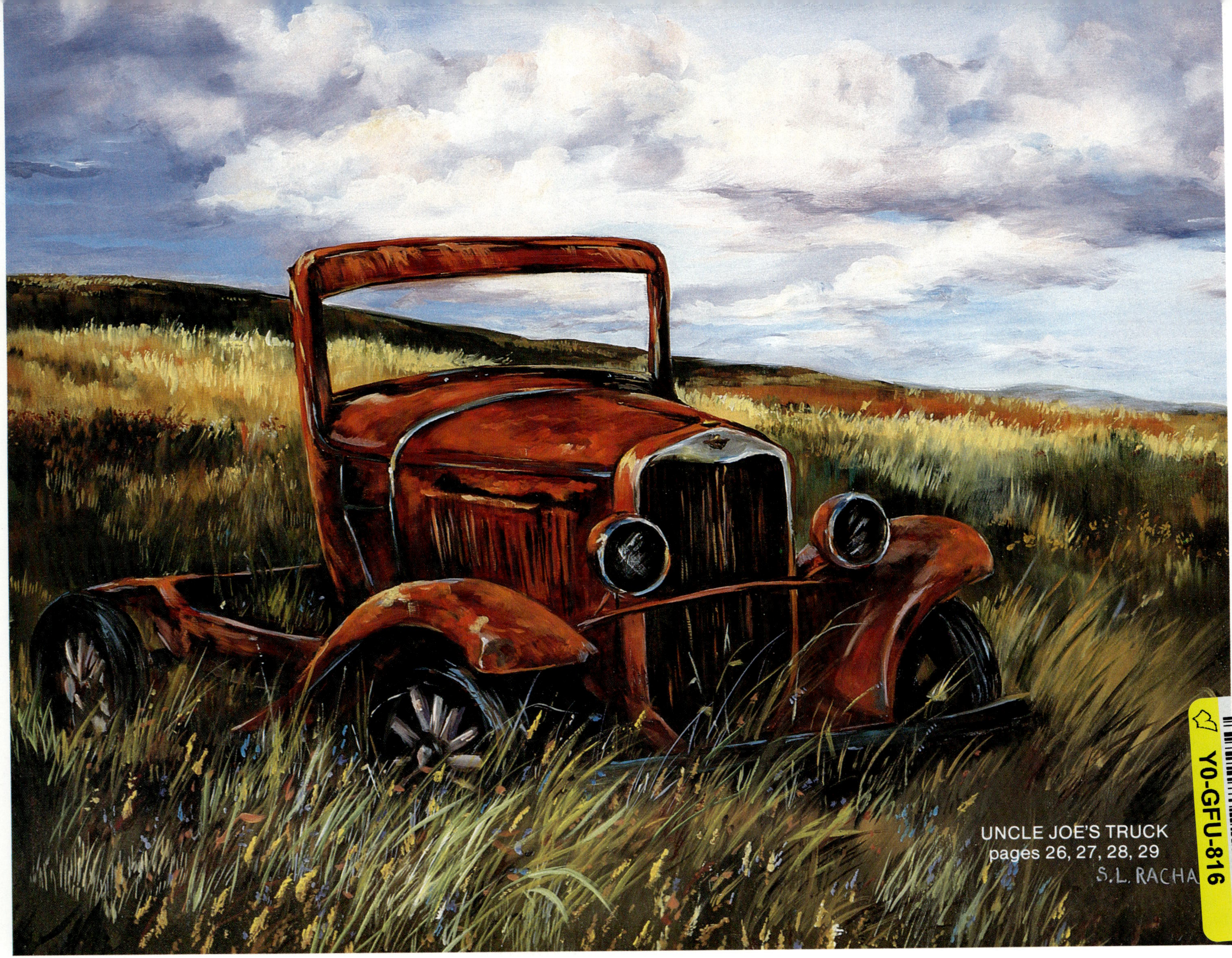
UNCLE JOE'S TRUCK
pages 26, 27, 28, 29
S.L. RACHA

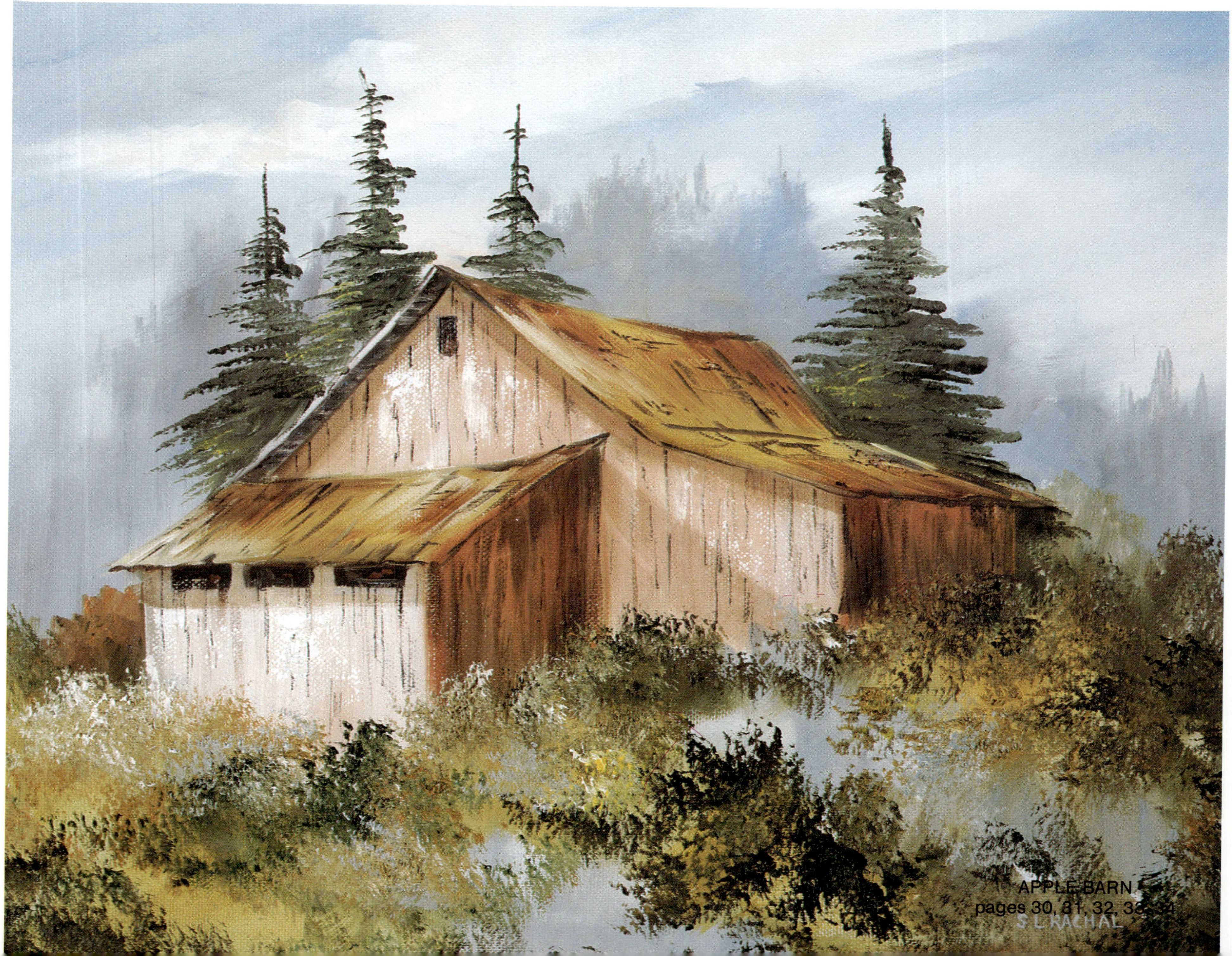

APPLE BARN
pages 30, 31, 32, 33, 34

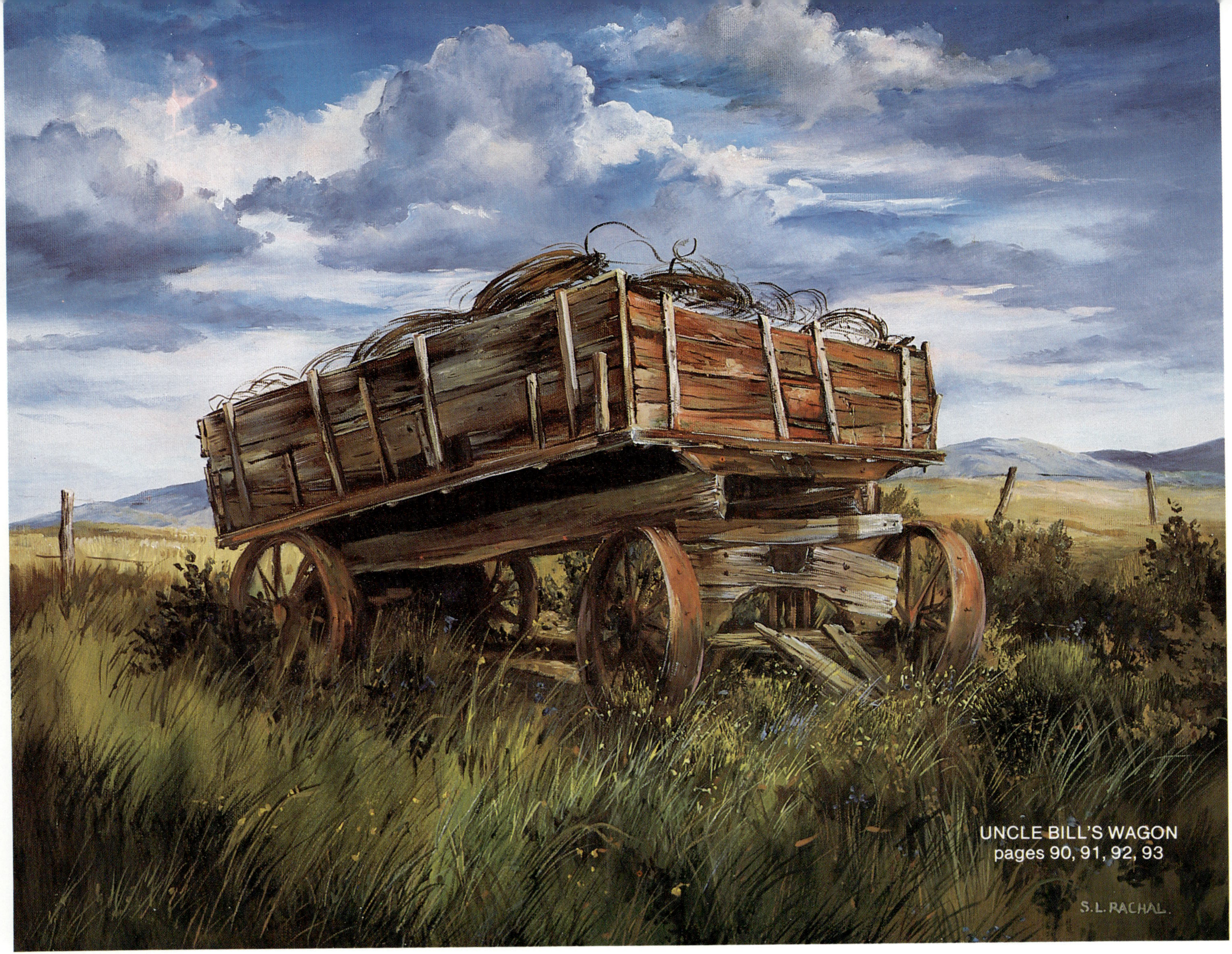

UNCLE BILL'S WAGON
pages 90, 91, 92, 93

MAY I?
pages 40, 41

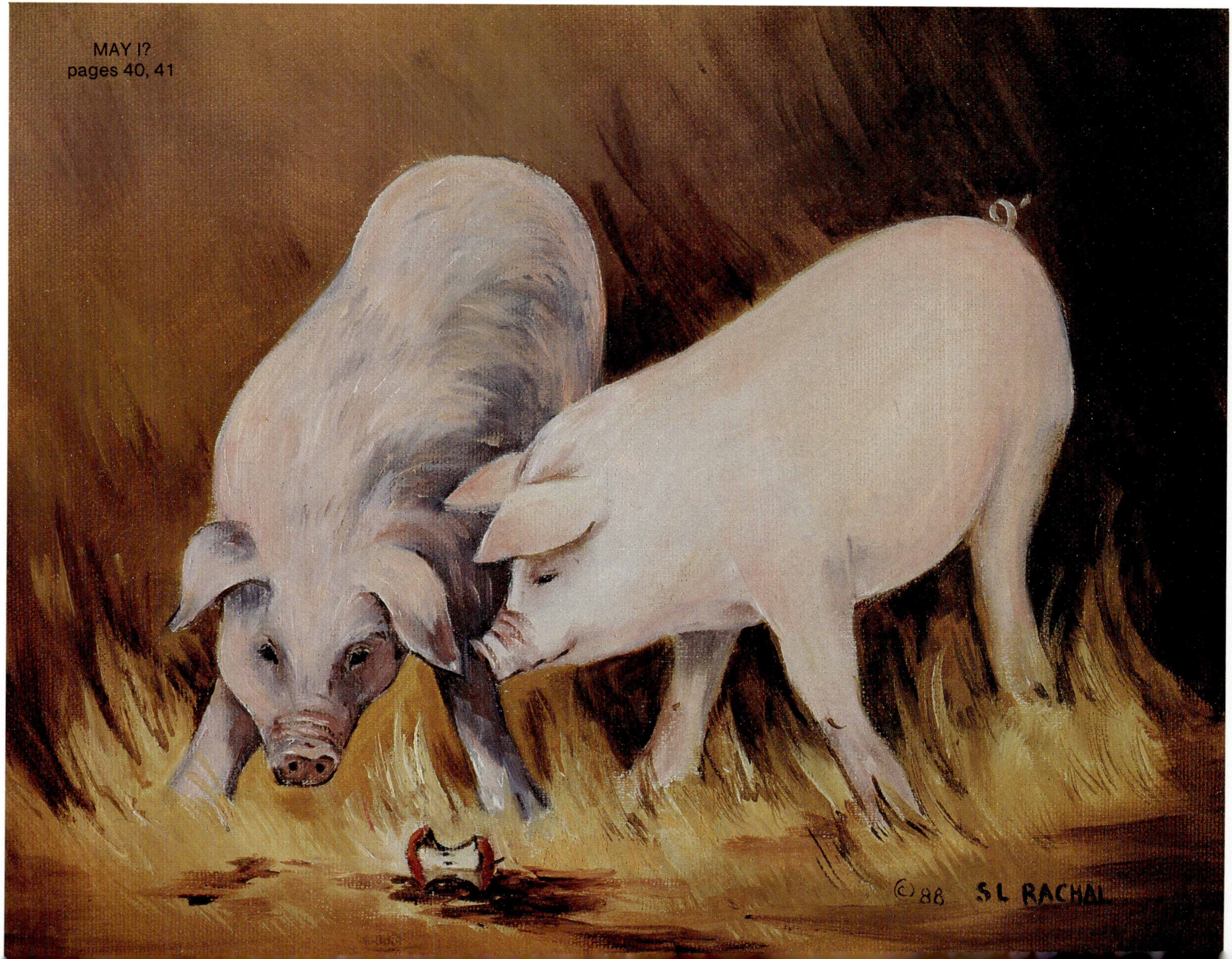

13435 NE Whitaker Way, Portland, Oregon 97230
Phone (503) 254-9100

ABOUT THE ARTIST

Sharon Rachal, a traditional artist, is a master of pen and ink, watercolor and oil. Inspriation for most of her work is acquired from the quiet rural area of Southern California nestled in the San Bernardino mountains.

The "Barn Lady" is what many of her students call her because of her award winning works of art depicting nostalgic rural scenes.

She is proud to be a recent recipient of the Grumbacher award for best use of color on "Blackie's Orchard", a 12 X 16 oil. Her painting entitled "Dawn's Early Light", an oil of an Oregon barn, is part of the permanent collection at the San Bernardino County Museum.

Rachal is founder of the Yucaipa Valley Art Association and an active member of the Fine Arts Institute of Redlands. She is the Editorial Artist for the News Mirror Newspaper, and teaches weekly classes in her studio in Yucaipa, California.

For more information on workshops and new videos, please write to Sharon L. Rachal, 33601 Yucaipa Blvd., Yucaipa, California 92399.

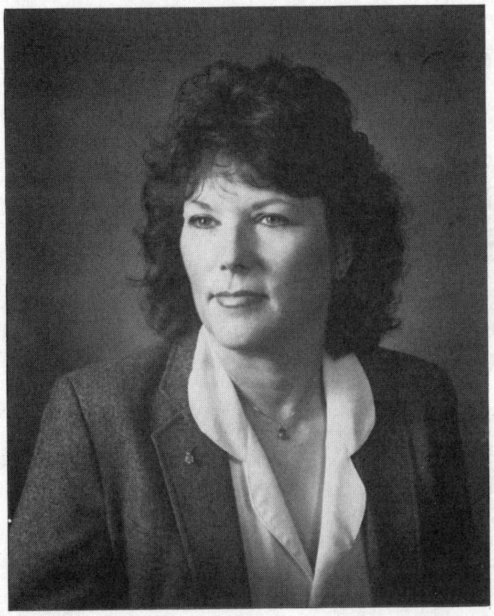

INTRODUCTION

We live such a fast paced life and really don't take the time to look at things around us. I believe that is why God made artists. An artist takes simple ordinary things and creates a picture so other people will take a moment to see the absolute beauty in them.

Artists are records of history. They are mind changers, and they stop time for a split second.

I wasn't born with a golden paint brush in my mouth, but I was born with a desire to express my artistic abilities. I can't ever remember not drawing, however, I wasn't the best or most talented either. That is why I believe anyone can learn to draw and paint if they desire to, because if I can, you can!

Hope you like the subjects which are included in this book. Tried to give a variety of things to paint. Each is a complete and unique lesson in itself. Know you will glean something new and different when doing each lesson plan.

DEDICATION

This book is dedicated to my students and readers because they have been such a source of encouragement. No sooner had Rustic Charms, Vol. I been released when I heard through cards, letters and word of mouth, "When will your next book be out?" Thanks to all of you for the inspiration.

SUPPLIES

My Regular Palette — Grumbacher Pre-Tested

Cadmium Yellow Light
Yellow Ochre
Cadmium Orange
Cadmium Red Light
Alizarin Crimson
Permanent Blue
Cobalt Blue
Cerulean Blue
Sap Green
Burnt Sienna
Burnt Umber
White

Additional Colors — Grumbacher Pre-Tested

Thalo Green
Naples Yellow
Raw Sienna
Thalo Yellow Green
Mars Violet
Black
Paynes Gray

Brushes —

Langnickel 5010 series (from #1 through #20) Flat Sable
Grumbacher 7357 #1 - Liner
Grumbacher 738 #1 - Round Sable
Peacock 145 #9 - Blending Brush. Sometimes referred to as Hake or Bunny Brush.
Fan Brush - Any small bristle fan.
#6 - Bristle Brush

Palette Knife — A trowel type can be used to mix paint and to paint with.

Palette — Refers to two things. One is the list of colors and two is the object which paint is placed upon to be mixed. There are several kinds of palettes on the market, wood, plastic and disposable paper. The disposable paper palette is the easiest to use. No clean-up, just tear off and throw away at the end of the lesson.

Medium — This refers to what is mixed into the paint to thin it. Copal painting medium is used most throughout this book. Turpenoid can be used as a medium also. Use it when painting flowers.

Brush Cleaners — There are many good products on the market today. Each and everyone seems to be good. Some are more expensive than others. I use odorless mineral spirits because it is less expensive. Fill a coffee can (metal container — not glass), one-half full. Wad a paper towel up and place in the bottom. This will keep brush from being dipped into paint sediment which forms on bottom of can after much use. When dirty, pour off top into another clean metal container. Stop pouring when dirty color appears.

Canvas — Use a good grade of canvas. There is cotton and portrait. Cotton should be double primed and stretched over squared stretcher bars with no lumps or bumps. The bars should be smooth and rounded slightly on inside, so as not to make a mark on the canvas. Like it best for landscapes and barns. Portrait canvas is a synthetic material and is very smooth. The paint lays on the surface and does not sink in. It is my favorite for florals.

Masonite — This can be purchased at local lumber yards. Make sure it is untempered. It comes in large sheets. Some lumber yards will cut it, others won't, so if you purchase it, make sure you have a way of getting it cut. Wonderful to use for glazing techniques. Gives the painting a different look.

Wood — Always sand and seal with wood sealer before using. Any of the paintings in this book can be painted on wood.

Miscellaneous:

Graphite — Used to transfer pattern. Place shiny side down, pattern over top and trace on to painting surface.

Tracing Paper — Thin transparent paper used to trace over patterns. Also used to draw lines on then transferred to painting surface.

Paper Towels or Rags — Used to wipe brushes off with.

Ruler — Keep ruler in paint box for measuring.

Vine Charcoal — For sketching.

Easel — There are many kinds on the market. Can use stand up type or table. This is to hold canvas on while painting or drying.

Note Pad and Pencil — For taking notes. Get into the habit of making notes of color mixes, etc.

Art Box — Somethina to carry supplies in. A utility box works nicely.

Palette of Colors:

I work basically with a limited palette. This means with just a few colors. My palette is layed out the same way each time. Start with Yellows on the left side, Orange, Reds in center, Blues, Greens, Brown on right side and White at the very bottom. Leave the center area clean. This is for mixing the colors. Get into this habit. It will save a lot of confusion, because colors will always be in the same place each time.

Color Combinations Used Through This Book:

Always mix first two colors before adding third.

1. Warm White — White with just a hint of Cadmium Yellow Light.
2. Pink — White + a pin point of Alizarin Crimson.
3. Soft or Pale Blue — White + Cerulean Blue.
4. Mauve — Cobalt Blue + Mars Violet + White.
   Alizarin Crimson + Cobalt Blue + White.
5. Dark Green — Sap Green + Burnt Sienna.
   Sap Green + Cadmium Red Light
   Cobalt Blue + Yellow Ochre + a touch of Alizarin Crimson.
6. Olive Green — Sap Green + Cadmium Orange.
   Cadmium Yellow Light + Black
7. Raw Sienna — Yellow Ochre + Burnt Sienna.
8. Black — Burnt Umber + Cobalt Blue.
   Alizarin Crimson + Thalo Green.
9. A very deep Black — Thalo Green + Alizarin Crimson + Permanent Blue.
10. Fake Cobalt Blue — Cerulean Blue + Permanent Blue + White.
11. Grays — Cadmium Orange + Cerulean Blue + White.
    Cobalt Blue + Burnt Umber + White.
    Cerulean Blue + Burnt Umber + White.

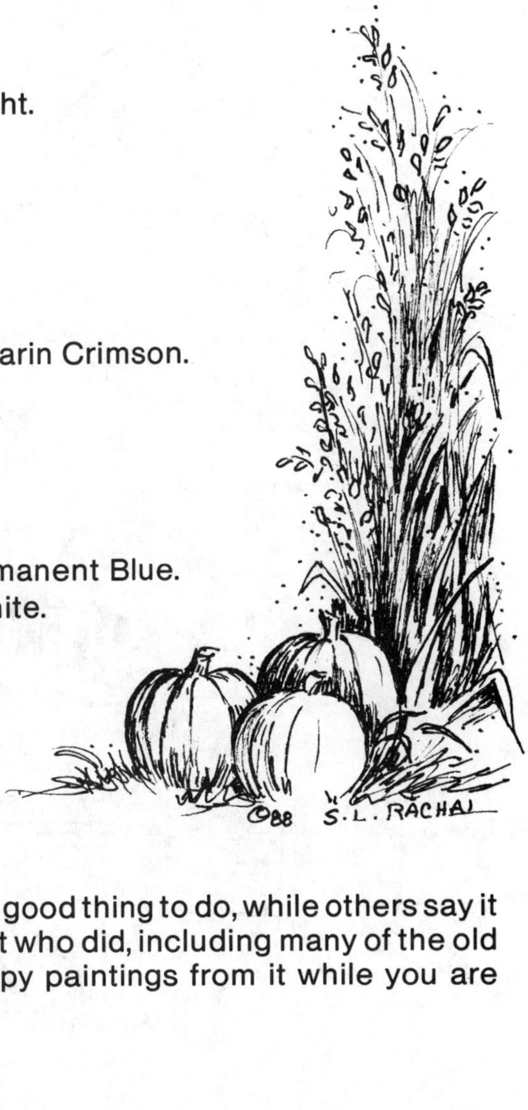

COPYING

There are many pro's and con's about copying. some say it is a good thing to do, while others say it is a bad thing to do. I learned by copying and I know many an artist who did, including many of the old masters. That is why this book was published, so you could copy paintings from it while you are learning to paint.

LEARNING TO PAINT

May I suggest that you start learning to create by painting the paintings in this book. Read all it says, everything, don't miss a word. It will be helpful. Study it! Digest it! Then do it! After you have completed a painting, try another, only this time use the colors from the painting you just finished but with your own composition. Your composition could come from the family photograph album, or you could make up something or even set up your own still life. Start out this way and continue until you are comfortable enough to do your own work. This is the way I started, copy pictures, create the next, using the palette from the previous copied picture. You will learn a lot about color this way as well as learn to rely on oneself and be creative.

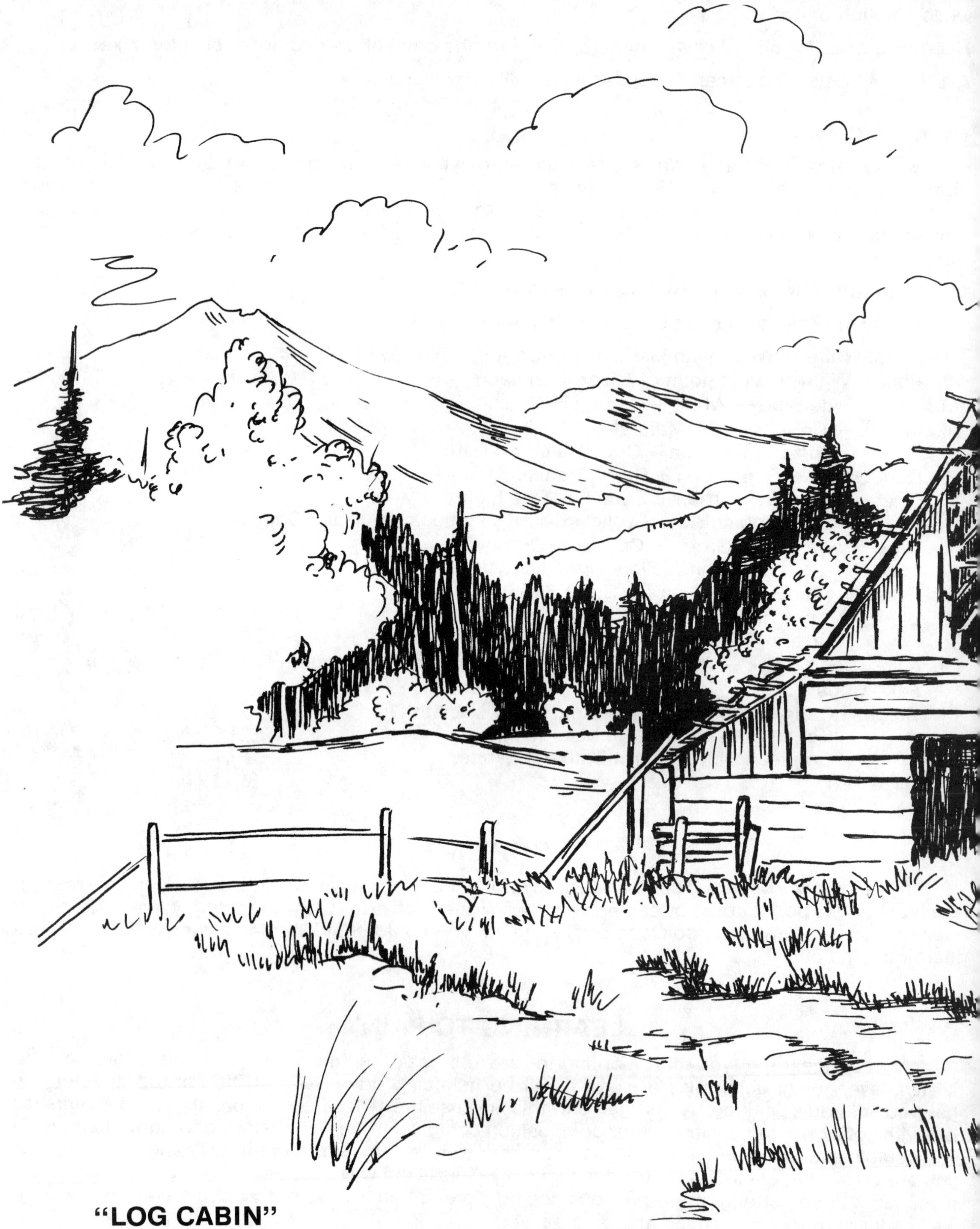

"LOG CABIN"

Instructions on pages 12, 13

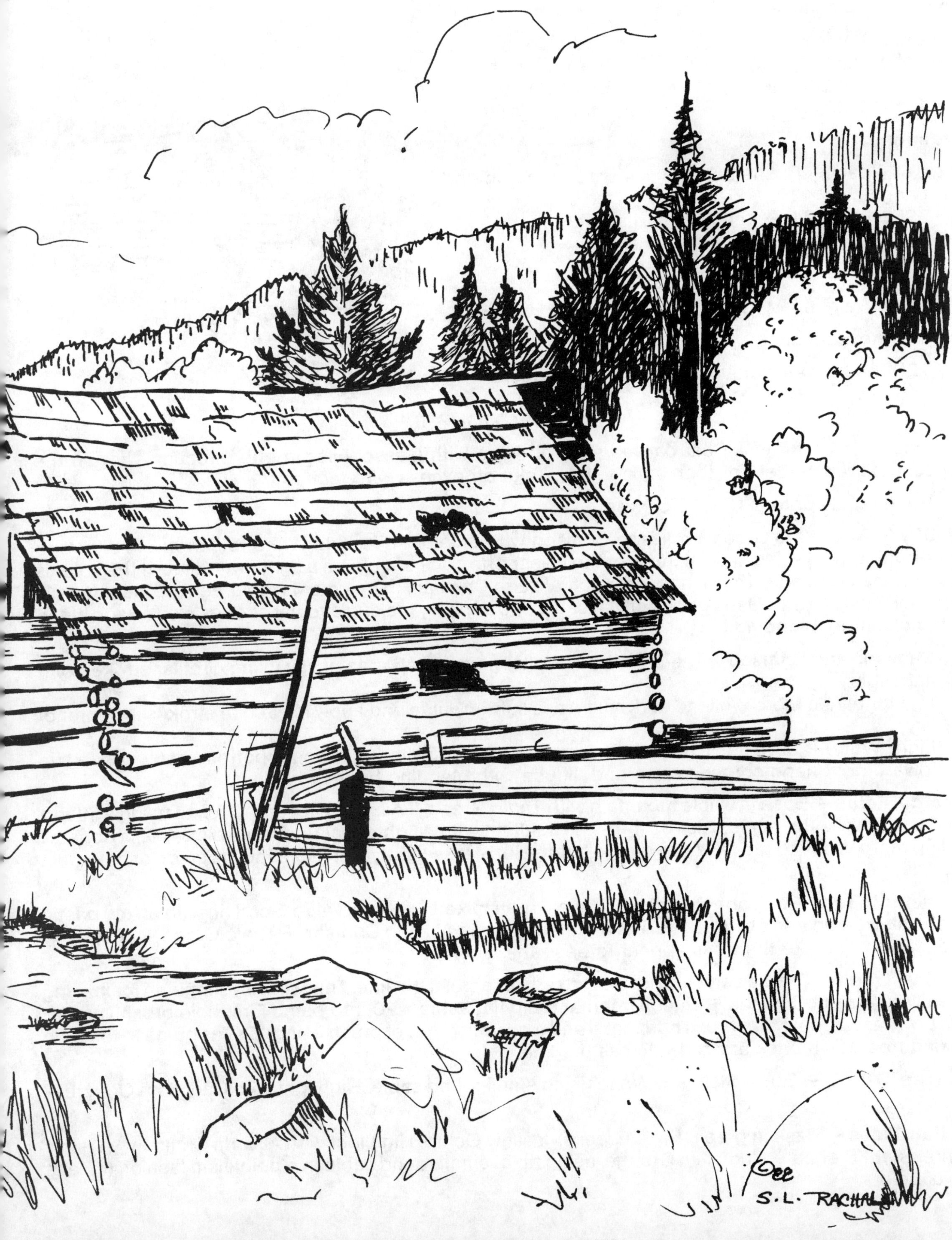
©82
S.L. RACHAL

"LOG CABIN"

This is one of my favorite paintings. It hangs over my couch in my living room.

Palette: Grumbacher Pre-Tested

Cadmium Yellow Light
Yellow Ochre
Cadmium Orange
Alizarin Crimson
Thalo Green
Burnt Sienna
Burnt Umber
Titanium White

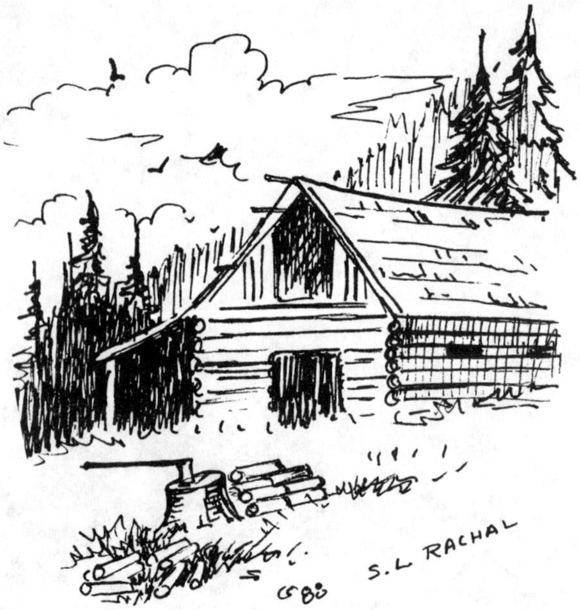

Brushes:

#6 Filbert — Bristle brush which is rounded on end.
Langnichel #20 — Flat sable.
7357 Liner #1 — Long pointed sable.
Peacock 134 #9 - Blending brush.

Medium:

Copal Painting Medium.

Miscellaneous:

12 X 16 canvas, palette paper, palette knife.

DIRECTIONS

This step is optional. Coat canvas several times with Gesso. First in one direction, then in the opposite direction. Let dry, then sand lightly. Take off excess with tack rag.

1. Trace lightly onto a 12 x 16 canvas.

2. **Sky** — Mix Thalo Green + Alizarin Crimson with palette knife. Add White to corner of mixture to lighten value. (Save this dark mixture for the trees). The color should be a light gray value. If the color is more on the violet side, then it has too much Alizarin Crimson. If the color is too greenish, then there is too much Thalo Green. Use a good soft flat sable and apply by making circular strokes. Soften and blend with a clean dry blending brush.

   Dark: Alizarin Crimson + Thalo Green + White in upper left area of sky using circular strokes with flat sable.
   Mid-tone: Add more White to dark mixture to lighten value and apply in circular strokes in center of sky.
   Light: White + just a dot of Alizarin Crimson to make a pink hue, starting at bottom of sky working up toward right hand corner. Soften and diffuse with blending brush.

3. **Mountains** — Base in whole mountain with Thalo Green + Alizarin Crimson + White using a Filbert #6 brush. This is the same color as the sky. Highlight with a lighter value of sky color. This is done by adding more White to gray mixture on the right side. Stroke lightly with flat sable from top of mountain towards the bottom.

4. **Distant Trees** — Alizarin Crimson + Thalo Green mixed to a dark value. Scrub in with an old bristle brush using an up and down stroke. Let dry then glaze in Alizarin Crimson + Thalo Green + White (sky color). This will make the trees appear to be in the distance.

5. **Pine Trees** — Draw a vertical line and make "Z's" across the line. This will be your guide for making trees. Mix Alizarin Crimson + Thalo Green and dip flat sable #20 into paint. First hold brush vertical, press on canvas, next turn brush horizontal and work off corner of brush using "Z's" as guide to follow in making trees. Dab back and forth across the line.

6. **Tree Trunks** — Burnt Sienna + White using small round sable. Highlight with Cadmium Orange + White.

7. **Fall Trees** — Base in green, Thalo Green + Yellow Ochre. Highlight with Alizarin Crimson + Yellow Ochre. Burnt Sienna + Cadmium Orange, using tip of small round sable in a pointilism fashion (means dot of color).

8. **Sunlit Ground** — Cadmium Yellow Light + Thalo Green. Blend into Burnt Sienna with side stroke of flat sable brush working from outside and blending lightly into sunlit area.

9. **Log Cabin** — Base in roof with Alizarin Crimson + Thalo Green + White (sky color) with #6 Filbert brush. Detail using small round brush with Burnt Umber + Burnt Sienna in short choppy strokes following parallel of roof. Dark holes in roof, Alizarin Crimson + Thalo Green.

10. **Logs and Fence** — Base in from dark to light using flat sable.

Dark: Burnt Umber and some of the sky color (Alizarin Crimson + Thalo Green).
Mid-tone: Burnt Sienna.
Light: White + Cadmium Orange. White + Yellow Ochre.

11. **Ground** — Horizontal strokes with #6 Filbert brush.

Dark: Burnt Sienna and Burnt Umber on bottom of ground. This will help frame the picture.
Mid-tone: Burnt Sienna + White.
Light: White + Cadmium Orange.

12. **Rocks** — Base in shape with Burnt Umber with Filbert brush. Highlight with White + Burnt Umber. Use dry brush to mush colors slightly.

13. **Grass** — Use liner brush, thin paint with Turpenoid to a soupy mixture. Hold brush straight up and using sweeping light strokes.

Dark: Alizarin Crimson + Thalo Green. Burnt Sienna.
Mid-tone: Cadmium Orange.
Light: Cadmium Orange + White. White + Yellow Ochre.

Extra pattern

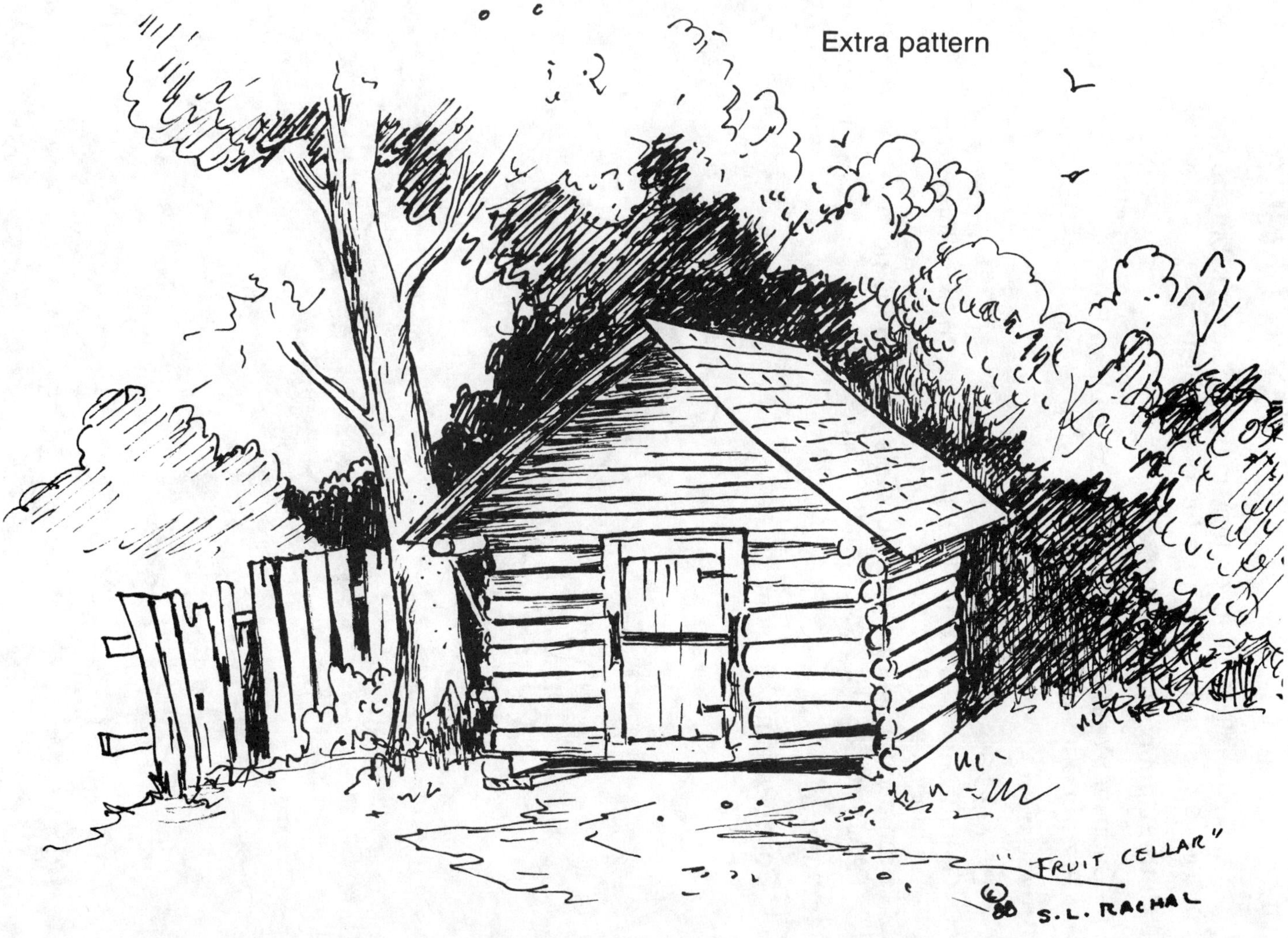

CAT 'N DAISIES

I am not really a cat lover, they make me sneeze, but they are such fun to paint. They can look so angelic as this one does, or be full of mischief.

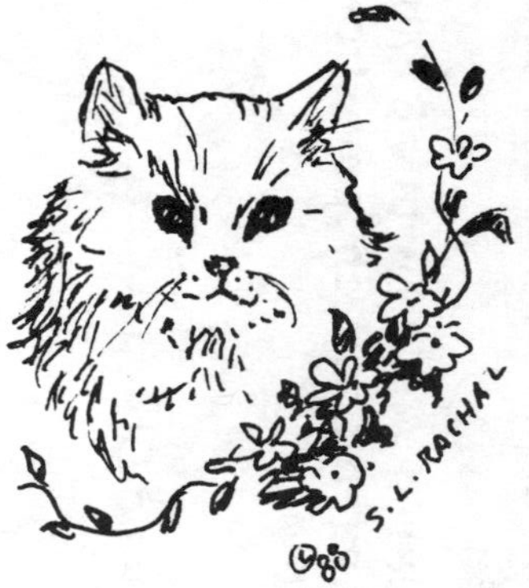

Palette: Grumbacher Pre-Tested

Cadmium Yellow Light
Alizarin Crimson
Cerulean Blue
Sap Green
Paynes Gray
Titanium White

Brushes:

Langnickel 5010 #4, #20 - flat sable
Grumbacher 7357 #1 - liner, red sable with extra long point
Grumbacher 1060 #3 - fan
Grumbacher 178 #1 - round sable with a good point
Peacock 145 #9 - soft blending brush

Medium:

Copal Painting Medium.

Miscellaneous:

12 X 16 canvas, Turpenoid, palette knife, paper towels, graphite.

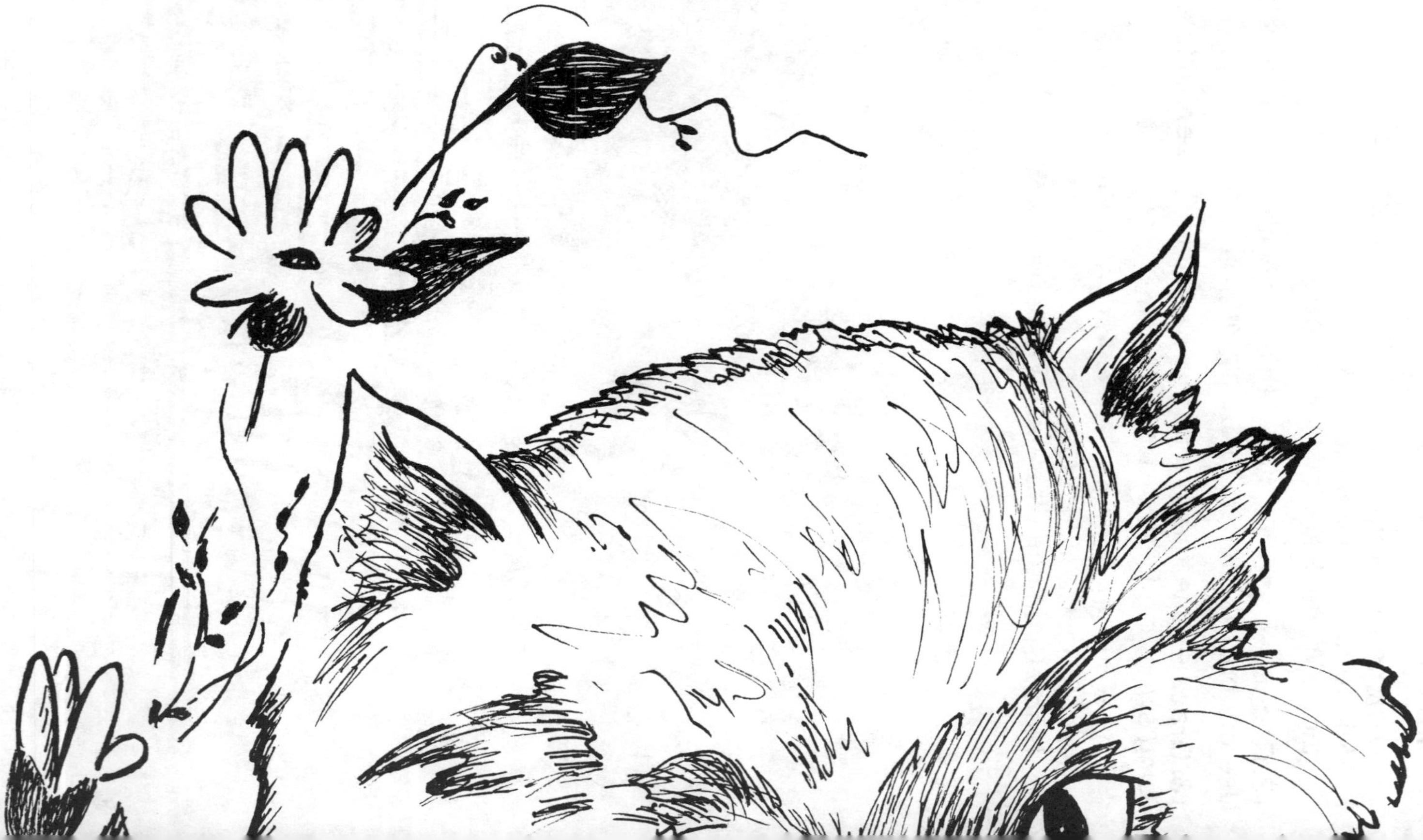

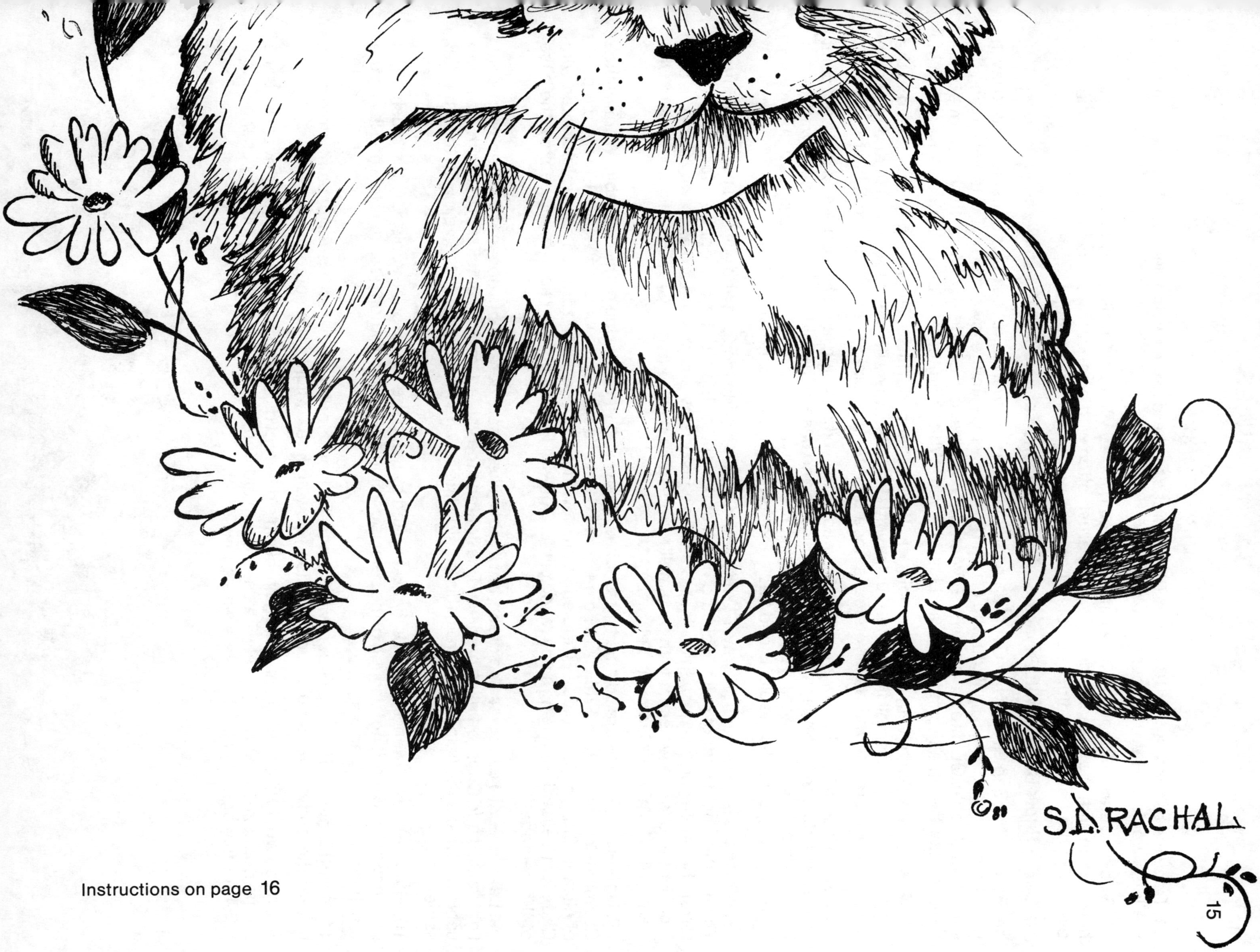

Instructions on page 16

CAT 'N DAISIES

DIRECTIONS

1. Trace the cat onto a 12 x 16 canvas. Do not press too hard when tracing because the cat is light and the lines would be hard to cover.

2. **Background** — Blend in with a flat sable using mixed White + Cerulean Blue, which is a pale blue hue. Soften with the blending brush, wiping brush often with a paper towel. Try to have color nice and even. (Let the background dry completely before painting the next step.)

3. **Cat** — Pupil: Base in with Paynes Gray in an almond shape using the small round sable.

4. **Eye** — Thin Sap Green with Copal painting medium. This will make the color transparent and lay in with the small flat sable. Highlight with Cadmium Yellow Light in the lower portion of the eye using the small round sable. Outline the eye with Paynes Gray using small round sable. Want to see the eye come to life? Take the small round sable and just dot with White on the left side of the pupil. Neat huh?

5. **Nose** — Mix White with just a pin point of Alizarin Crimson. This will make a pink hue. Blend in the nose with pink using small flat sable. Outline with Paynes Gray with small round brush and pat some over the nose area. If you want your cat's nose brighter and pinker, just eliminate this step.

6. **Fur** — Base in the shadow areas with Paynes Gray + White using large flat sable. Add just a pin point of Alizarin Crimson to White to make a soft pink hue and base in the mid-tones. Softly blend with the fan brush using short over-lapping strokes. Highlight with warm white which is White + Cadmium Yellow Light with the small flat sable. Blend back and forth with dry fan brush.

7. **Whiskers** — Thin Paynes Gray + White with Copal painting medium and roll the liner brush into it. The liner will hold a lot of paint. Hold the brush at the end of the handle. (Do not hold too close to the ferrule because you will get a thick line). Start the whiskers by pulling outward and away from the cats face. Dot above the whiskers with the small round sable using Paynes Gray. Highlight whiskers with warm white, White + Cadmium Yellow Light.

8. **Daisies** — Strokes are comma type strokes, push - pull - lift with side of the flat sable. Warm white - Cadmium Yellow Light + White. On some of the petals I added pink, which is White + just a pin point of Alizarin Crimson, and blue — Cerulean Blue + White. Centers — Alilzarin Crimson, highlighted with Cadmium Yellow Light using small round sable. Dot with Paynes Gray on tip of round sable at the base of the centers.

9. **Leaves** — All I used was Sap green, but it looks like I used more colors doesn't it? Whenever I want light value, I add Copal painting medium. This lightens the value. Draw the outside of leaf with the round sable and make the vein. Stroke from this outside line towards the center of the vein with the small flat sable.

10. **Fillers** — Sap Green + Burnt Umber is applied by using the small round sable. Lay the brush on its side, now lift upward. If not enough of the color is coming off the brush, then push harder when laying the brush down on the canvas.

11. **Scroll Lines** — Thin Sap Green with Turpenoid. Roll liner brush in it so it is full of paint. Hold brush toward the end of the handle and make long flowing lines. Might take some practice.

If you would like to paint this cat again, but in a different direction, just flip the tracing over and trace on the opposite side. Now you have a cat looking a different way. The flowers could be changed to a different flower and you will have a whole new painting.

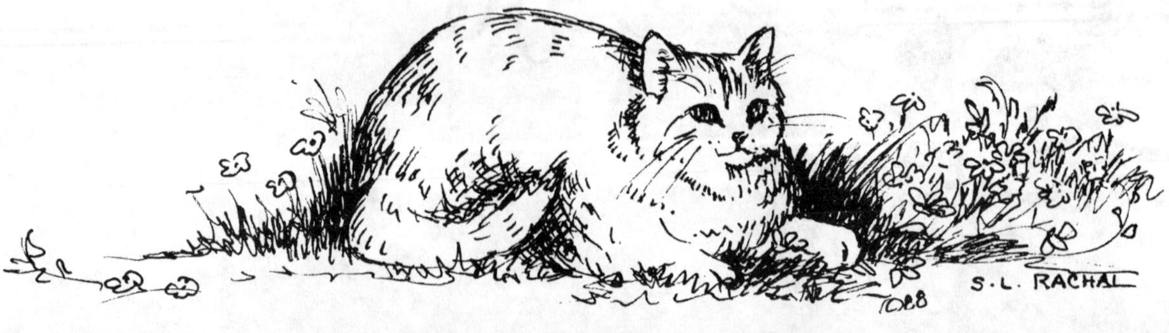

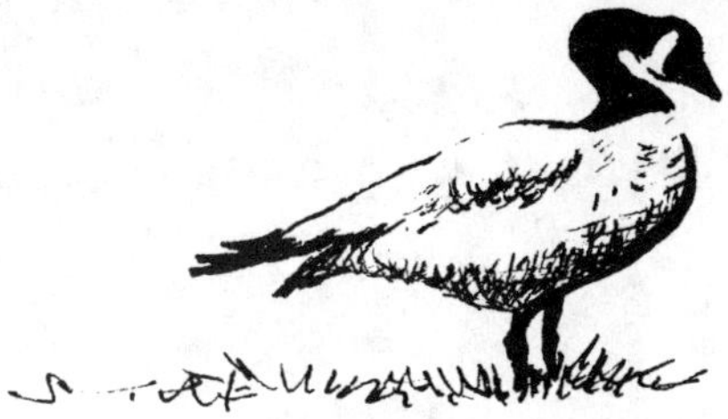

CANADA GOOSE

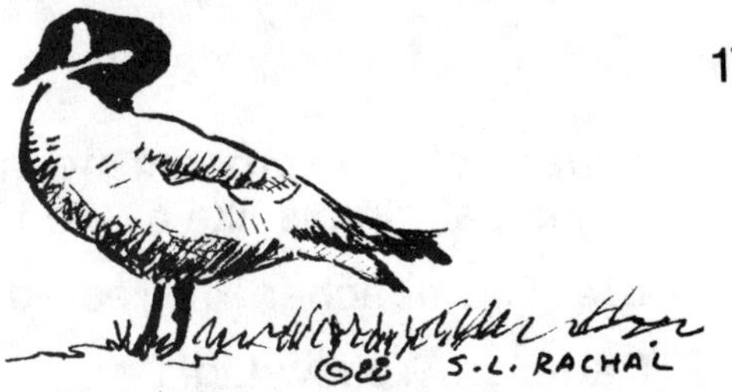

DIRECTIONS

A glazing technique is used exclusively in this painting. A glaze is a thin transparent layer of paint, made by thinning the paint with Copal painting medium. Make sure each layer of paint is completely dry before applying any additional layer of paint. Keep in mind that the feathers must look soft, not hard and the water must look real. This is done by constantly softening and blending the glaze, after it has been applied, with a soft blending brush.

1. Trace the goose onto a 12 X 16 canvas or masonite. If using masonite, coat it two times with Gesso and sand lightly before using. Very important — when preparing painting surface with Gesso, make sure it is nice and smooth. This means no lumps or bumps.

2. **Water** — Remember water has no color of its own, it only reflects what is around it. Think of a checker board when applying water, first blend vertically and then across horizontally. Mix three values of green from dark to light with palette knife.

   Dark: Sap Green + Cobalt Blue. Add just a hint of Burnt Sienna for darker areas, it also adds warmth.
   Mid-tone: Sap Green + Yellow Ochre. This may be lightened by adding White.
   Light: White + Cobalt Blue. White + Cerulean Blue. White + Yellow Ochre.

   Apply with large flat sable. The reflection of the goose is painted at the same time the bird is painted, using all the same colors and brushes. Let dry completely, then float White + Cobalt Blue, which has been thinned with Copal painting medium, in a horizontal brush stroke with the large flat sable. Soften with the soft blending brush. Ripples are Cerulean Blue + White and Cobalt Blue + White applied with small round sable.

3. **Goose** — Use small flat sables when applying paint and remember to soften and blend with the soft blending brush. The round sable is used for the detail areas of the bird. Apply paint from dark to light.

4. **Head** — Dark: Cobalt Blue + Burnt Umber.
   Mid-tone: Cerulean Blue + White.
   Light: White + Mars Violet

   Same colors repeated on neck area.

5. **Eye** — Dark: Cobalt Blue + Burnt Umber applied with small round brush in a little circle. Highlight with White using the tip of the round sable and dot. Outline with White + Mars Violet around the eye.

6. **Side of Face** — White + just a hint of Yellow Ochre. Shadow with Cerulean Blue + White using small flat sable.

7. **Chest** — White + just a hint of Yellow Ochre. Shadow with Cerulean Blue + White.

8. **Feathers** — Dark: Cobalt Blue + Burnt Umber.
   Burnt Sienna + Mars Violet.
   Mid-tone: Cobalt Blue + Mars Violet + White.
   Light: White + Cadmium Yellow Light.
   White + Mars Violet.

9. **Back End** — White + hint of Yellow Ochre shadowed with Cerulean Blue + White, and Mars Violet + White. After dry, glaze in shadows with Cobalt Blue using small flat sable and then blend with dry flat sable.

10. **Tail** — Dark: Cobalt Blue + Burnt Umber. Highlight with Cerulean Blue and White + Mars Violet with round sable.

CANADA GOOSE

A friend of mine brought me this photograph because she thought I would want to paint it. She was right. This painting is like a good book, I hated to finish it.

Palette: Grumbacher Pre-Tested

Cadmium Yellow Light
Yellow Ochre
Mars Violet
Cerulean Blue
Cobalt Blue
Sap Green
Burnt Sienna
Burnt Umber
Titanium White

Brushes:

Langnickel 5010 #2, #4, #6, #20 - Flat sable.
Grumbacher 178 #1 - Small Round Sable which has good point.
Peacock 145 #9 - A soft blending brush.

Medium:

Copal Painting Medium or mix your own ⅓ Damar varnish, ⅓ Linseed Oil, ⅓ Turpenoid.

Miscellaneous:

12 X 16 canvas or masonite, Gesso only if painting on masonite, palette knife, paper towels and palette.

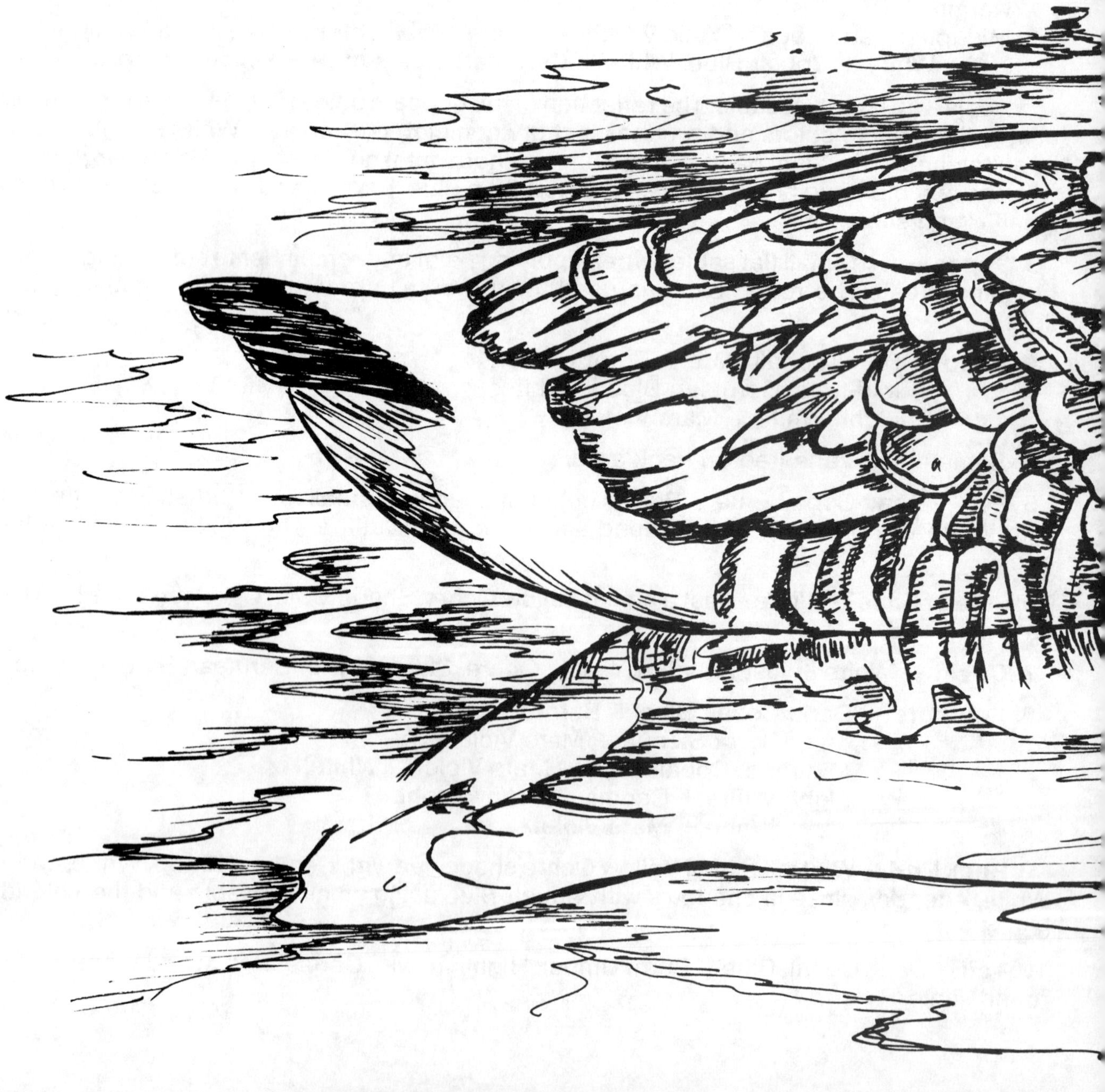

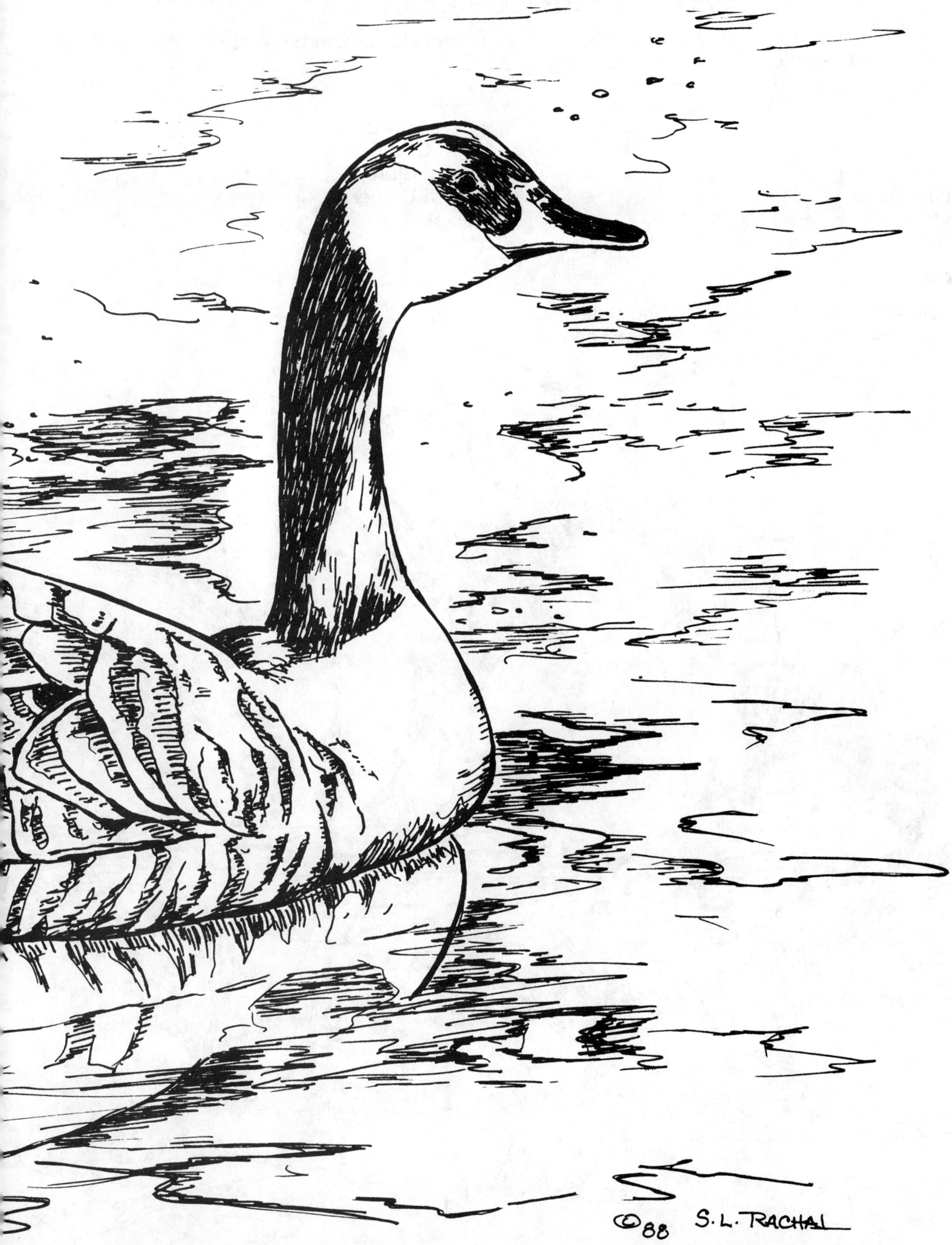

Instructions on page 17

"EVERYWHERE A CHICK-CHICK"

This painting is certainly filled with chicks, and they all seem to be doing something different. Could actually make many different paintings from this one.

Palette: Grumbacher Pre-Tested

White
Cadmium Yellow Light
Lemon Yellow
Yellow Ochre
Raw Sienna
Cadmium Orange (only a pin dot for beaks)
Cerulean Blue
Sap Green
Burnt Sienna
Burnt Umber
Black
Mauve

Brushes:

Langnickel 178 #1, — Small Round Sable
Langnickel 5010 #1, #5, #20 — Flat Sable
Peacock 145 #9 — Blending Brush

Miscellaneous:

9 X 12 canvas, palette.

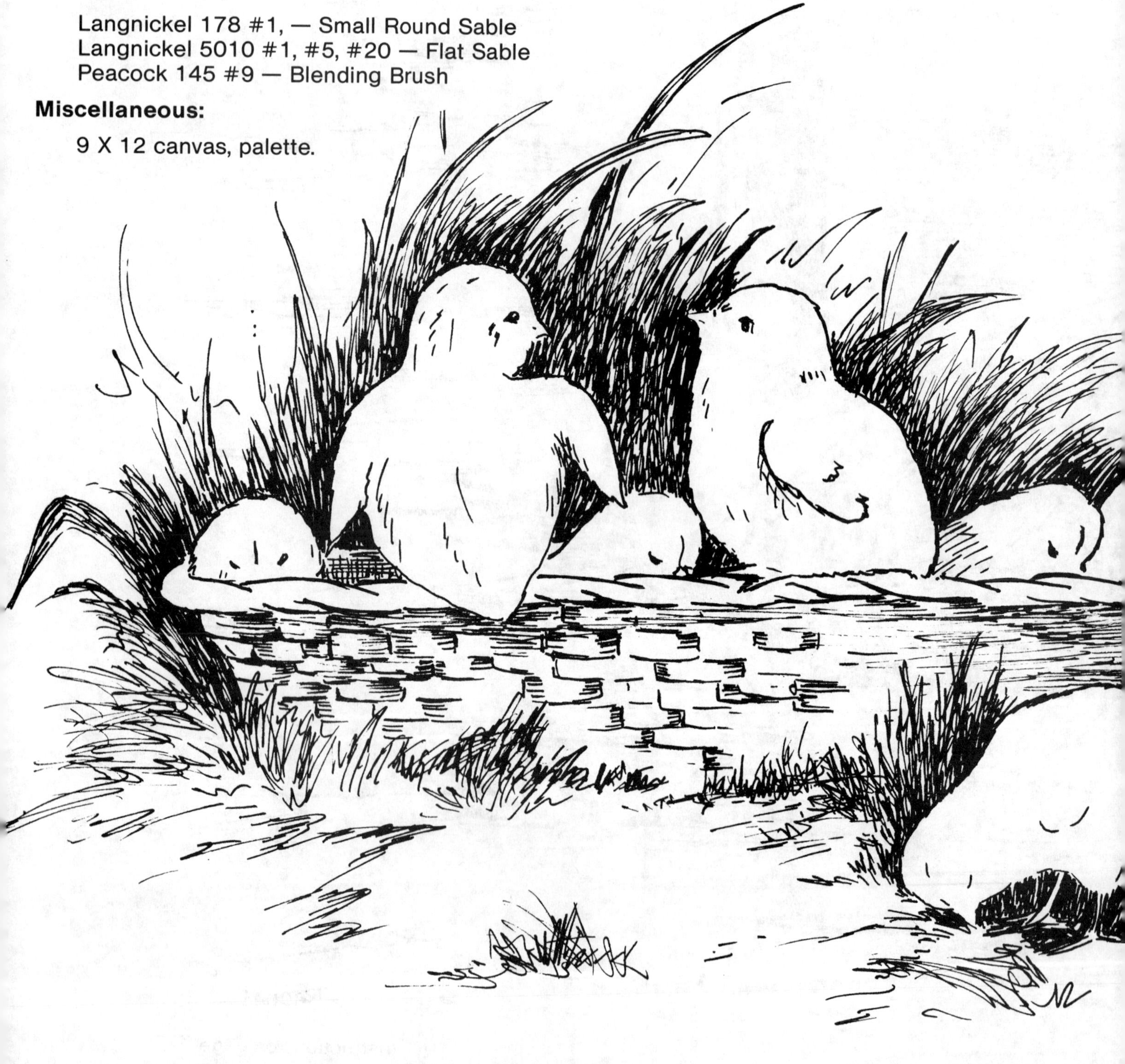

DIRECTIONS

All the colors have Copal painting medium mixed in. Keep a clean dry sable brush for blending colors. Formula is blend — wipe brush — soften.

1. Trace pattern onto a 9 X 12 canvas.

2. **Vignette** — A picture with no definite border, shading off gradually at the edges. Mix Cerulean Blue + White to a soft blue. Criss cross into vignette area with large flat sable. Soften with blending brush after color has set up and gotten a little tacky. Blend Cerulean Blue into each four corners and softly blend in a circular motion with blending brush. There should be no demarcation in color.

3. **Grass** — Use a flat sable and start at base of grass pulling upwards, twist and lift. First blend in Mauve behind grass. This can be a tube Mauve lightened by adding White. This color is used to give depth to the grass.

   Dark: Sap Green + Burnt Umber
   Mid-tone: Sap Green + just a touch of Cadmium Orange
   Light: Sap Green + Lemon Yellow

4. **Weeds** — Use a light touch with small round brush to get a light line. If too much pressure is applied, the line will be thick.

   Dark: Burnt Umber
   Mid-tone: Yellow Ochre - highlight with Cadmium Yellow Light + White
   Light: Pale Orange - Cadmium Orange + White

5. **Basket** — Base in with Burnt Sienna using large flat sable. Highlight weave with Cadmium Orange + White using flat edge of medium size flat sable. Shadows and outline weave with Burnt Umber using small round sable.

6. **Ground** — Base in light brown which is White + Burnt Sienna. Highlight with a peach mixture of White + Cadmium Orange. Drag some of the grass color down into ground and blend across lightly with flat sable. This will soften color.

7. **Chicks** — Body - Base in Yellow Ochre + just a hint of Cadmium Orange with medium size sable (#5). Blend color so there are no hard edges. Shadow under wings and on side of head with Burnt Sienna thinned with Copal painting medium.

8. **Feathers** — Short strokes with small round brush. Soften and diffuse color with clean dry sable. Apply Lemon Yellow and Cadmium Yellow Light to light areas. Highlight with White + Cadmium Yellow Light.

9. **Eye** — Notice some of the eyes are open wide, and some are nothing more than slits. Use a round sable with Black. Give the eye life by adding just a pin point of White with small round brush.

10. **Beak and Feet** — Base in with Cadmium Orange using small round sable brush. Highlight with Lemon Yellow. Shadow with just a hint of Burnt Umber.

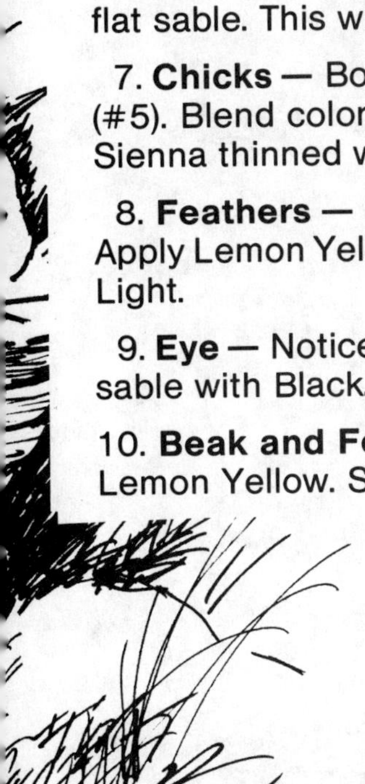

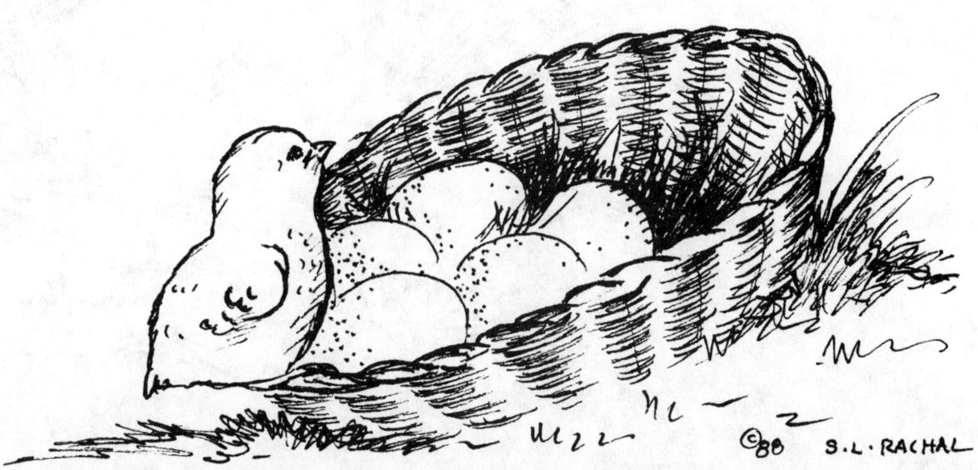

S. L. RACHAL

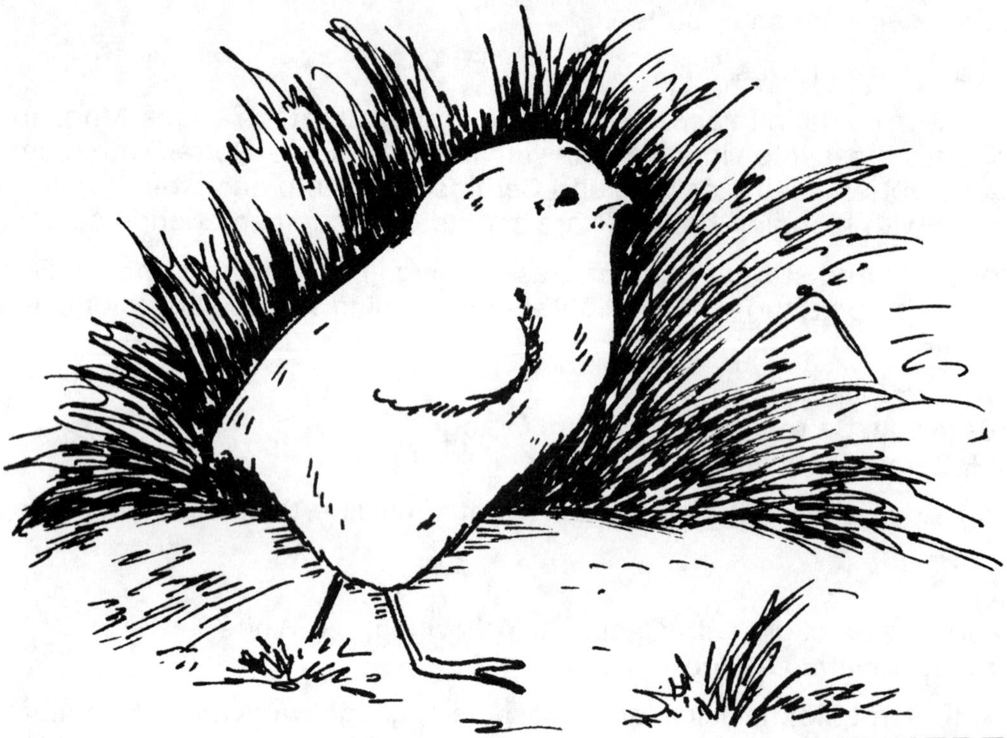

"HERE CHICK·

©88 S.L RACHAL

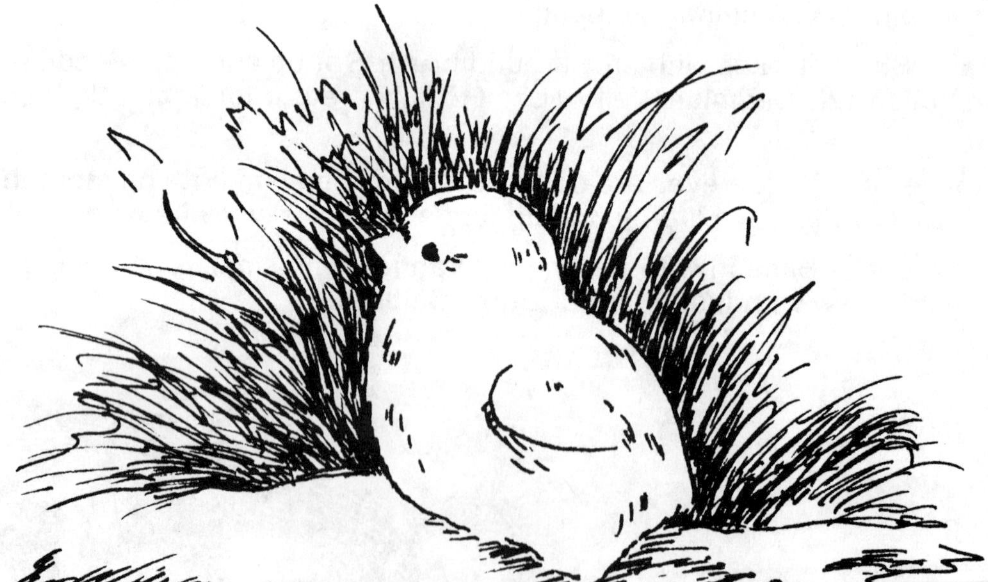

THERE CHICK"

©88 S.L. RACHAL

"HERE CHICK — THERE CHICK"

These two paintings were painted as a pair at the same time so the colors would match. Background color could be changed to whatever you prefer.

Palette: Grumbacher Pre-Tested

Lemon Yellow (Zinc Yellow)
Cadmium Yellow Light
Yellow Ochre
Cadmium Orange (just a pin dot is needed)
Cadmium Red Light (just a pin dot is needed)
Cerulean Blue
Sap Green
Burnt Sienna
Burnt Umber
Black (just a pin point)
Titanium White

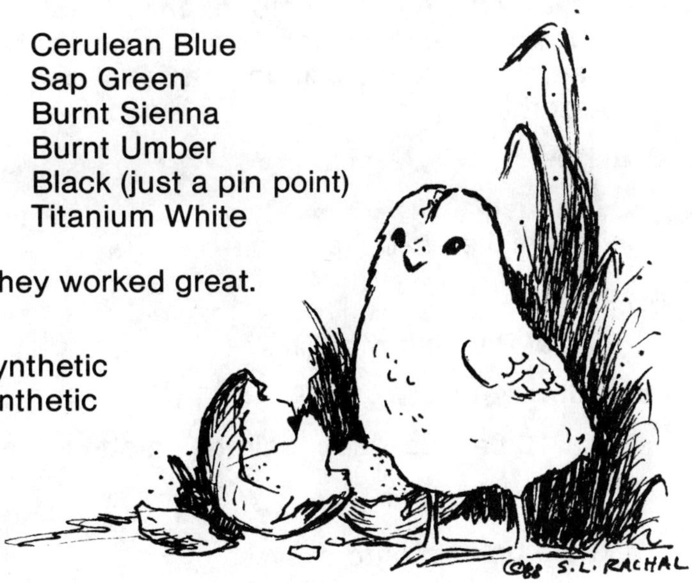

Brushes:

Tried some new synthetics for this painting and they worked great.

Langnickel 5010 #1, #20 — Flat Sable
Langnickel 2040 #0 Sunburst — Small Round Synthetic
Langnickel 2010 #4, Sunburst — Flat Shader Synthetic
(Any old brush for blending in background.)

Medium:

Copal Painting Medium.

Miscellaneous:

5 X 7 canvas for each picture, palette knife for mixing, palette and paper towels.

DIRECTIONS

1. Trace pattern on to 5 X 7 canvas very carefully.

2. **Vignette** — This is the outside area around design. Mix White + Cerulean Blue to a pale blue with palette knife and apply with large flat sable. Blend and smooth, wiping brush often with paper towel so as not to have any edges.

3. **Grass** — Base in with Sap Green using small flat shader. Darken this value by adding a touch of Burnt Sienna. Lighten value by adding Cerulean Blue + White. Start stroke from bottom of grass, twisting brush — lifting upward with small round brush.

4. **Ground** — White + Burnt Sienna based in with flat sable. Highlight with a peachy mixture of White + Cadmium Orange. Blend some of the grass into ground with small sable.

5. **Chick** — Body is Yellow Ochre + just a hint of Cadmium Orange. Base in using flat shader. Blend in shadows with Burnt Sienna. Be sure to continually wipe brush and soften color.

Feathers — Short strokes with small round brush. Apply Lemon Yellow and Cadmium Yellow Light to light areas. Then soften and diffuse color using flat shader. Highlight with warm white, White + Cadmium Yellow Light, in light short stroke with small round brush.

Eye — Just dot the eye with Black using tip of round brush. Highlight with just a pin point of White.

Beak — Base in with Cadmium Orange using small round brush and highlight with Lemon Yellow. Shade with just a hint of Burnt Umber.

Feet — Cadmium Orange, highlight with Lemon Yellow and shadow with Burnt Umber using small round brush.

6. **Lady Bug** — Do you see it? Just a dot of Cadmium Red Light on blade of grass and dot head with Burnt Umber using small round brush. DO NOT MAKE TOO BIG — A LADY BUG IS VERY SMALL.

©88 S.L. RACHAL

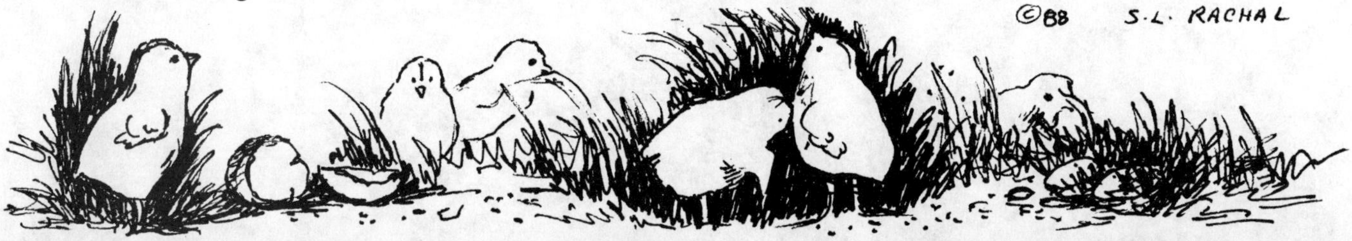

MAILBOX AND BASKET OF APPLES

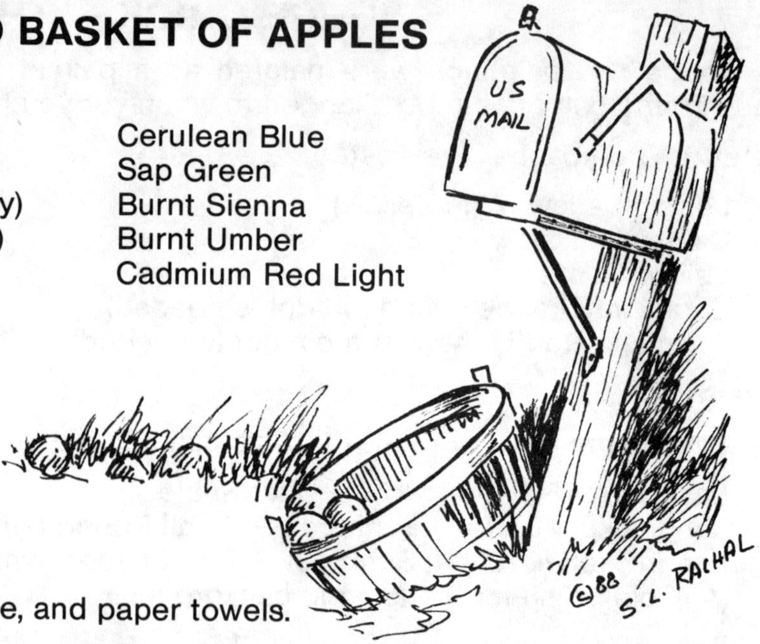

Palette: Grumbacher Pre-Tested

White
Yellow Ochre (small amount only)
Cadmium Yellow Light (small amount only)
Cadmium Orange (pin point amount only)
Alizarin Crimson
Cerulean Blue
Sap Green
Burnt Sienna
Burnt Umber
Cadmium Red Light

Brushes:

1" Brush
Langnickel #20 Flat Sable

Medium:

Copal Painting Medium.

Miscellaneous:

8 X 10 canvas, paper palette, palette knife, and paper towels.

DIRECTIONS

1. Trace pattern onto canvas.

2. **Vignette** — Criss-cross White + Cerulean Blue around outside area of picture with large flat sable. Paint with Copal painting medium so it will flow nice and easy.

3. **Atmosphere** — Violet, Cerulean Blue + Alizarin Crimson + White. Place behind mailbox and tree. This color will add depth to the painting.

4. **Trees** — Sap Green + Burnt Sienna dabbed on with 1" brush. Highlight with Yellow Ochre. Blend in some of the atmosphere color at edge of horizon.

5. **Ground** — Base in with Burnt Sienna + White. Highlight with lighter value of Burnt Sienna.

6. **Post** — Burnt Umber + White. Shadow with Burnt Umber.

7. **Mailbox** — White shadowed with Cerulean Blue + violet. (A mixture of Cerulean Blue + Alizarin Crimson + White.)

8. **Basket** — Stroke in curve of basket with flat sable.

   Dark: Burnt Sienna
   Mid-tone: Yellow Ochre
   Light: Cadmium Yellow Light

   Lines on basket are Burnt Umber.

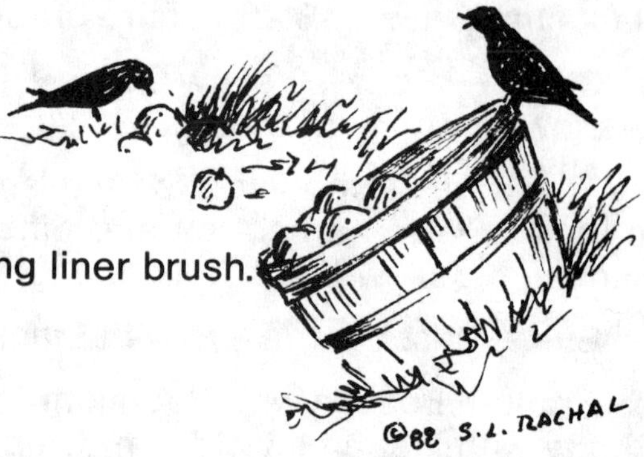

9. **Grass** — Sap Green. Highlight with Sap Green + White using liner brush.

10. **Apples** —

    Dark: Alizarin Crimson based in on all apples.
    Mid-tone: Cadmium Red Light. Follow curve of apple.
    Light: Cadmium Orange. Highlight with just a touch of orange.

11. **Birds** — Add life to the painting by adding birds. The birds are nothing more than a "V" stroke. Fill the liner brush with Burnt Umber thinned with Turpenoid.

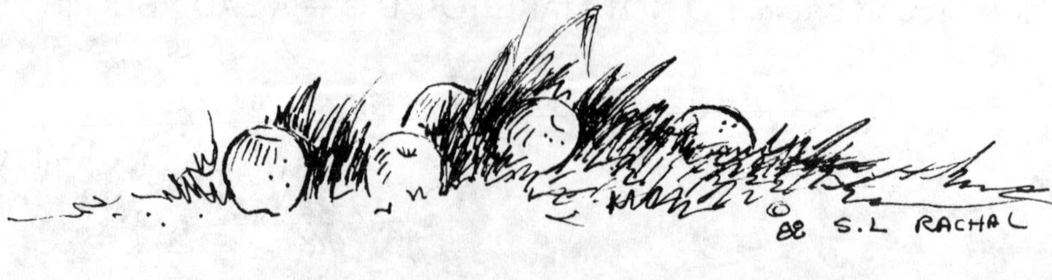

MAILBOX AND BASKET OF APPLES

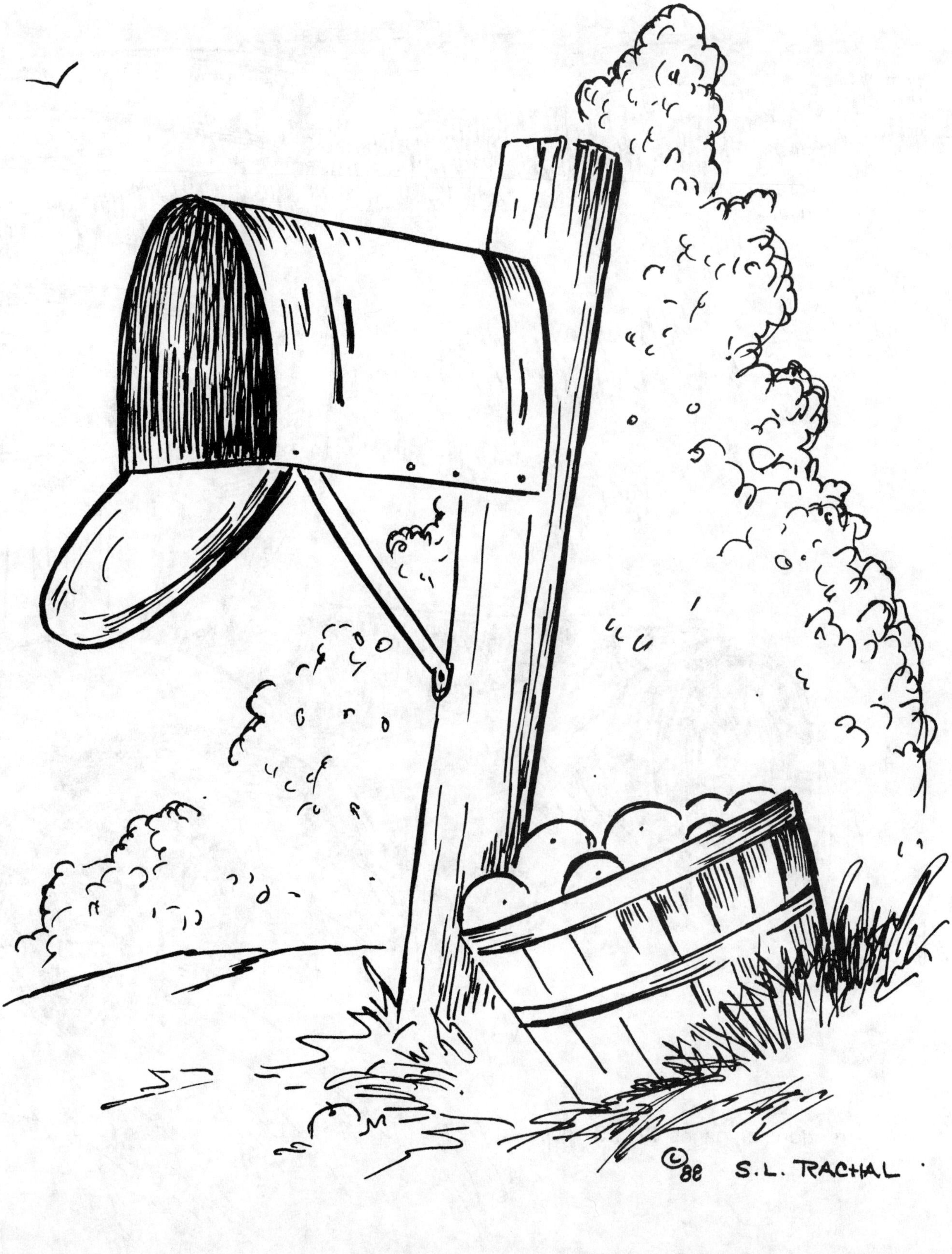

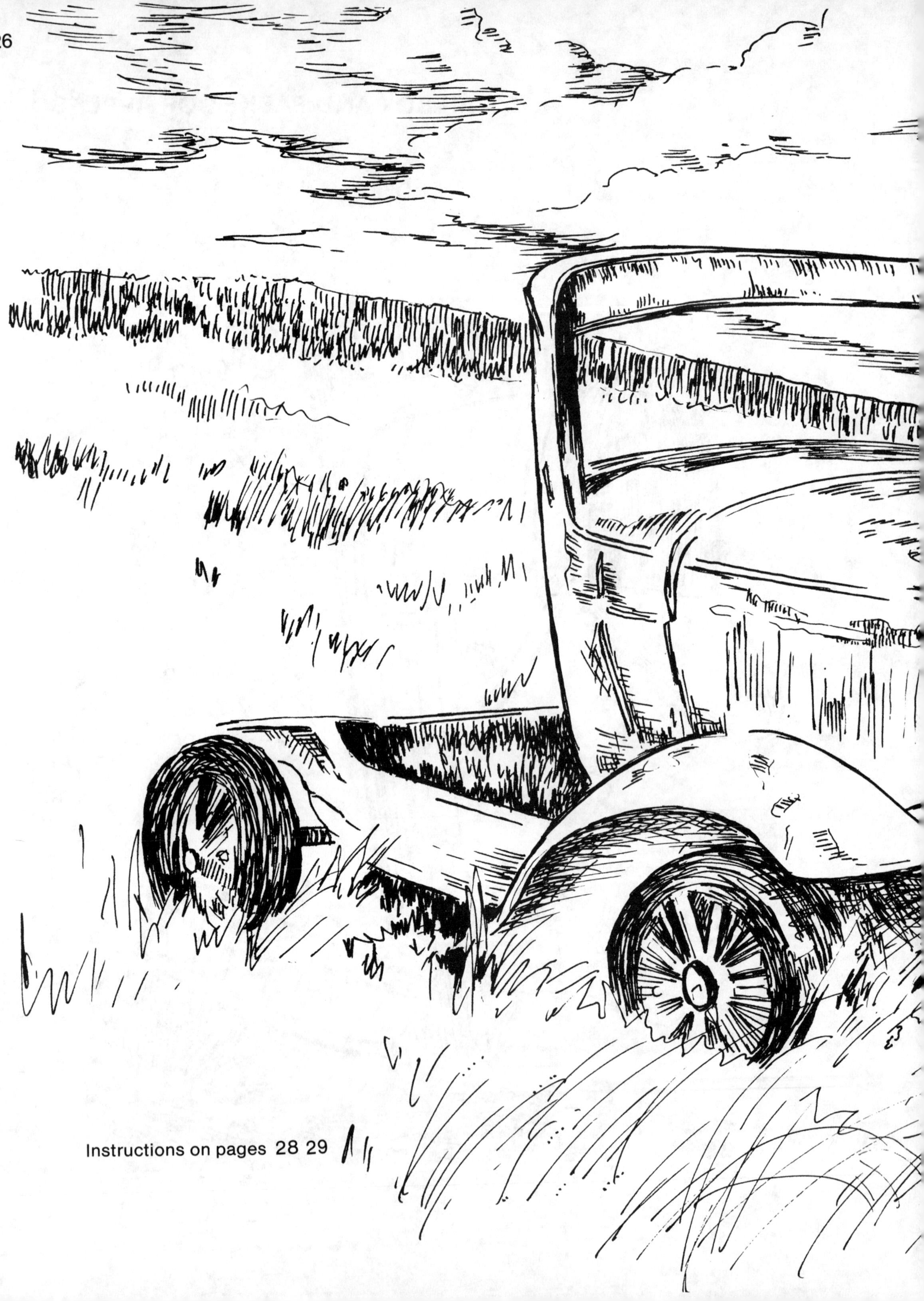

Instructions on pages 28 29

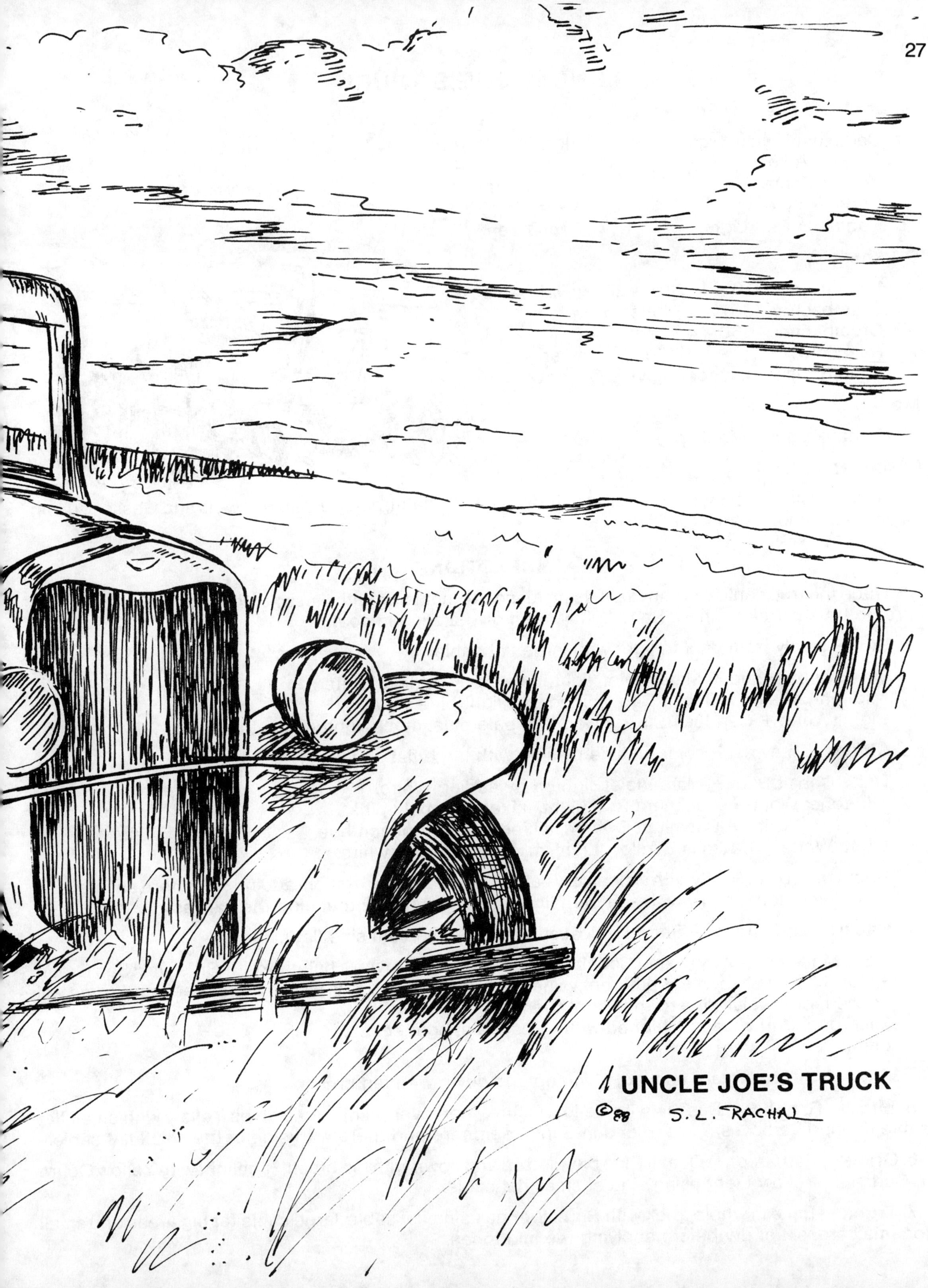

UNCLE JOE'S TRUCK

©88 S. L. RACHAL

UNCLE JOE'S TRUCK

Palette: Grumbacher Pre-Tested

Cadmium Yellow Light
Naples Yellow
Yellow Ochre
Cadmium Orange
Cadmium Red Light
Alizarin Crimson
Cerulean Blue
Cobalt Blue
Mars Violet
Sap Green
Burnt Sienna
Burnt Umber
Titanium White

Brushes:

Langnickel 5010 #1, #10, #20 — Flat Sable
Grumbacher 7357 #1 - Liner
Grumbacher 1060 #4 - Fan
Peacock 145 #9 - Soft blending brush
Foam Brush - only for applying Gesso

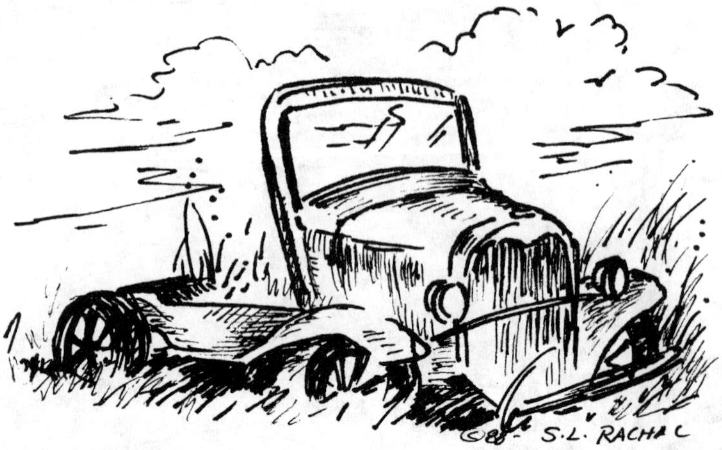

Medium:

Copal Painting Medium.

Miscellaneous:

12 X 16 Canvas or masonite, palette knife for mixing paint, palette, paper towels and Gesso (if using masonite), retouch varnish.

DIRECTIONS

1. Trace the truck onto the canvas. If using masonite, coat first with Gesso using a foam brush, making sure no brush strokes show. Sand lightly, then give a second coat.

2. **Sky** — Apply from dark to light with large flat sable.

   Dark: Cobalt Blue + Mars Violet, lighten value by adding White.
   Mid-tone: White + Cobalt Blue mixted to a light blue value.
   Light: White + Cerulean Blue, mixed to a pale blue, much lighter than the mid-tone.

3. **Clouds** — Lay each color on side by side with large flat sable.

   Dark: Cobalt Blue + Mars Violet, lighten by adding White.
   Mid-tone: White + Cadmium Red Light, mixed to a pale pink
   White + Cadmium Orange, mixed to a soft peach hue.
   Light: White + Cadmium Yellow Light, mixed to a warm white.

   Blend the colors lightly with a clean dry flat sable in a circular motion, adding color here ant there as needed. Blend horizontally with soft blending brush, just barely touching the canvas.

4. **Background Grass** — Short vertical strokes with medium size flat sable.

   Dark: Make a green by mixing Cobalt Blue + Yellow Ochre with a palette knife. Brush mix Sap Green + Burnt Sienna to achieve different values of green. Some areas will be more green and some will be warmer in value due to the Burnt Sienna.
   Mid-Tone: Burnt Sienna thinned with Copal painting medium.
   Light: Yellow Ochre.

   After all the colors are applied, blend up and down with fan brush.

5. **Middle Ground** — Base in with Yellow Ochre, then over paint with Naples Yellow with small flat sable in short vertical strokes. Blend in Sap Green here and there with side of the small flat sable.

6. **Grass** — Sap Green + Cobalt Blue blended up and down with fan brush. Highlight with Yellow Ochre + Cadmium Yellow Light using side of small flat sable.

7. **Truck** — Base in whole truck with Burnt Sienna using flat sable, large sable for big areas and small for small areas. Let dry before applying the mid tones.

Dark: Apply the dark areas with Burnt Umber using flat sable under fenders, radiator, inside of lights and on spots on side of truck.
Mid-tones: Criss-cross over base paint with Cadmium Orange, then Cadmium Red Light using small flat sable. DO NOT COVER all of the Burnt Sienna. We want some of this to show through.
Light: White + Mars Violet, which is a pale pink.

Metal strips on side of truck and top of radiator: Mix White + Cerulean Blue. Gray this mixture with Burnt Umber and apply with flat sable. For light: White + Cerulean Blue and highlight with White + Cadmium Yellow Light using small round brush.

8. **Headlights** — Outline with small round sable using Cerulean Blue + White. Block inside of headlights in with small flat sable using Cobalt Blue + Burnt Umber. Highlight with Cerulean Blue + Cadmium Yellow Light using small round brush.

9. **Tires** — Base in with Cobalt Blue + Burnt Umber with medium size flat sable. Apply treads with Cerulean Blue using small round sable.

10. **Spokes** — Burnt Umber + White using small round sable.

After truck is painted and completely dry, I glaze the same colors over existing colors. This really enhances the colors and gives much more life to the subject.

11. **Weeds** — Thin paint with Turpenoid using a liner brush.

Dark: Burnt Umber + Cobalt Blue
Mid-tone: Cadmium Red Light. Cadmium Orange.
Light: Yellow Ochre. Cadmium Yellow Light.

Stroke with long flowing strokes from bottom of weeds upwards. Dot some of the tips of the weeds.

12. **Blue Flowers** — Dot in cone shape with Cobalt Blue and highlight with Cerulean Blue with small round sable.

13. **Yellow Flowers** — Dot with Yellow Ochre and highlight with Cadmium Yellow Light using small round sable.

14. After painting has dried, give several light misty coats of retouch varnish. In six months give several misty coats of Damar Varnish for the final varnish.

Bonus pattern

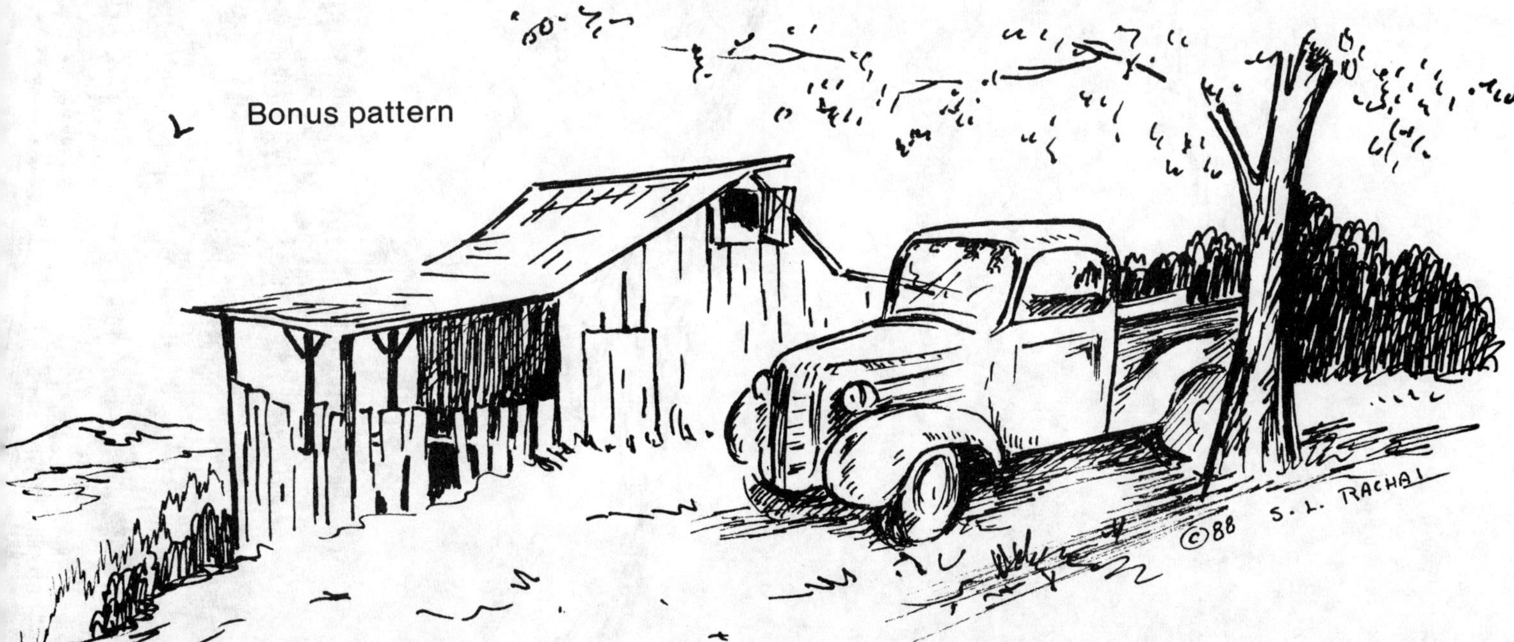

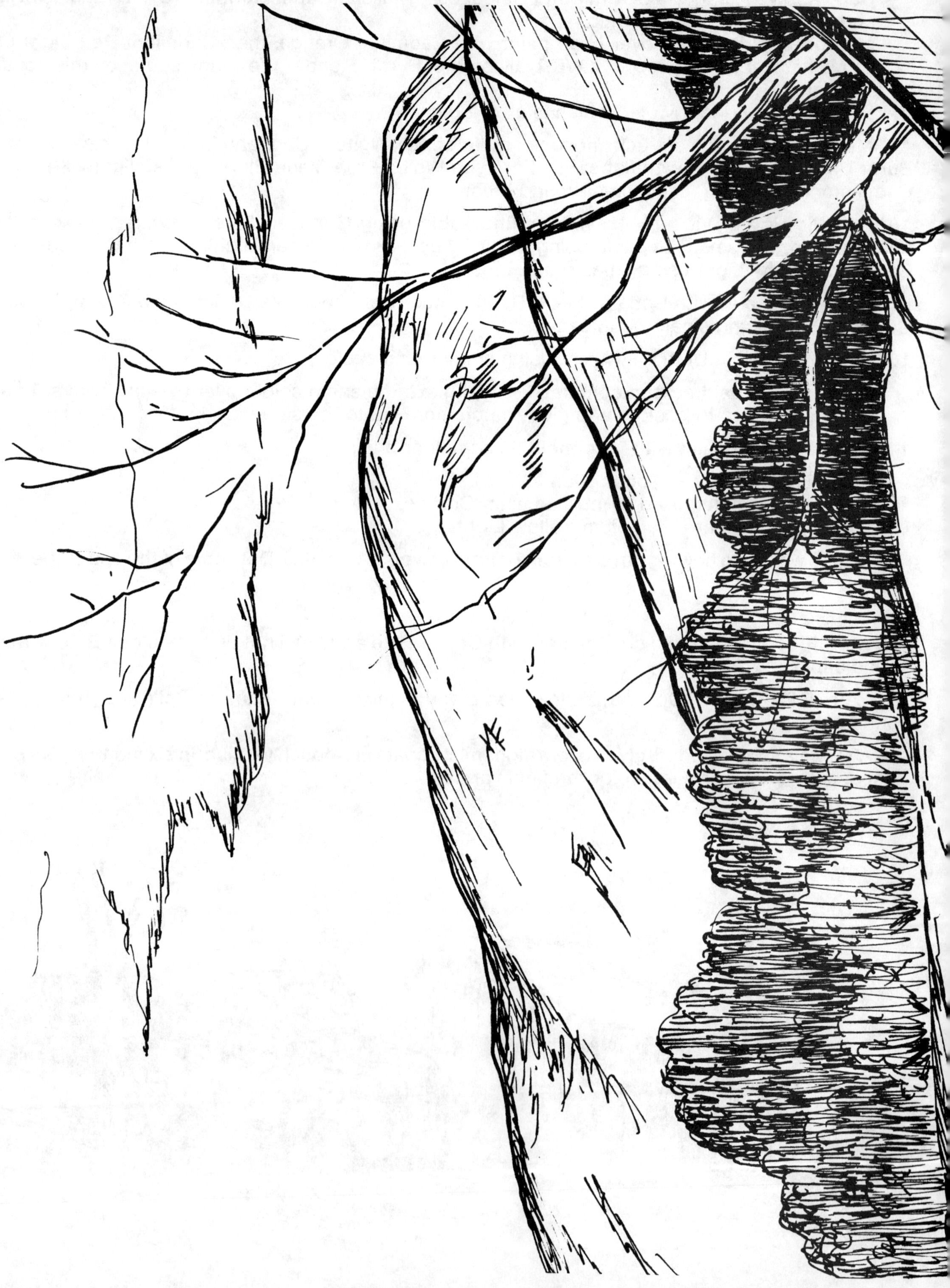

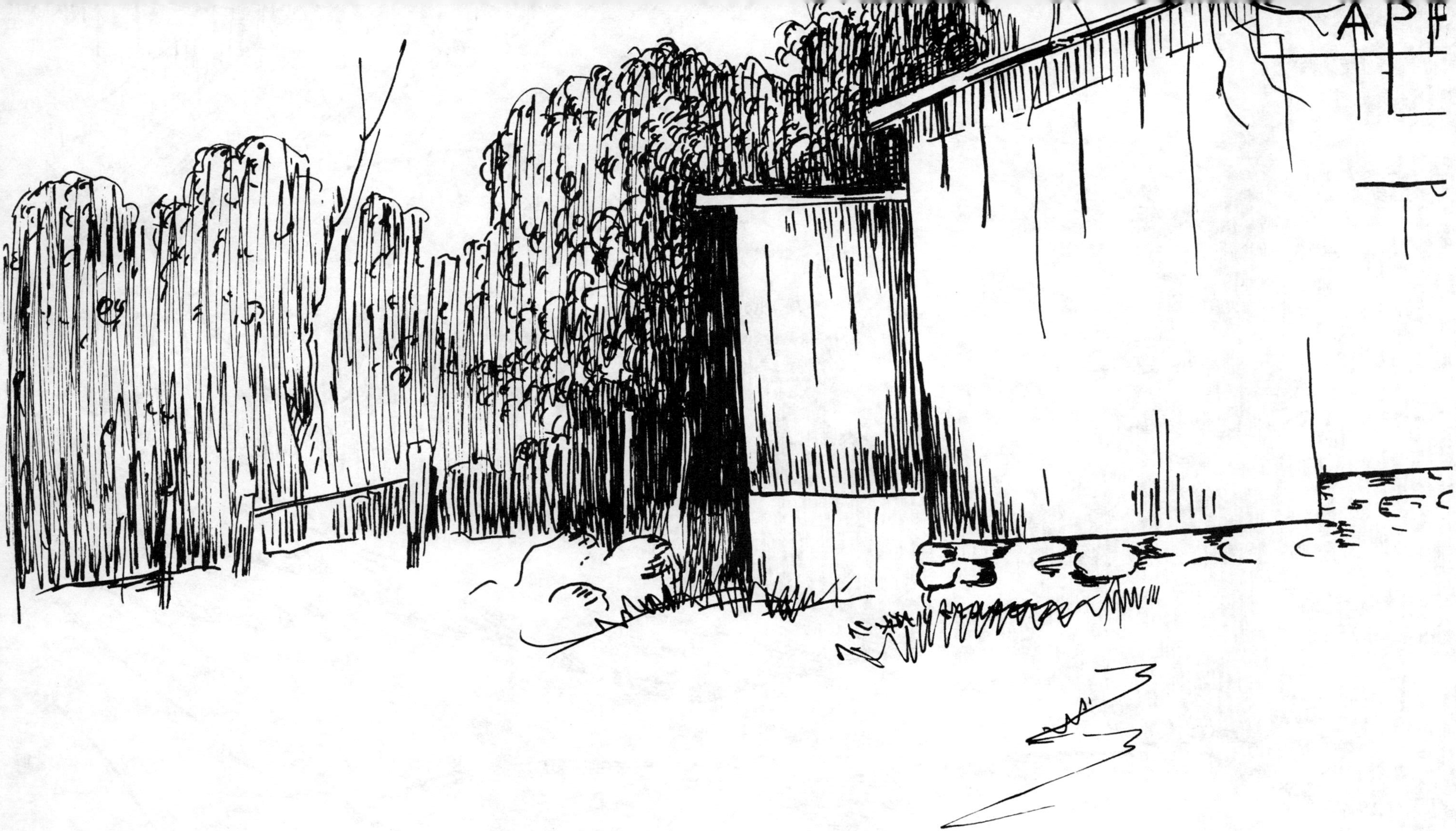

APPLE BARN

Left section of the painting guide.

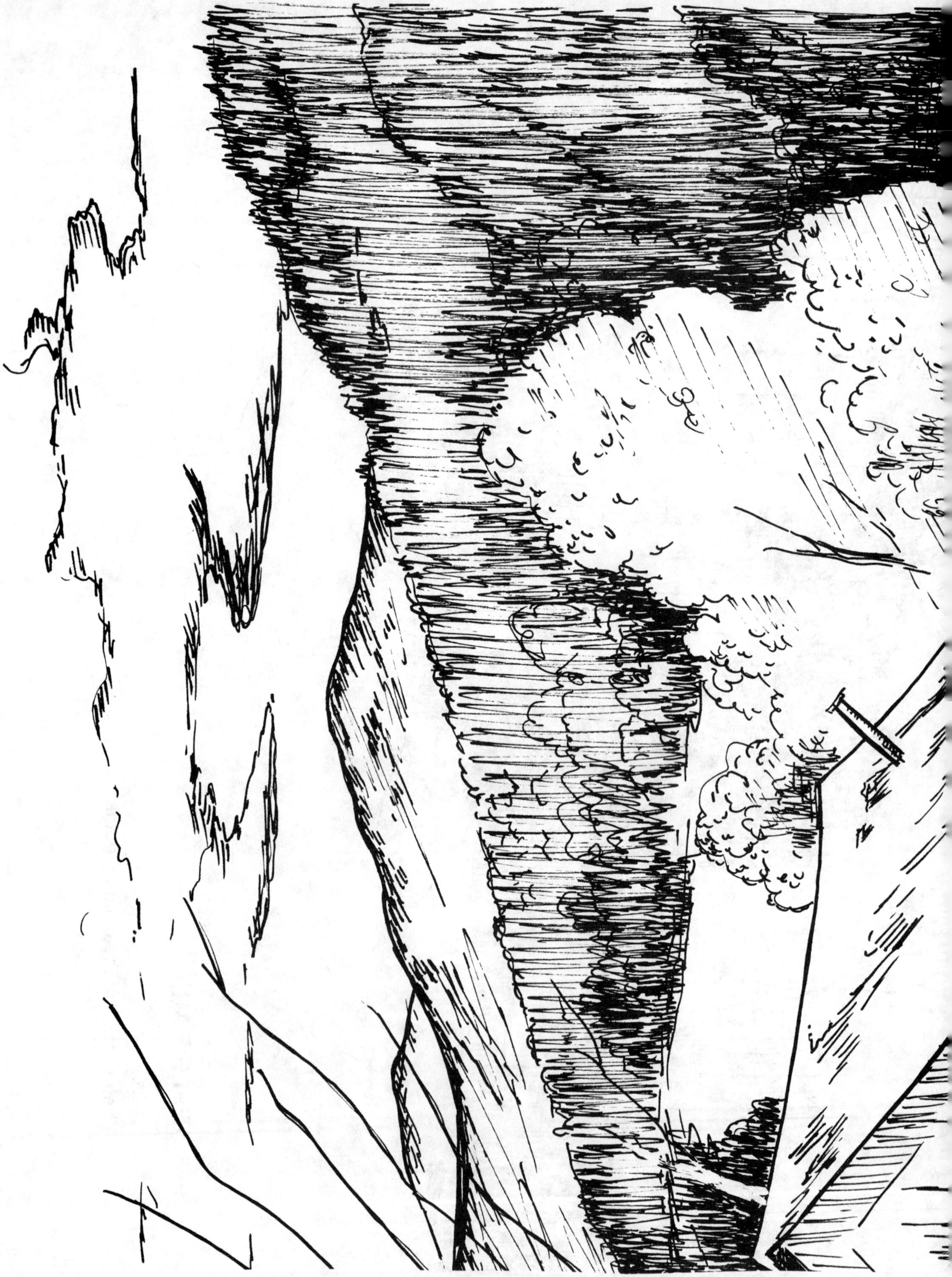

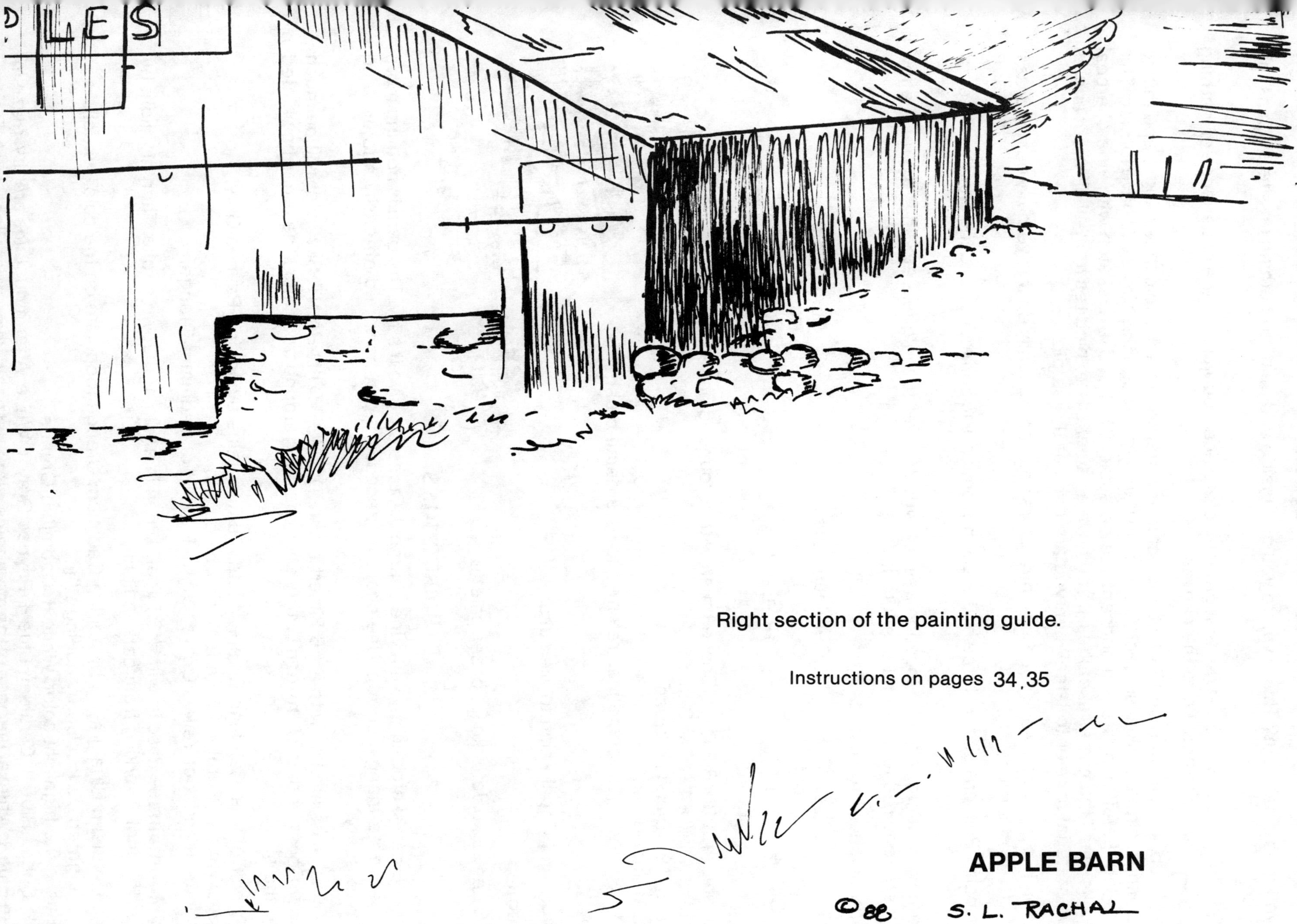

Right section of the painting guide.

Instructions on pages 34, 35

APPLE BARN

©88 S. L. RACHAL

APPLE BARN

Have you tried a paint out? This is where you go outside and paint something on site, such as this barn.

It is lots of fun. Even if you don't get that great masterpiece, you will gain the experience of learning to look at color and try to apply it to the canvas.

Before set up, walk around and look at subject from different angles. Hold index finger and thumb together forming a circle. Look at subject you plan on painting through this circle you have formed. This blocks out a lot of stuff and lets you concentrate on subject better. Next, sketch with vine charcoal lightly, or make small thumb nail sketches. If you have a camera, take pictures from all different angles so you have material to refer to later when you are back at the studio.

After sketch is in, mentally ask yourself what colors you see. I usually do this verbally out loud, as it helps me to think clearer.

Lay out paint. Plan on painting three hours and no longer. The sun moves and the shadows change rapidly.

This barn was painted right on location using a wet into wet technique. Later in the studio, a few touch ups were required to give that spark to it.

Palette: Grumbacher Pre-Tested

White
Cadmium Yellow Light
Yellow Ochre
Cerulean Blue
Cobalt Blue
Sap Green
Burnt Sienna
Burnt Umber
Paynes Gray

Brushes:

Grumbacher 4229 #6 Filbert (Bristle brush with a rounded-flat end)
Langnickel #14, #4 - Flat Sable
Hake 145 #9 - Blending brush
735 #1 - Liner brush
178 #1 - Round sable, sometines referred to as a detail brush.

Medium:

Turpenoid and Copal Painting Medium.

Miscellaneous:

12 X 16 canvas, palette knife, paper palette.

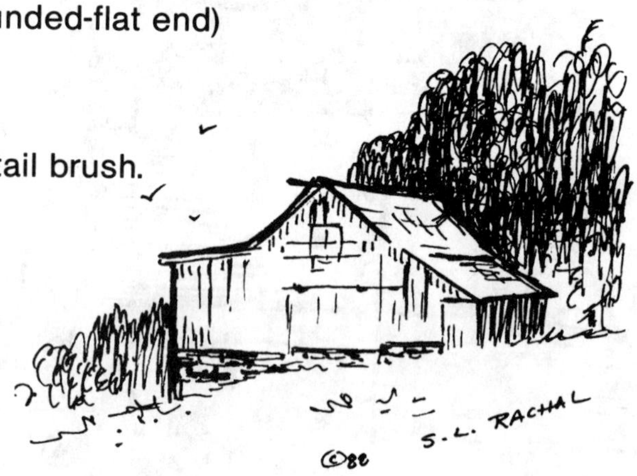

DIRECTIONS

1. Trace or you can sketch lightly with vine charcoal. Come on, give it a try. The barn is nothing more than a square with a triangle on top. Use charcoal because it can be wiped off easily and drawing changed if necessary.

2. **Sky** — Criss-cross strokes with a #6 Filbert brush. DO NOT THIN PAINT. Sky color will be much richer this way. Cover whole sky and don't worry about painting around tree limbs. These can be painted in later over the sky.

Dark: Cobalt Blue + Cerulean Blue + White. Darken value by adding Paynes Gray.
Mid-tone: White + Cerulean Blue for a soft blue.
Light: White + a hint of Yellow Ochre. White + a hint of Cadmium Orange.

3. **Distant Mountains** — Base in with #6 Filbert brush in an up and down stroke. Then highlight by stroking in a 45° angle working from dark to light.

#1 Dark: Cerulean Blue grayed by adding Cadmium Orange (opposite on the color wheel).
Mid-tone: Lighten dark value by adding White.
Light: This is the highlight color. White + Cadmium Orange.
#2 Dark: Cobalt Blue + Cerulean Blue + Paynes Gray + White. After mountains are dry, glaze in Cerulean Blue + White at the base of the mountains with a flat sable using a very light touch. Diffuse so that a line of demarcation does not show with a dry clean sable. This will push the mountains back and give depth to the painting.

4. **Trees** — Use old worn out sable for this, or make a tree brush by beating an old sable with a hammer so that some of the bristles break. It will make neat tree foliage.

Dark: Sap Green + Burnt Sienna.
Mid-tone: Add Yellow Ochre to dark mixture.
Light: Cadmium Orange at base of trees patted in while paint is still wet.

5. **Distant Land** — Underpaint with Yellow Ochre. Then glaze in a Paynes Gray + White + Cobalt Blue with flat sable, letting some of the underpainting show through.

6. **Old Tree** — Use liner brush, roll into Burnt Umber + White, a gray value, which is thinned with Turpenoid. Pull from the base up, twisting brush as lifting up. Add White to lighten value. Add depth by putting in accents of real darks with Paynes Gray.

7. **Trees Behind Barn** —

Dark: Sap Green + Burnt Sienna + Paynes Gray.
Mid-tone: Sap Green + Cadmium Orange.
Light: Sap Green + Cadmium Yellow Light.

8. **Barn** — First lay in underpainting using #6 Filbert. After dry, glaze in different colors with flat sable using Copal painting medium.

Front: White. After dry, glaze in Burnt Sienna, then glaze in Burnt Umber.

Woodgrain: Burnt Umber with small round sable.

Side: Underpaint in Yellow Ochre. Glaze in Burnt Sienna + Burnt Umber.

Roof: Base in Burnt Sienna. Drag Cerulean Blue + White over this following angle of roof.

Tip of roof: White + Cadmium Orange.

Stones: Paynes Gray + White using small flat sable #4. Highlight with White + Yellow Ochre.

After barn is dry, glaze in shadows with Burnt Umber. Then soften with clean dry sable. With this method it will give more life and luminous to the painting.

9. **Fence** — Burnt Umber + White. Highlight with White + Cadmium Orange, using small round detail brush.

10. **Grass** — Use Hake 145 #9. Dip into paint then lift up. Use Sap Green + Burnt Sienna and Sap Green + Cadmium Yellow Light. Blend some of the grass at a slight angle with Cadmium Yellow Light + Sap Green. This will give feeling of a hill. Use blending brush (145 #9) and dip into paint — do not thin. Push brush into canvas, and flip upward with Sap Green + Burnt Sienna.

11. **Sign** — Outline with a green, Cobalt Blue + Yellow Ochre. Place an index card on canvas. With the chiseled edge of sable brush follow edge of card. This will help to make a straight line. "Apples" is printed with red and outlined with Paynes Gray using small round brush.

"BLACKIE'S ORCHARD"

e. **Robe box:** (The bottom right box).

Top - Cobalt Blue + Mars Violet + White. Highlight with White + Cadmium Yellow Light.
Side - Cobalt Blue + Burnt Umber.
Front - Lines - Burnt Sienna + Burnt Umber.
Label - White - and glaze in Cerulean Blue.
Letters - Yellow Ochre - outline with Burnt Umber.

Glaze in all shadows with Ivory Black, then soften with blending brush.

If you want to paint a mate to this, just use one of the boxes, add a few strands of grass and a couple of apples.

"BLACKIE'S ORCHARD"

This is a very interesting subject, boxes with various labels on them with a landscape in the background.

Palette: Grumbacher Pre-Tested

Cadmium Yellow Light
Yellow Ochre
Cadmium Orange
Cadmium Red Light
Titanium White

Alizarin Crimson
Mars Violet
Cobalt Blue
Cobalt Blue
Cerulean Blue

Burnt Sienna
Burnt Umber
Ivory Black

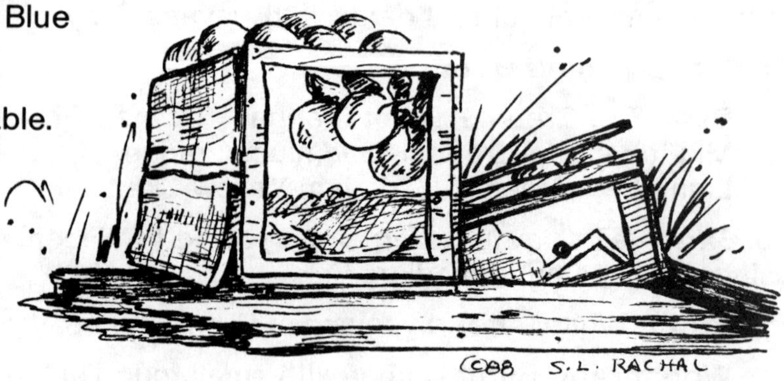

Brushes:

Langnickel 5010 #4, #6, #8, #20 - Flat Sable.
Grumbacher 178 #1 - Round Sable.
Peacock 145 #9 - Blending Brush.
Foam Brush

Medium:

Copal Painting Medium.

Miscellaneous:

12 X 16 untempered masonite or 12 X 16 canvas, Gesso if using masonite, palette knife, tack cloth.

DIRECTIONS

This painting has a lot of detail in it — don't hurry, just enjoy!

1. Trace pattern onto a 12 x 16 canvas or masonite. (If using masonite, prepare by giving two coats of Gesso with foam brush. First coat in a vertical direction, then coat in a horizontal direction. Sand lightly, and tack off with tack cloth.

2. **Sky** — Mix White + Cerulean Blue with palette knife to a soft blue hue, and apply using large flat sable in a circular motion. Add peachy value, White + Cadmium Orange, near horizon. Soften with blending brush.

3. **Distant Trees** — Thin paint to a glaze consistency by adding Copal painting medium. The colors will be transparent. To make irregular edges of trees, use the corner of a flat sable twisting and turning brush as dabbing. By using various sizes of sables, the edges will appear different.

   Dark: Mars Violet + Cerulean Blue + White
   Mid-tone: White + Cerulean Blue
   Light: White + Mars Violet

4. **Distant Trunks** — A soft gray value, Burnt Umber + Cerulean Blue, lightened by adding White, thinned with Copal painting medium. Hold round brush just like a pencil and draw in trunks. Blot trunks with a rag or paper towel. This will soften value. Highlight with a soft mauve, White + Mars Violet.

5. **Path** — Important — use horizontal brush strokes. This will make the path appear to lay down. Lay in with a warm brown, Burnt Sienna + White, using medium size flat sable (#8) near the horizon. Blend in some of the sky color, White + Cerulean Blue. Highlight with White + Cadmium Orange. Shadow edge of path with Burnt Umber thinned with Copal painting medium blended and patted in with a small flat sable.

6. **Grass** — Mix a green value, Yellow Ochre + Cerulean Blue. To lighten value add White. Short horizontal strokes with flat sable (#8). This will make it appear to lay down.

7. **Rocks** — Double load a small flat sable (#4). Place Burnt Umber on one side and a peachy White, White + Cadmium Orange, on the opposite side of brush. Short side stroke, the light will be at the top and the dark will be at the bottom. One stroke will do it.

8. **Leaves** — Mix three values of green. Apply with corner of small flat sable (#4) moving brush from left to right as dabbing, overlapping strokes.

Dark: Cobalt Blue + Yellow Ochre + touch of Burnt Umber
Mid-tone: Cobalt Blue + Yellow Ochre
Light: Cadmium Yellow Light + Cerulean Blue

9. **Limb** — Base in with Burnt Sienna, using small round brush. Highlight with Cadmium Orange.

10. **Boxes** — Base in all boxes with Yellow Ochre with flat sable #20, leaving the labels unpainted. Let dry then apply layers of glazes using various sizes of flat sables and small round sable for the details. Use two brushes for glazing, one for applying color and one for softening color. Make sure the softening brush is clean and dry.

a. **Clove box:** Cobalt Blue + Burnt Umber + White glazed over Yellow Ochre underpainting with flat sable #6.

Label: Base in White + Cerulean Blue. Let dry.

Letters: Spell CLOVE with Yellow Ochre and outline with Burnt Umber using small round brush.

Shadows: Glaze in with Black and Copal painting medium.

b. **Oak Glen Apples: box.**

Dark: Cobalt Blue + Burnt Umber + White glazed over underpainting of Yellow Ochre.
Mid-tone: Mars Violet + Cobalt Blue + White using small flat sable.
Light: White + Cadmium Orange on top of box and the right front edge using small round sable.

Everything listed below is on the label.

Label: **Sky** - White + Cerulean Blue
Trees - Yellow Ochre + Cobalt Blue. Lighten value by adding more Yellow Ochre. Shadow with Cobalt Blue.
Lower edge of label - Yellow Ochre.
Apples - Underpaint with Yellow Ochre. Glaze in Cadmium Red Light following contour of apple. Shadow with Alizarin Crimson. Highlight with Cadmium Orange + White + Burnt Umber.
Leaves - Cobalt Blue + Yellow Ochre. Highlight with Cadmium Yellow Light.
Oak Glen Apples - Print letters with small round sable in White, outline and stripe with Burnt Umber.
Line on label across bottom - Cadmium Red Light highlighted with Cadmium Orange, using small round sable and ruler as a guide.
Shadow - After completely dry, glaze in shadows with Ivory Black.

c. **Blackie's Box:** Burnt Sienna. Outline letters (Blackie) is Burnt Umber using small round brush. Shadows - Burnt Umber + Cobalt Blue using flat sable #6.

Label: **Light** - Cerulean Blue fused into Cobalt Blue.
Dark - Cobalt Blue.
Pears - Cadmium Yellow Light. Shadow - Burnt Sienna, Cobalt Blue.
Pear Label - Yellow Ochre with just a touch of Cadmium Orange. Outline letters (Pear) with White. Glaze in shadows with Ivory Black.

d. **Bottom box:** (front bottom box).

Side - Cobalt Blue + Burnt Umber glazed in with flat sable.
Front - White + Cadmium Yellow Light blended softly.
Label - Burnt Sienna thinned to a glaze consistency. Highlight with White + Cadmium Orange.
Letters - Burnt Umber using small round brush. The letters were supposed to be blended - only cut the bottom half of letters off.
Trees - Cobalt Blue + Cadmium Yellow Light dabbed in with the corner of flat sable #4.
Letters - White + Burnt Umber.

continued on page 35

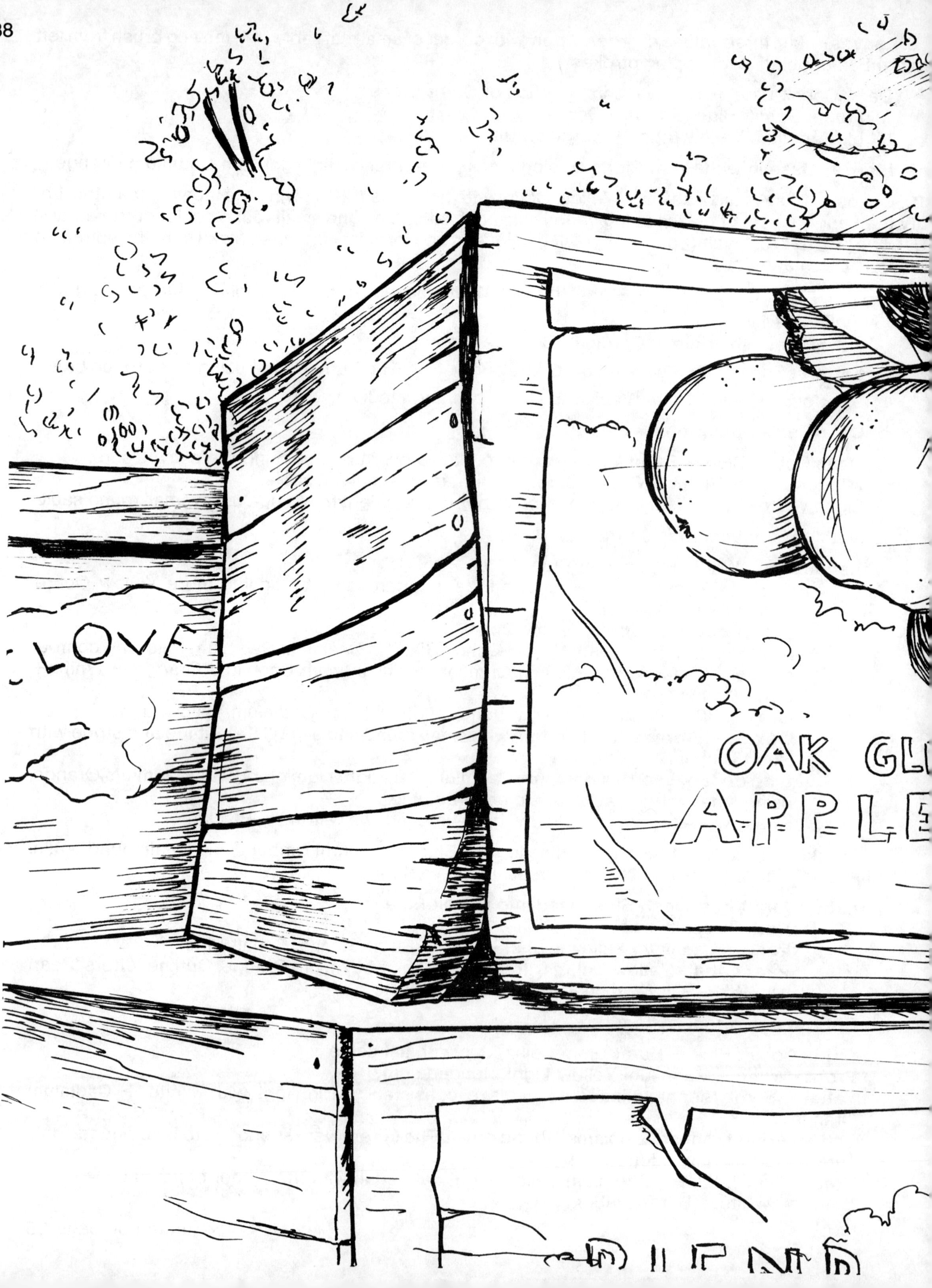
LOVE
OAK GL
APPLE

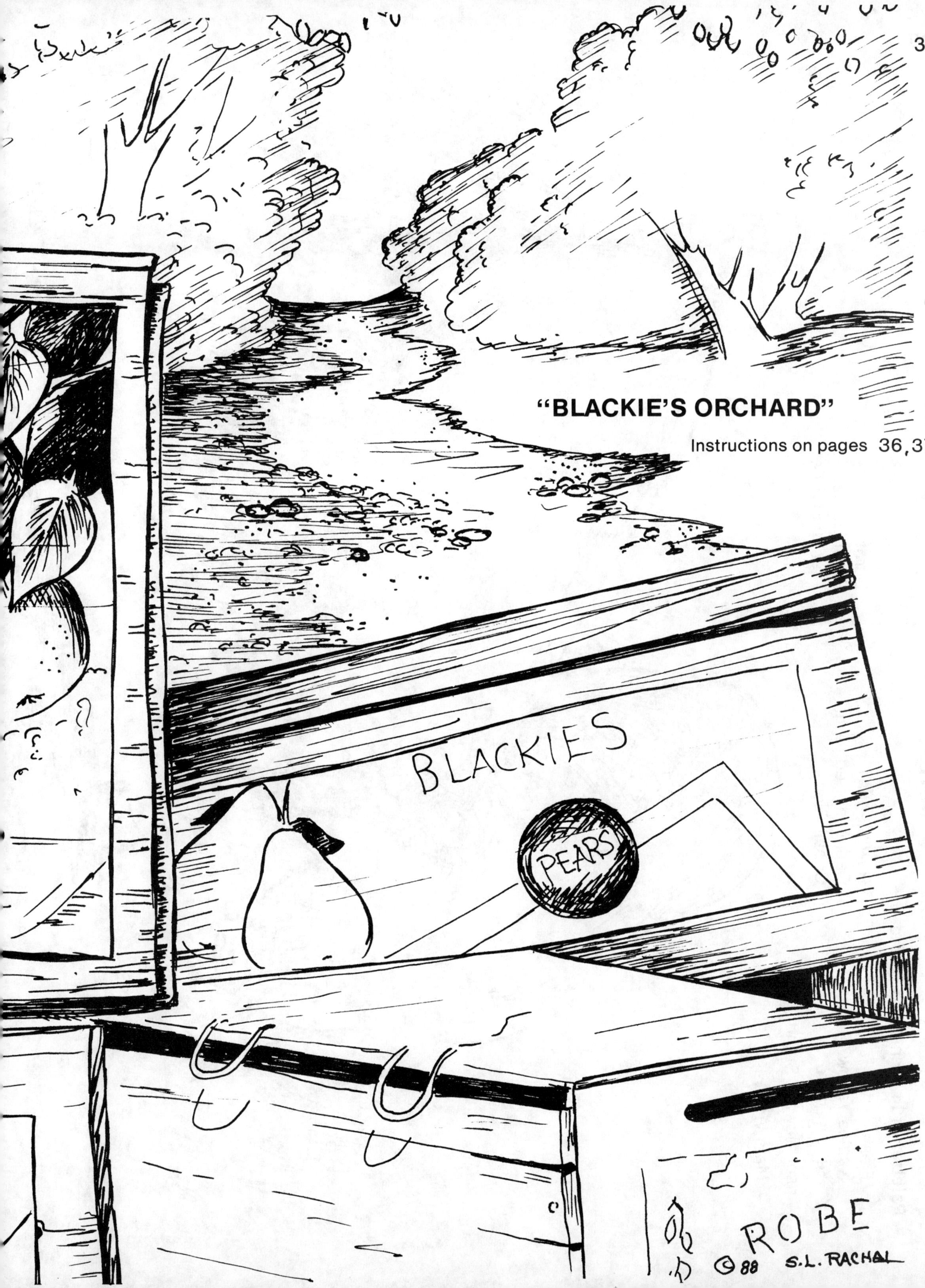

"BLACKIE'S ORCHARD"

Instructions on pages 36,37

MAY I?

Palette: Grumbacher Pre-Tested

Flesh	Raw Sienna	Burnt Sienna
Naples Yellow	Cadmium Red Light	Burnt Umber
Yellow Ochre	Cobalt Blue	Titanium White

Winsor Newton Brand

Mars Violet

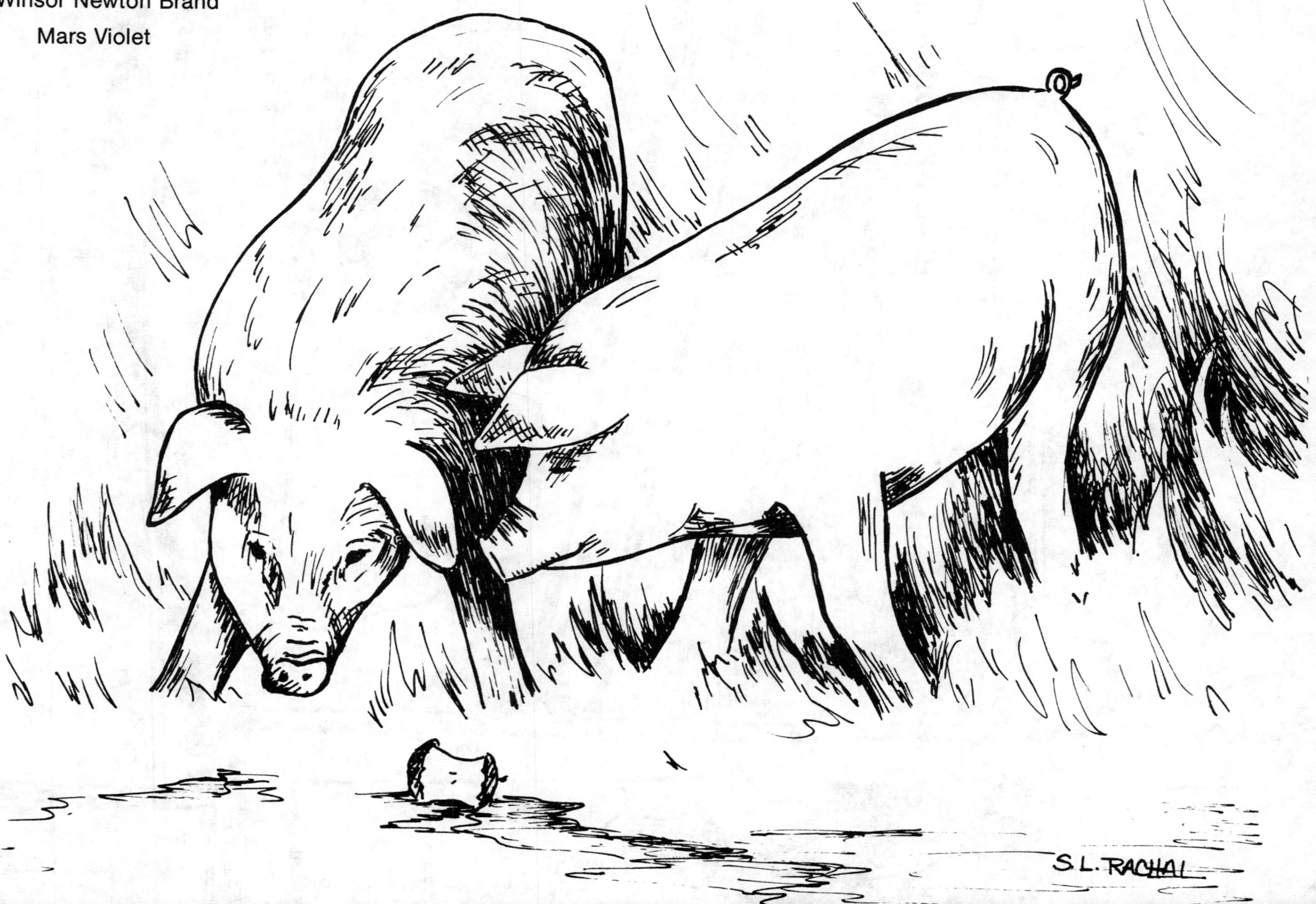

Brushes:

Langnickel 5010 #4 referred to as small flat sable, #20 referred to as large flat sable.
Grumbacher 178 #1 - Small Round Sable which has good point.
Peacock 145 #9 - A soft blending brush.

Medium:

Copal Painting Medium.

Miscellaneous:

8 X 10 canvas palette paper, paper towels, palette knife.

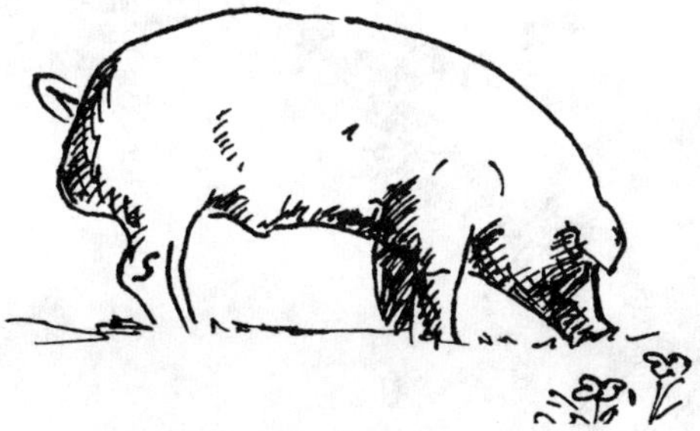

DIRECTIONS

1. Trace the pigs and apple core onto an 8 X 10 canvas. This painting would look cute on a wood piece, or back of an old shovel.

2. **Background** — Lay in each color side by side from dark to light at a slight angle with large flat sable.

Dark: Burnt Umber + Burnt Sienna
Mid-tone: Raw Sienna
Light: Yellow Ochre

Softly blend together with soft blending brush, letting some of the brush strokes show through.

3. **Dark Pig** — Apply colors from dark to light with large flat sable, following contour of pig.

Dark: Mars Violet + Cobalt Blue + White
Mid-tone: White + Flesh
Light: White + Cadmium Red Light, a light pink hue.

Eyes and Nostrils — Mix a dark value of Burnt Umber + Cobalt Blue with palette knife. Use small round sables to base in.

Eyelashes — Yes pigs have lashes. White + just a hint of Flesh, just a few short strokes with small round sable will do it.

Snout — Outline with Mars Violet using small round brush.

Ears — Mars Violet + Cobalt Blue + White. Highlight with White + Flesh.

4. **Light Pig** — Mix White + Flesh with palette knife, and base in with large flat sable. Blend in shadow areas with a light value of Mars Violet + Cobalt Blue with small sable.

Eye — Burnt Umber + Cobalt Blue, a dark brown value — almost black, using small round sable.

Mouth and Snout — Outline with Mars Violet and highlight with pink, White + Cadmium Red Light using small round sable.

5. **Grass** — Use chisel edge of flat sable, stroking sideways to suggest grass.

Dark: Raw Sienna
Mid-tone: Yellow Ochre
Light: Naples Yellow
Highlight: White + Naples Yellow

Blend lightly with soft blending brush, using short strokes and let some of the brush strokes show.

6. **Apple Core** — Use small round sable.

Inside of apple: White + Yellow Ochre.

Seeds: Two short dots of Burnt Umber.

Outside: Cadmium Red Light — shadow with Burnt Umber.

7. **Ground** — To make ground lay down, stroke in a horizontal brush stroke using flat sable with Raw Sienna.

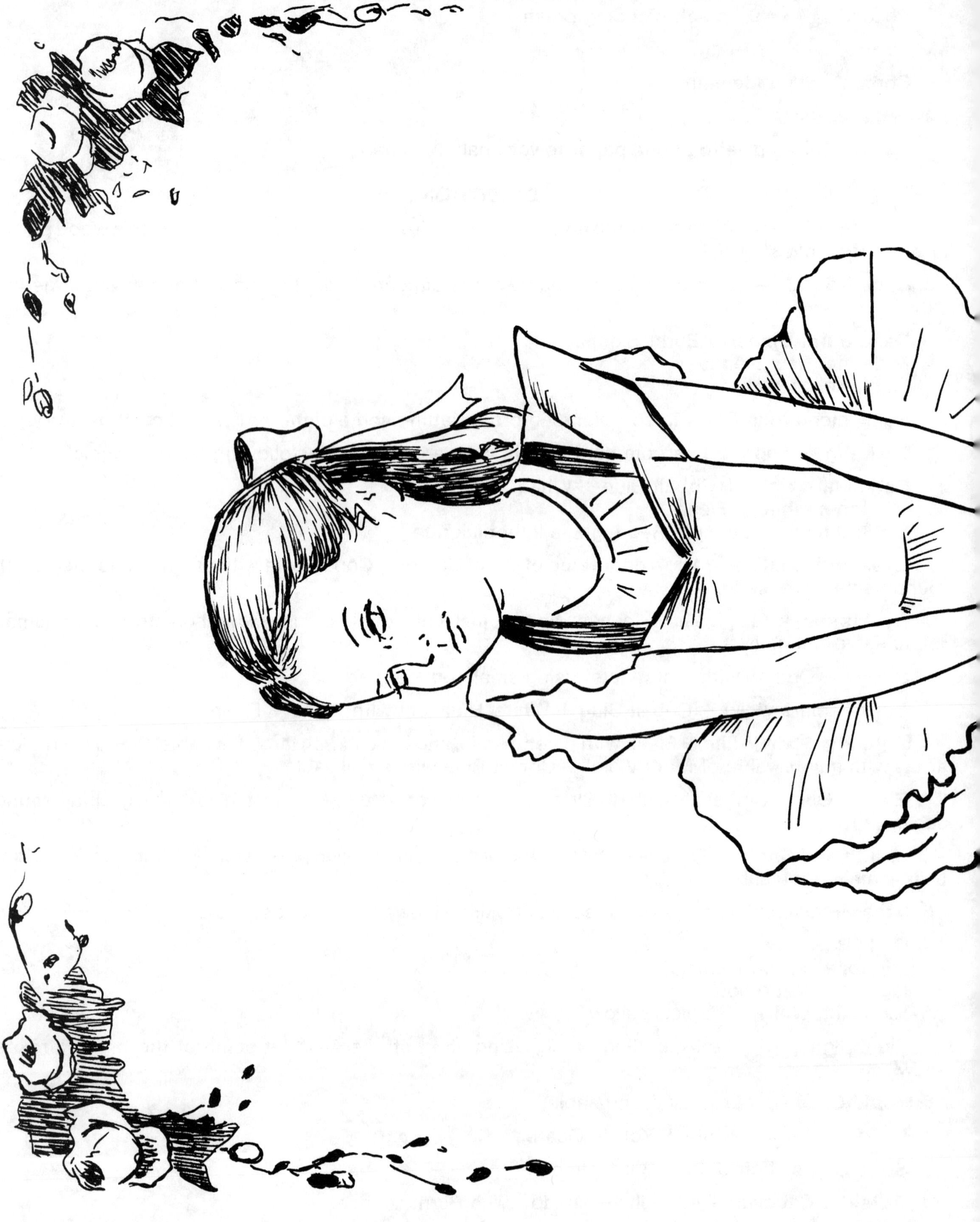

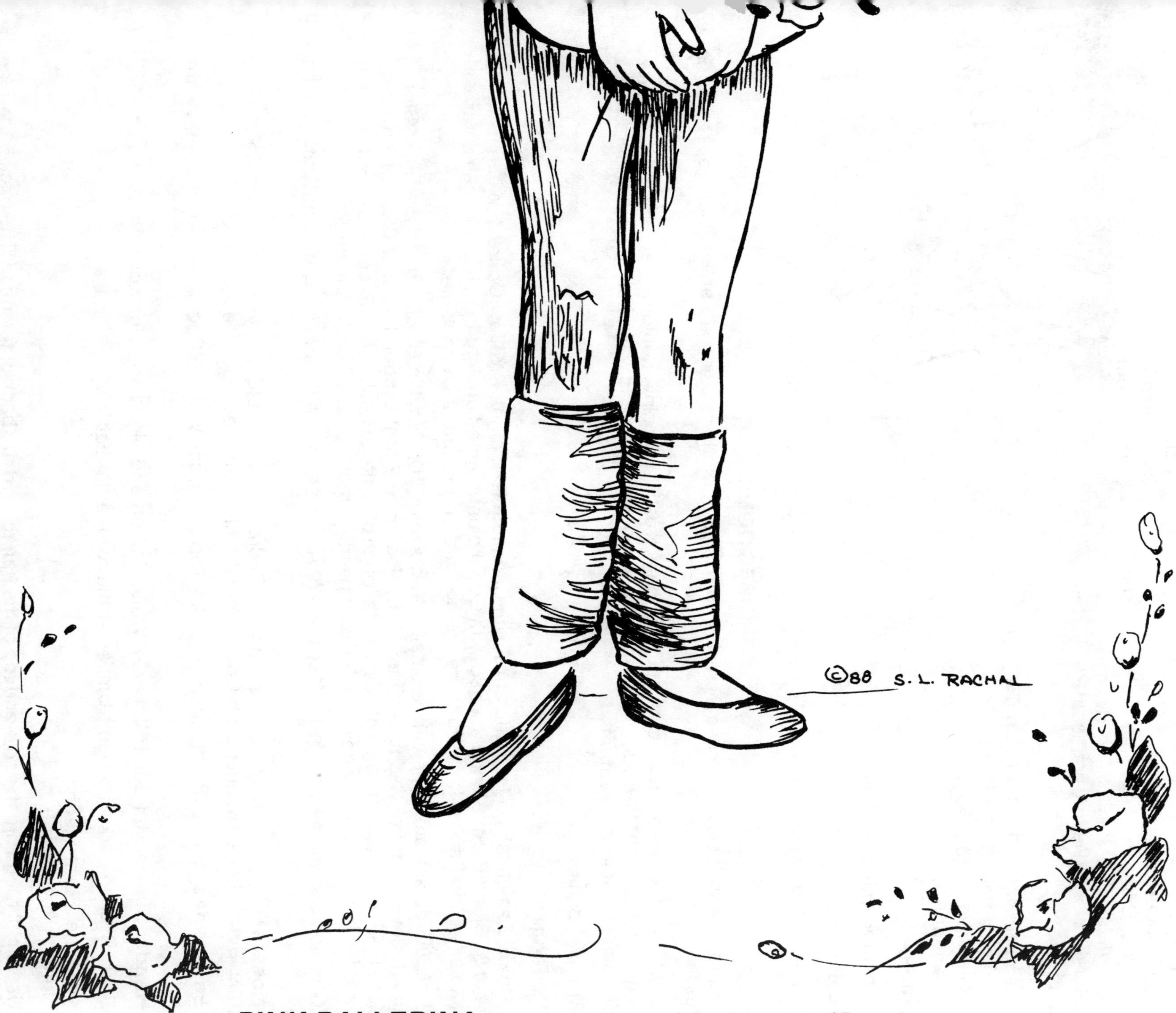

PINK BALLERINA Instructions on pages 44, 45

PINK BALLERINA

Palette: Grumbacher Pre-Tested

Titanium White
Cadmium Yellow Light (small amount)
Yellow Ochre
Cadmium Red Light
Alizarin Crimson
Cerulean Blue
Acrylic Ivory - Delta Ceramcoat
Cobalt Blue
Sap Green
Thalo Yellow Green (small amount)
Burnt Sienna
Burnt Umber

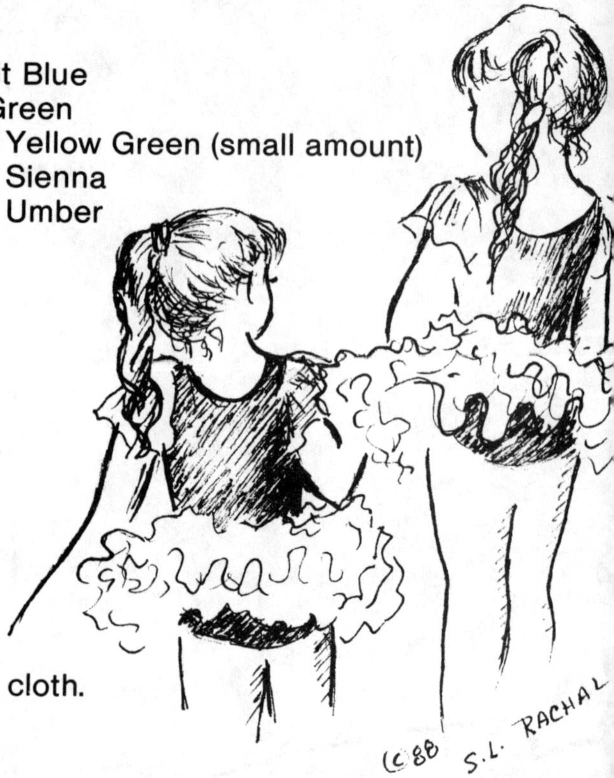

Brushes:

Langnickel 5010 #4, #6, #8 flat sable
Grumbacher 7357 #1 liner.
Grumbacher 738 #0
Foam brush.

Medium:

Copal Painting Medium.

Miscellaneous:

12 X 16 Wood piece or 12 x 16 canvas, palette, and tack cloth.

DIRECTIONS

1. Sand board, tack off excess particles with a tack cloth. If using a canvas, no preparation is necessary.

2. Coat board with Ivory acrylic paint using foam brush. The paint should be very smooth and even. If it is not, then give another coat. Wash foam brush out with soap and water immediately. Board should be dry before tracing pattern on.

3. Transfer pattern.

4. **Ballerina —**

Flesh: Base flesh on face and arms with Cadmium Red Light + Yellow Ochre + White using flat sable (#8). Blend Burnt Sienna thinned with Copal painting medium into the shadow flesh areas with flat sable (#6). Pat and diffuse so there are no hard edges with a clean sable.

Eye: All details are done with a small round sable (#0). Pupil is Black. The iris is Burnt Sienna highlighted with a dot of Cadmium Orange. Eyelashes — Burnt Umber + Cobalt Blue, which makes a black. Eyelids — a lighter value of flesh, add a touch of White to flesh color. Eyebrows — Burnt Sienna + Burnt Umber thinned way down with Copal painting medium and lightly brushed on.

Cheeks: Cadmium Red Light + just a hint of Alizarin Crimson floated on. Blend and pat using flat sable (#4).

Nose: Highlight with White + a touch of Cadmium Yellow Light, a warm white on tip of nose. Nostrils, Burnt Umber, thinned with Copal. Pat with cloth so they won't be too dark.

Ear: Inside a touch of Burnt Sienna + White. Top of ear, use White + Cadmium Yellow Light, a warm white.

Hands: Outline with Burnt Sienna + White. Soften and blend so color won't be too harsh.

Hair: Base in dark with Burnt Umber, stroke with a flat sable.

Mid-tone: Burnt Sienna.
Light: Yellow Ochre.

Use small round brush and blend top of the hair toward the back of the head. The back hair which hangs down is a slight "S" curve. A few short strokes for bangs.

Ribbon: Alizarin Crimson + White. Highlight with White while the paint is still wet using flat sable (#4).

Blouse and Leotards: Base in with White + Cerulean Blue, a pale blue using flat sable (#8). Shadow with Cobalt Blue + White + Burnt Umber. Next add a pale pink, Alizarin Crimson + White, on the right leg, and on the inside of the left leg with a flat sable (#8). Highlight with a warm white, White + Cadmium Yellow Light.

Tu-Tu and Leg Warmers: Alizarin Crimson + White, highlighted with White. Use straight Alizarin + Copal painting medium for shadow areas.

Shoes: Black highlighted with Cerulean Blue.

5. **Shadow** — A violet behind rose design, Cobalt Blue + Alizarin Crimson + White. Use a criss-cross stroke and soften with flat sable.

6. **Roses** — Base in Cadmium Red Light, using a "C' stroke with flat sable (#8). Shadow centers and under the bowl with Alizarin Crimson. Highlight with a "U" stroke using White + Cadmium Red Light.

7. **Rose Buds** — Base in Alizarin Crimson and highlight with Cadmium Red Light + White using small round brush.

8. **Leaves** — Sap Green highlighted with Thalo Yellow Green.

9. **Fillers** — Sap Green + Burnt Umber. Use small round brush. Lay flat against board, and push slightly then lift up.

10. **Lines** — Mix Copal painting medium into Sap green until soupy. Roll liner brush in this so it is full of paint. Use a free flowing stroke, holding brush by the end of the handle.

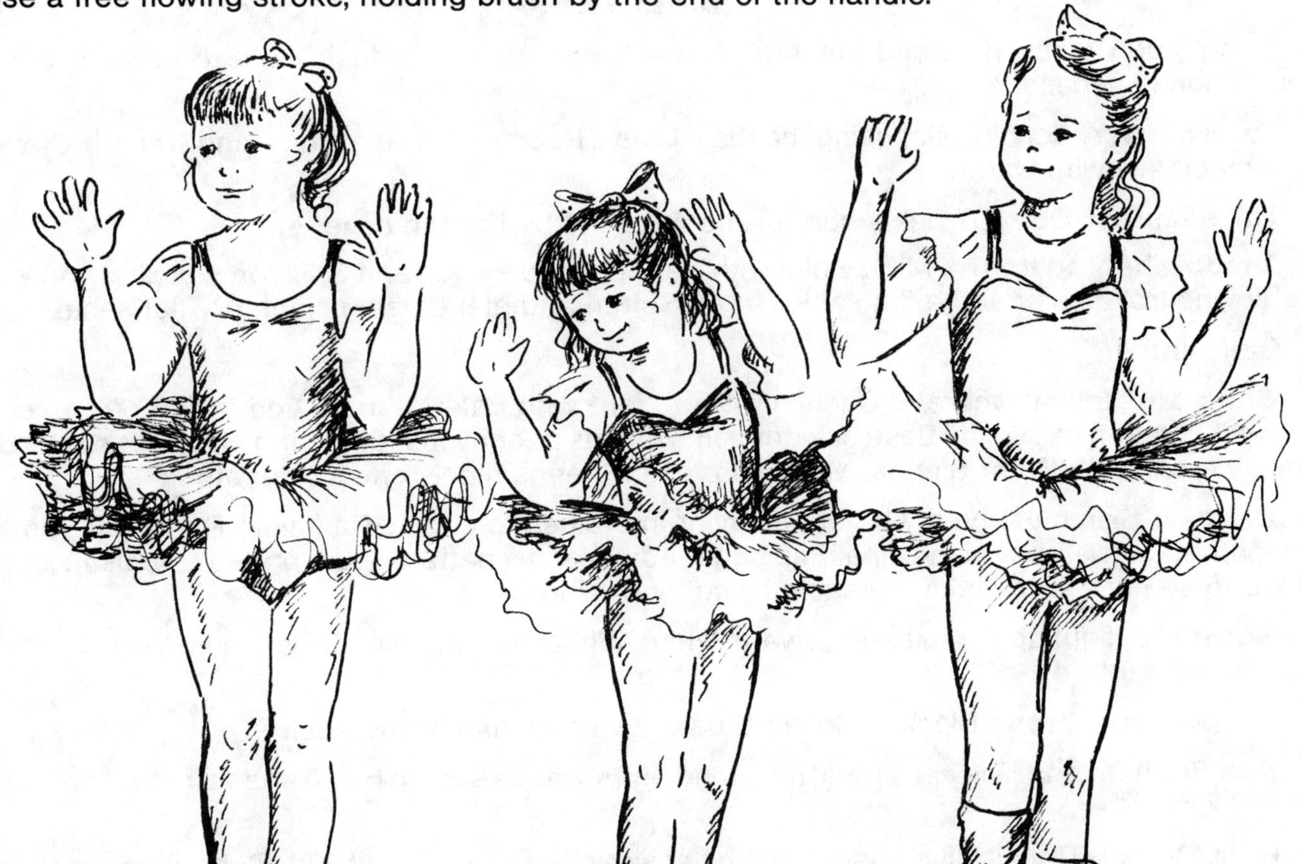

LITTLE BLUE BALLERINA

I visited a dance studio and took pictures of little girls dancing, wanting to get them while they were natural and not posing. Little did I know that when a little girl sees a camera there is a built in mechanism which says POSE!

Palette: Grumbacher Pre-Tested

Titanium White
Yellow Ochre
Cadmium Red Light
Alizarin Crimson
Acrylic Ivory - Delta Ceramcoat

Permanent Blue
Cerulean Blue
Sap Green
Thalo Yellow Green

Burnt Sienna
Burnt Umber
Ivory Black
Cobalt Blue

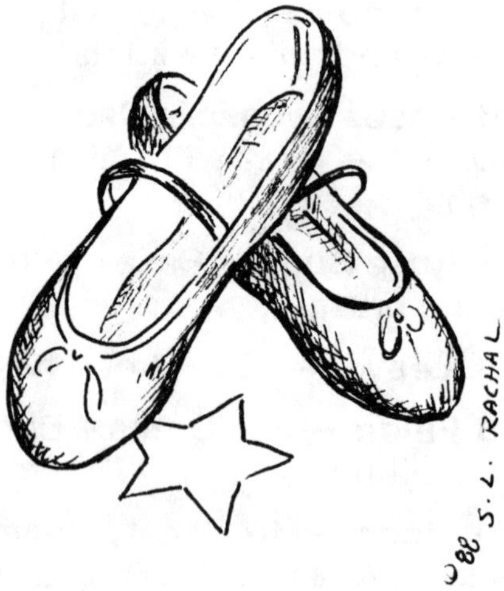

Brushes:

Langnickel 5010 (from #2 to #20), a variety of sizes.
Langnickel 2040 #0 Sunburst - synthetic small round brush.
Foam brush.
Grumbacher 7357 #1 liner.

Medium:

Copal Painting Medium.

Miscellaneous:

12 X 16 Wood piece or 12 x 16 canvas, palette, and tack cloth.

DIRECTIONS

1. Sand wood piece nice and smooth. Take off excess with a tack cloth. If using a canvas, no preparation is necessary.

2. Coat with Ivory acrylic paint using the foam brush. Kep brush strokes nice and smooth. Clean brush up immediately with water.

3. Trace pattern. Do NOT press hard or the lines will be hard to cover up.

4. **Shadow behind figure.** Mix a violet with Cerulean Blue + Alizarin Crimson + White. Apply in an up and down stroke using large flat sable (#20). Soften and blend using clean dry flat sable.

5. **Ballerina —**

Skin: Mix Yellow Ochre + Cadmium Red Light with palette knife. Add White off the corner of mixture to lighten the value. Base skin tone in with this peachy mixture using small flat sable. Blend in shadow areas with Burnt Sienna. Make sure color blends nicely one into another.

Cheeks: Skin must be dry before applying the blush to cheek. Cadmium Red Light thinned to a transparent consistency with Copal Painting Medium softly patted, and blended using small flat sable (#2). Diffuse edge with clean dry sable by softly patting.

Nose: Highlight tip of nose with a warm white, White + a pin point of Cadmium Yellow Light, using small round sable.

Eyelash and Brow: Black + Cobalt Blue drawn on using round sable.

Ear: Burnt Sienna. The ear should not stand out, so make sure to blend and soften with round sable, wiping brush often.

Hair: Black + Cobalt Blue based in with flat sable (#14). Highlight with Cerulean Blue with round sable using short strokes flowing the direction the hair flows.

Hair Clips: Just dots of warm white, White + Cadmium Yellow Light on tip of round sable.

Blouse and Leotards: A pale white, White + Cerulean Blue, based in with flat sable (#16). After dry, glaze in shadow with Cerulean Blue + Copal Painting Medium.

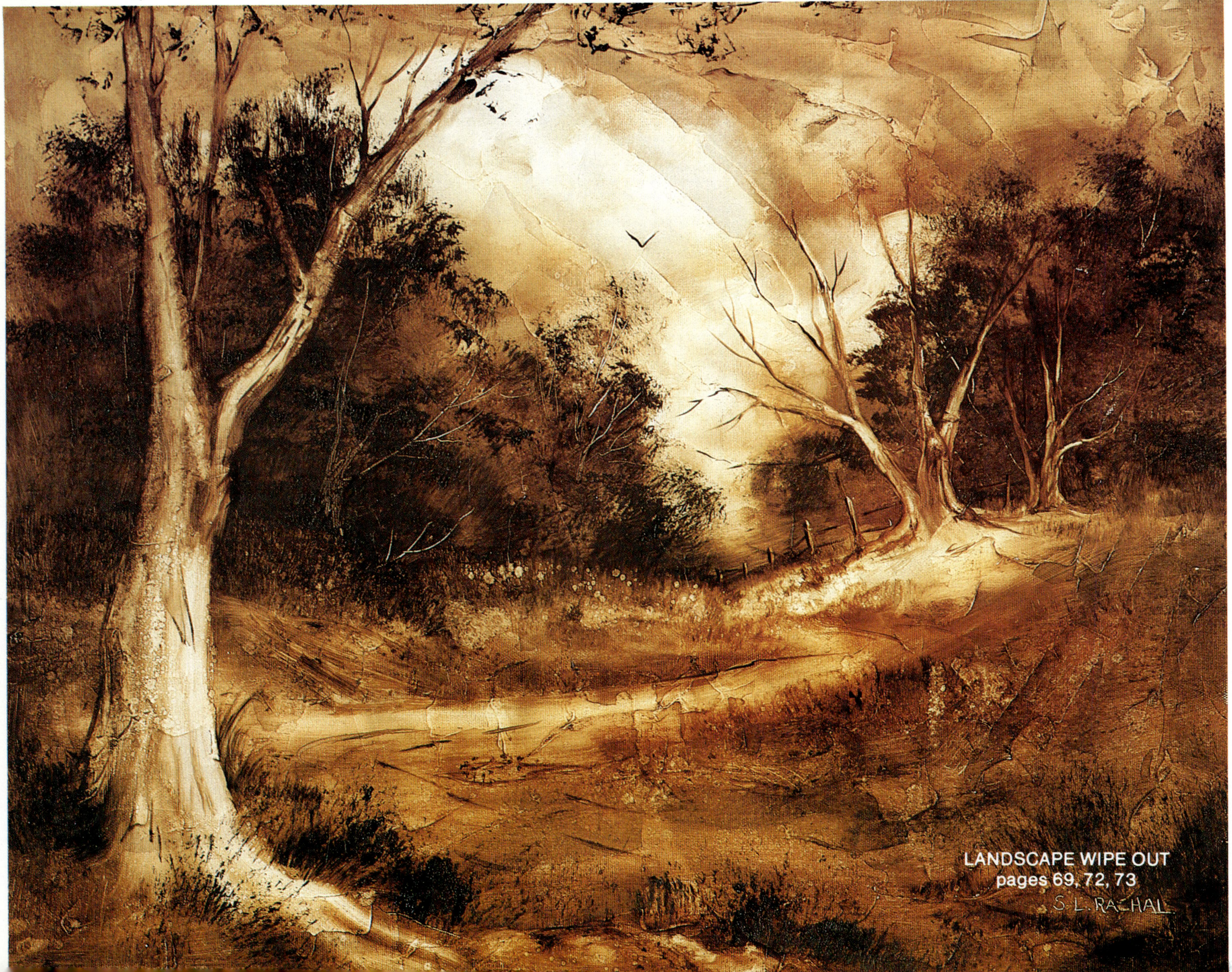

LANDSCAPE WIPE OUT
pages 69, 72, 73

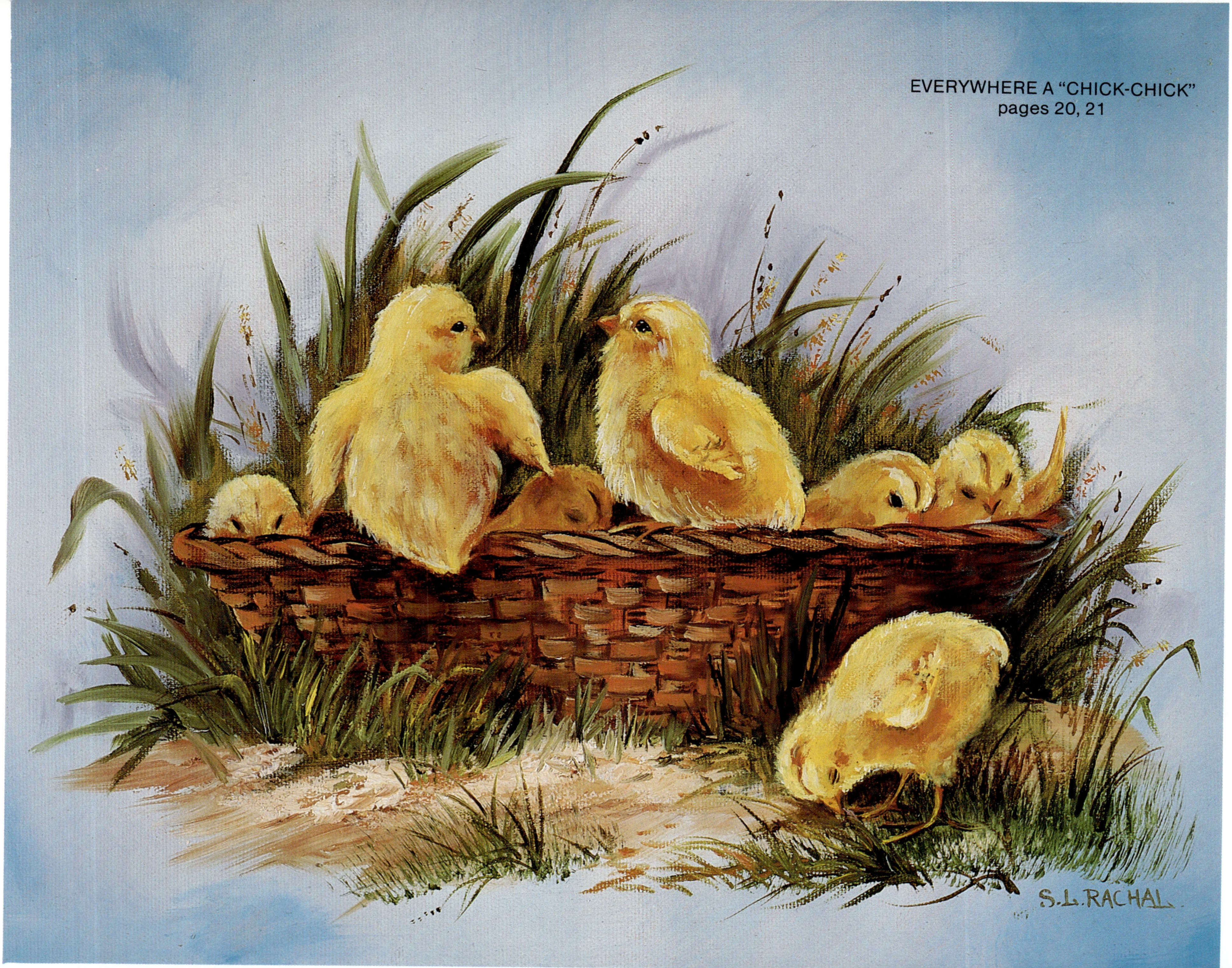

EVERYWHERE A "CHICK-CHICK"
pages 20, 21

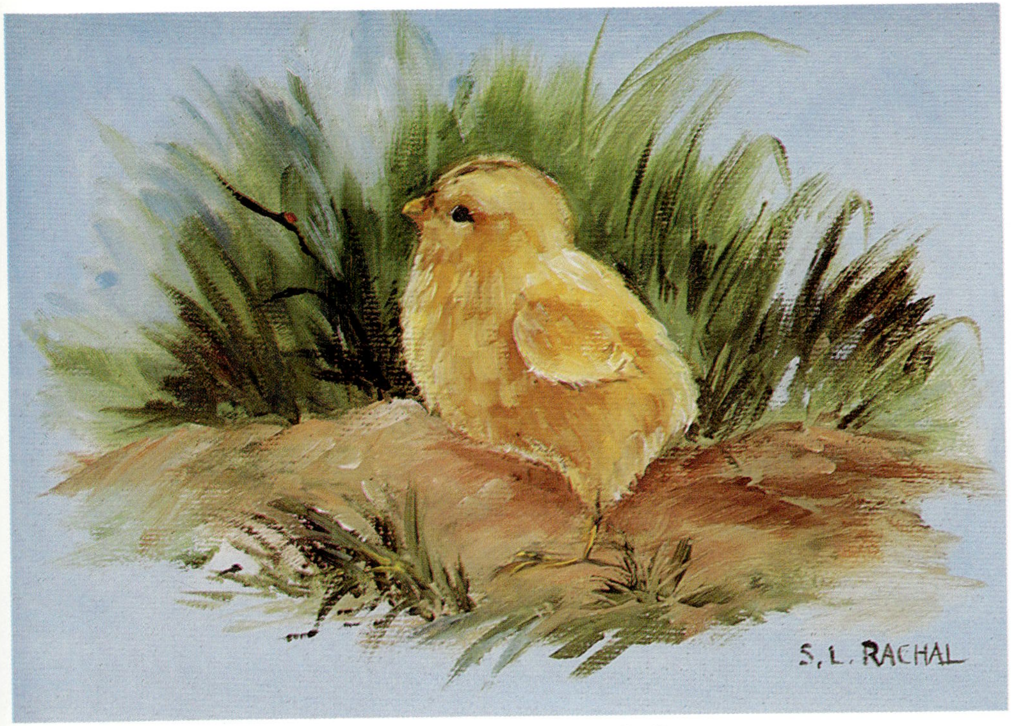

"HERE CHICK-THERE CHICK"
pages 22, 23

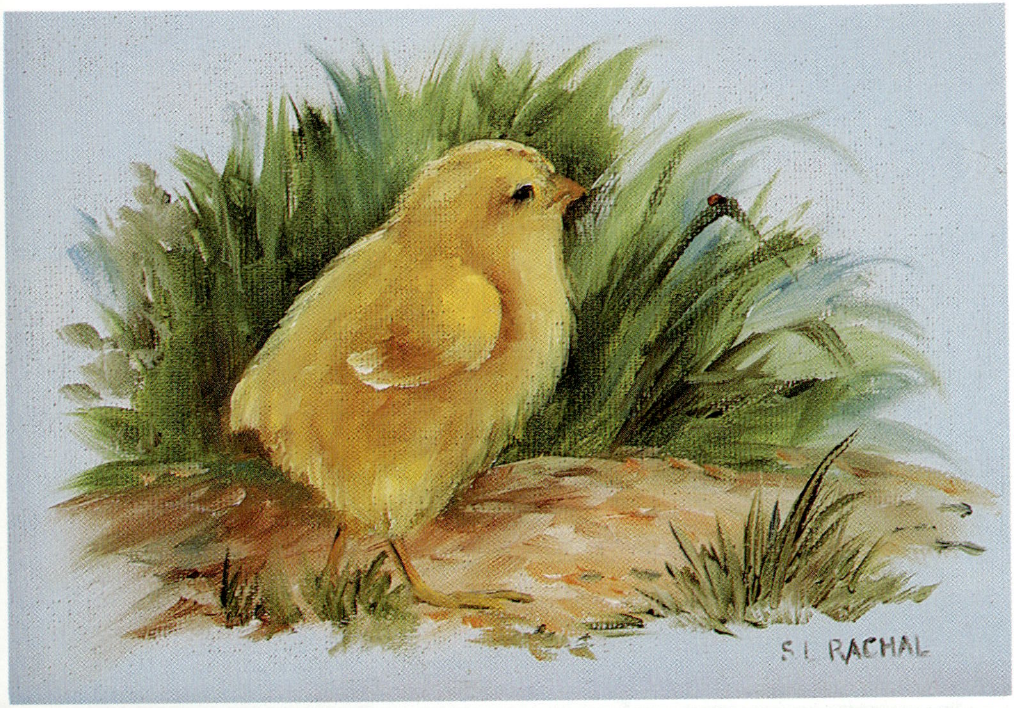

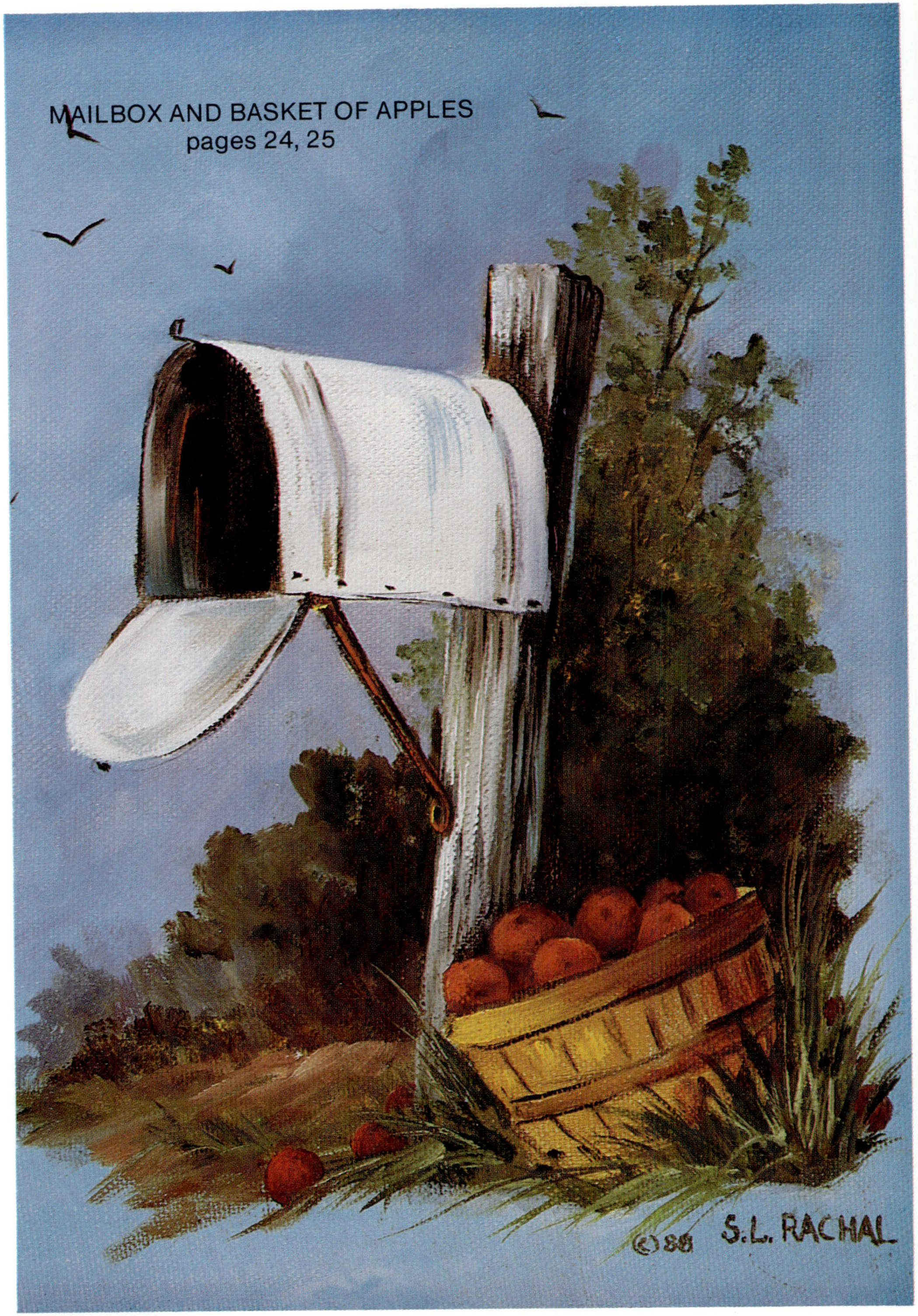

MAILBOX AND BASKET OF APPLES
pages 24, 25

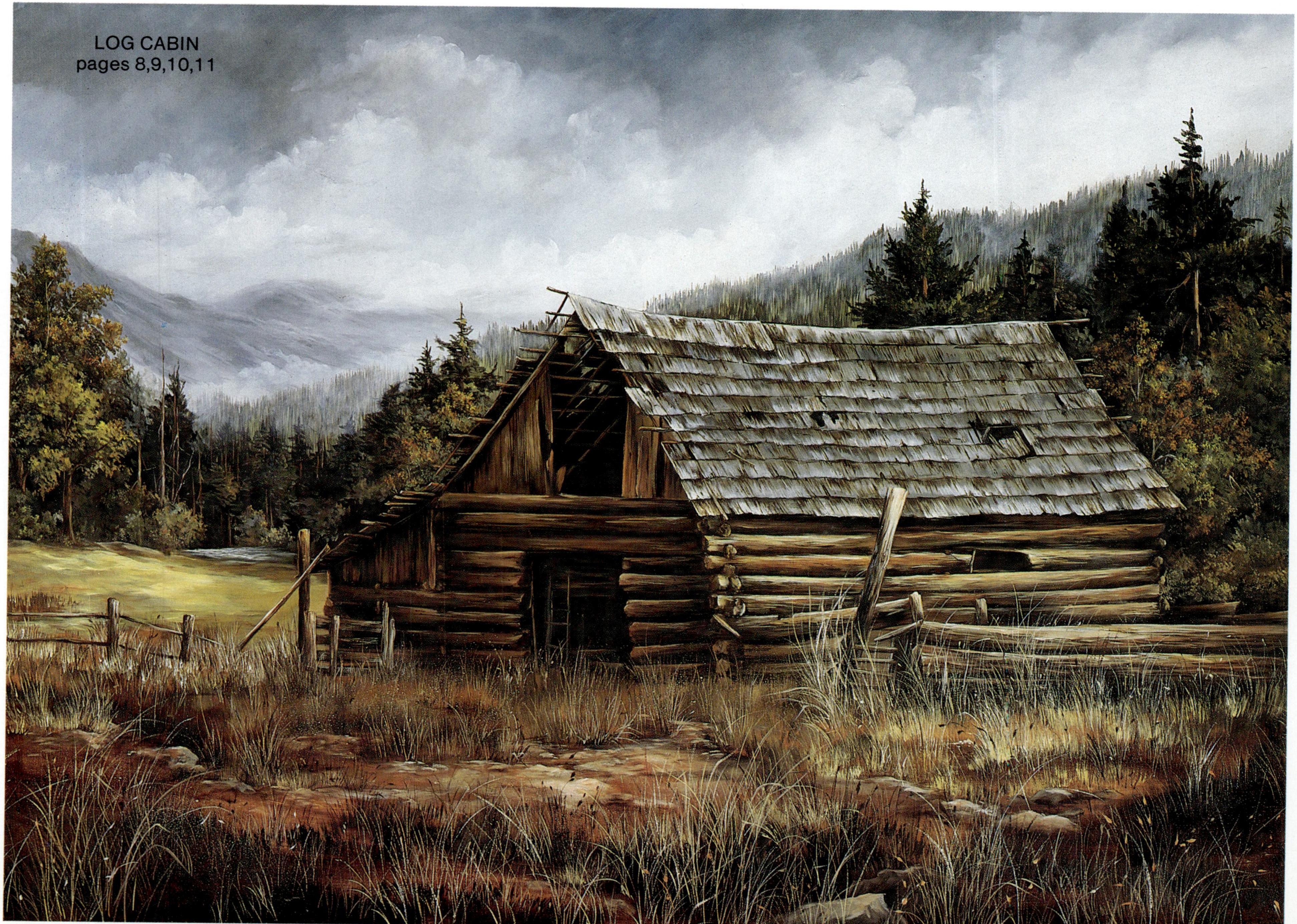

LOG CABIN
pages 8,9,10,11

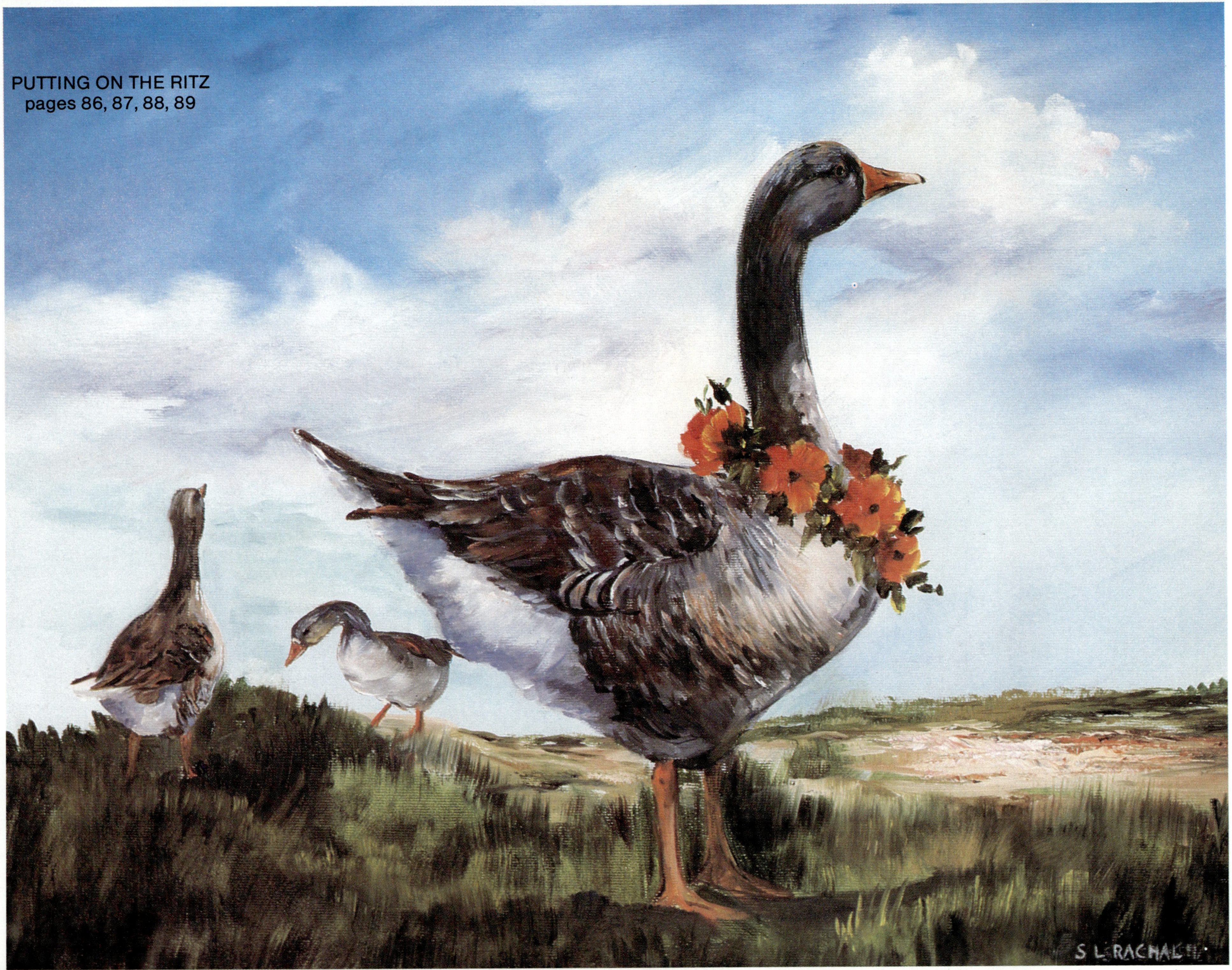

PUTTING ON THE RITZ
pages 86, 87, 88, 89

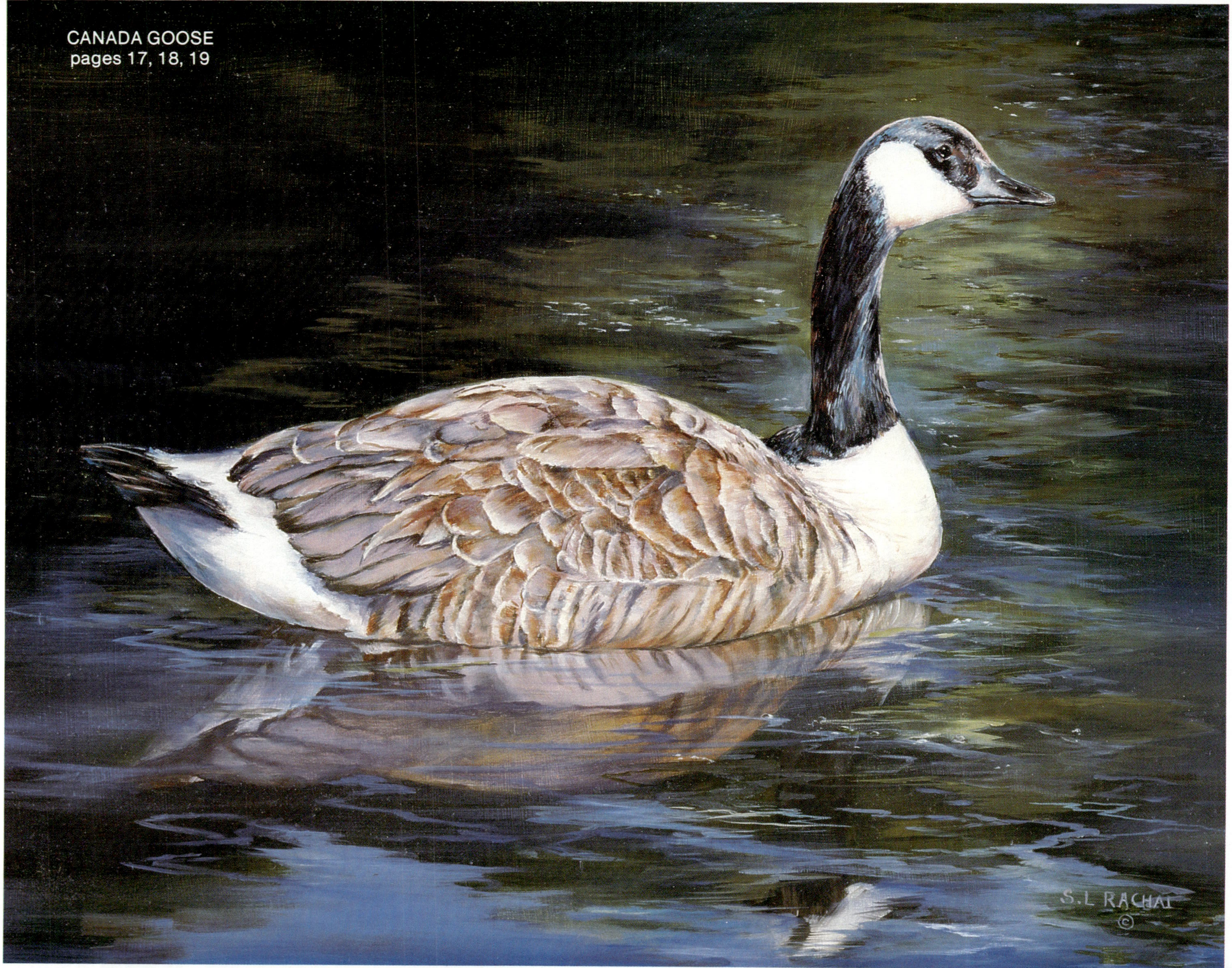

CANADA GOOSE
pages 17, 18, 19

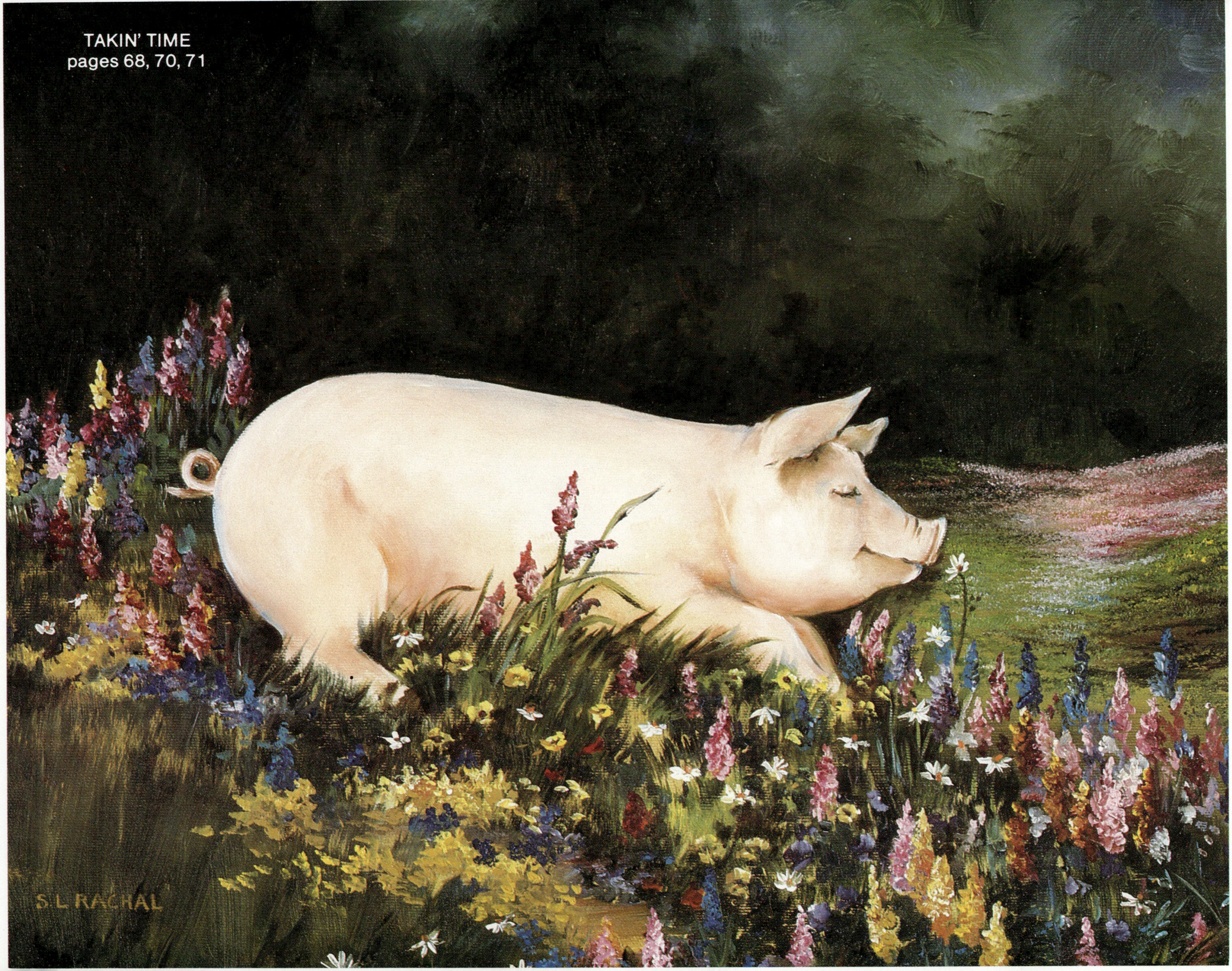

TAKIN' TIME
pages 68, 70, 71

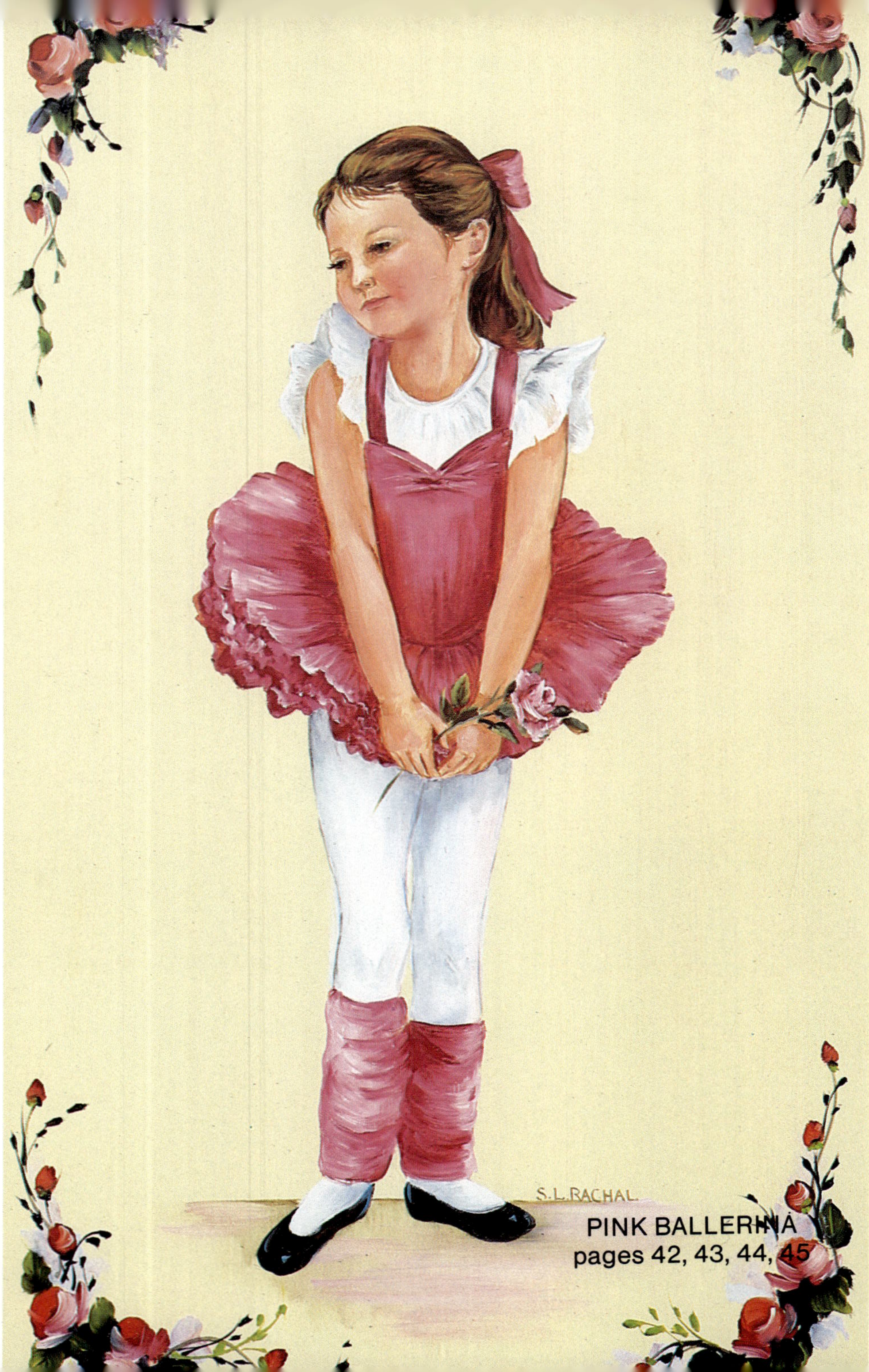

PINK BALLERINA
pages 42, 43, 44, 45

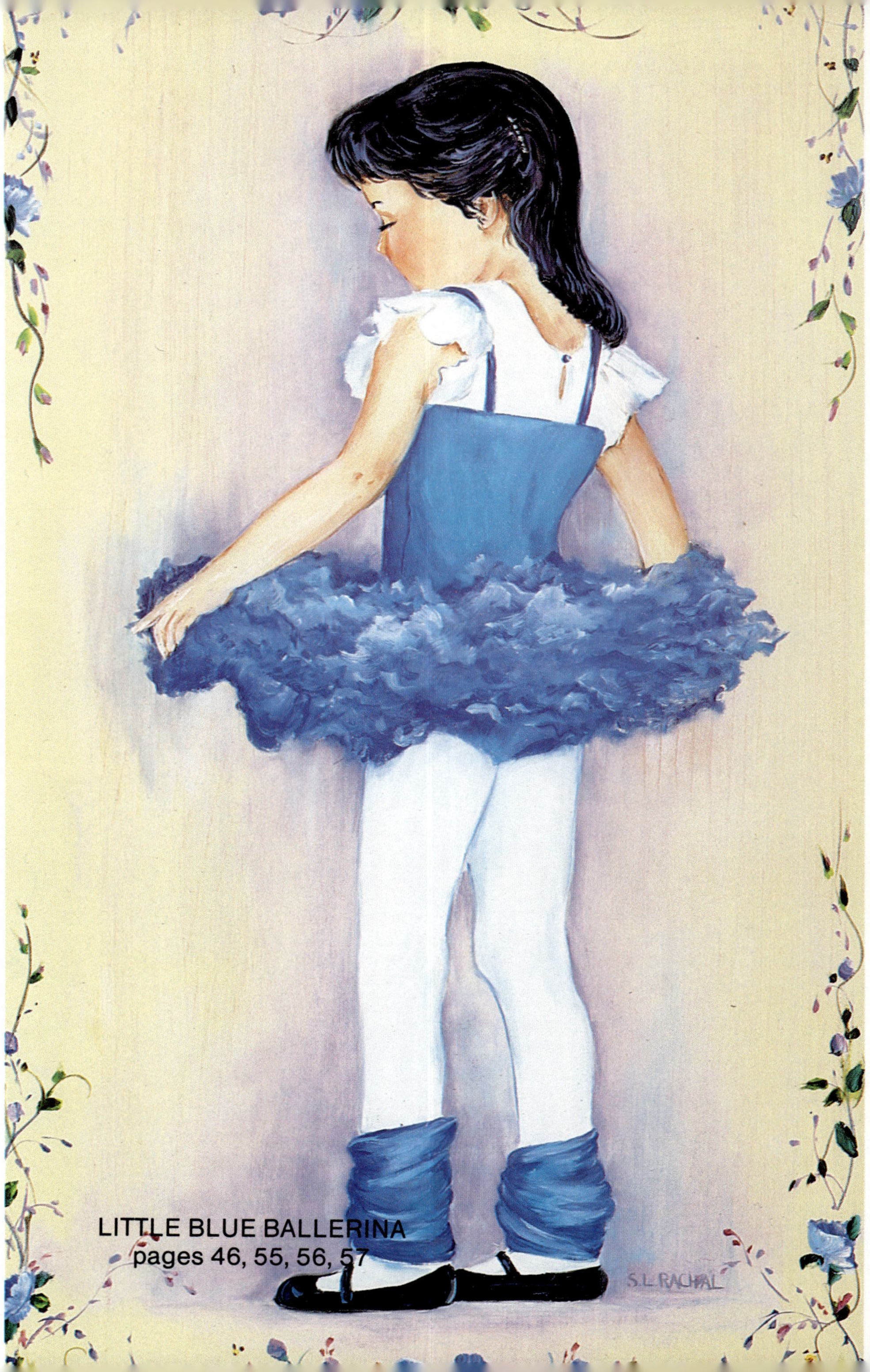

LITTLE BLUE BALLERINA
pages 46, 55, 56, 57

Leg Warmers: Use #16 flat sable.
Dark: Permanent Blue.
Mid-tone: Cerulean Blue.
Light: White + Cerulean Blue.

Top of Tu-Tu: Base in top of tu-tu with Cerulean Blue and shadow with Permanent Blue using #14 sable.

Tu-Tu: Work off corner edge of flat sable, like making "U's" up down and up down.

Dark: Permanent Blue.
Mid-tone: Cerulean Blue.
Light: White + Cerulean Blue.

Shoes: Black and highlight with Cerulean Blue.

6. **Flowers on Edges** — Underpaint with Permanent Blue in half circles. Top petal is White + Cerulean Blue. Start on outside of petal and stroke down toward inside of flower using small flat sable. This takes a very light touch.

7. **Leaves** — A push-pull-lift stroke with a small round sable. Use Sap Green highlighted with Thalo Yellow Green.

8. **Liner Work** — All liner work is done with soupy paint. Thin paint with Copal Painting Medium, and roll liner brush in it. Hold brush at end of the handle using free flowing strokes. Sap Green + Burnt Umber. Violet mixture, Cerulean Blue + Alizarin Crimson + White. Don't worry if you make a mistake, just wipe off with a rag, and start all over.

9. **Little Pink Flowers** — These are a dot of pink, White + Cadmium Red Light, using tip of small round sable.

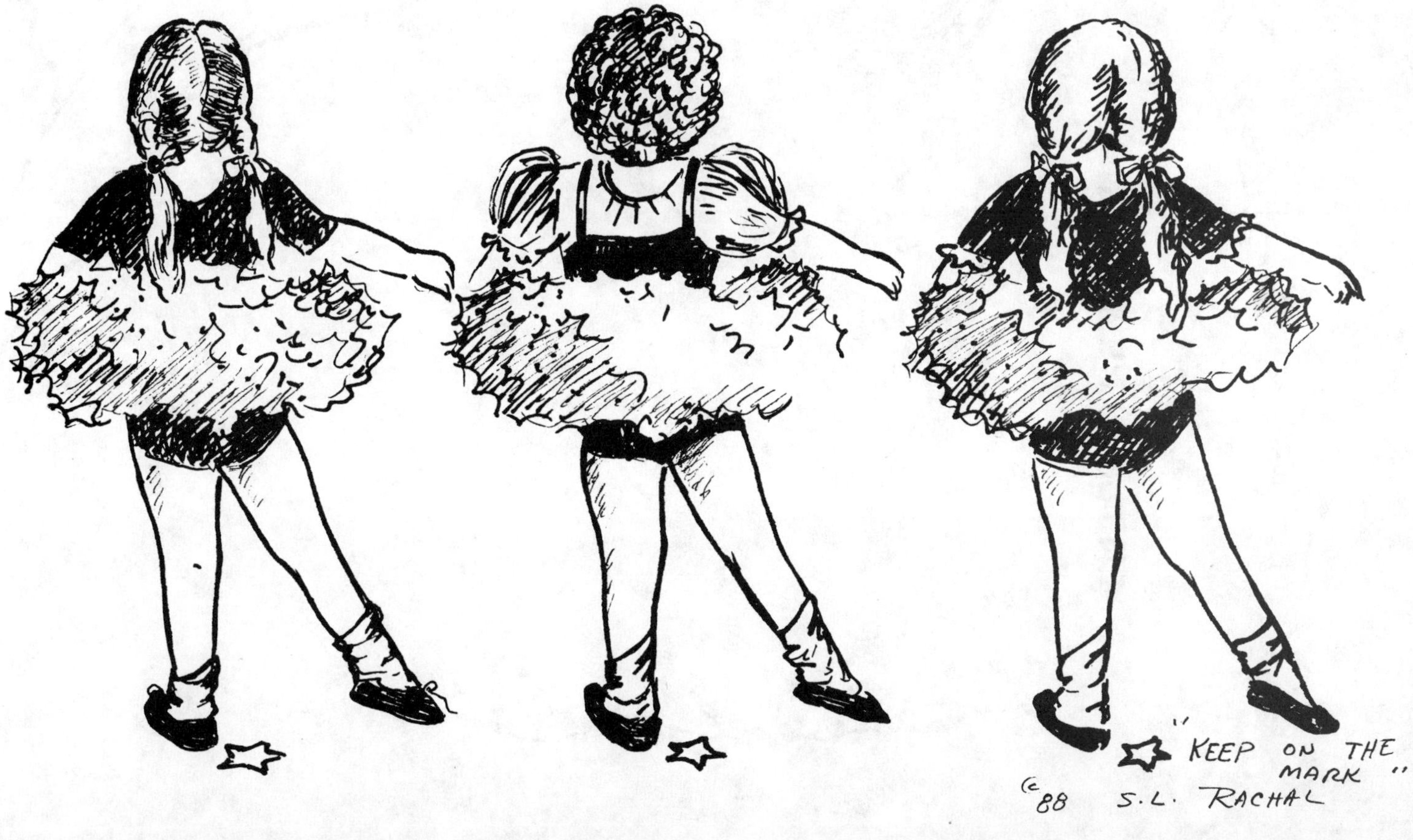

LITTLE BLUE BALLERINA

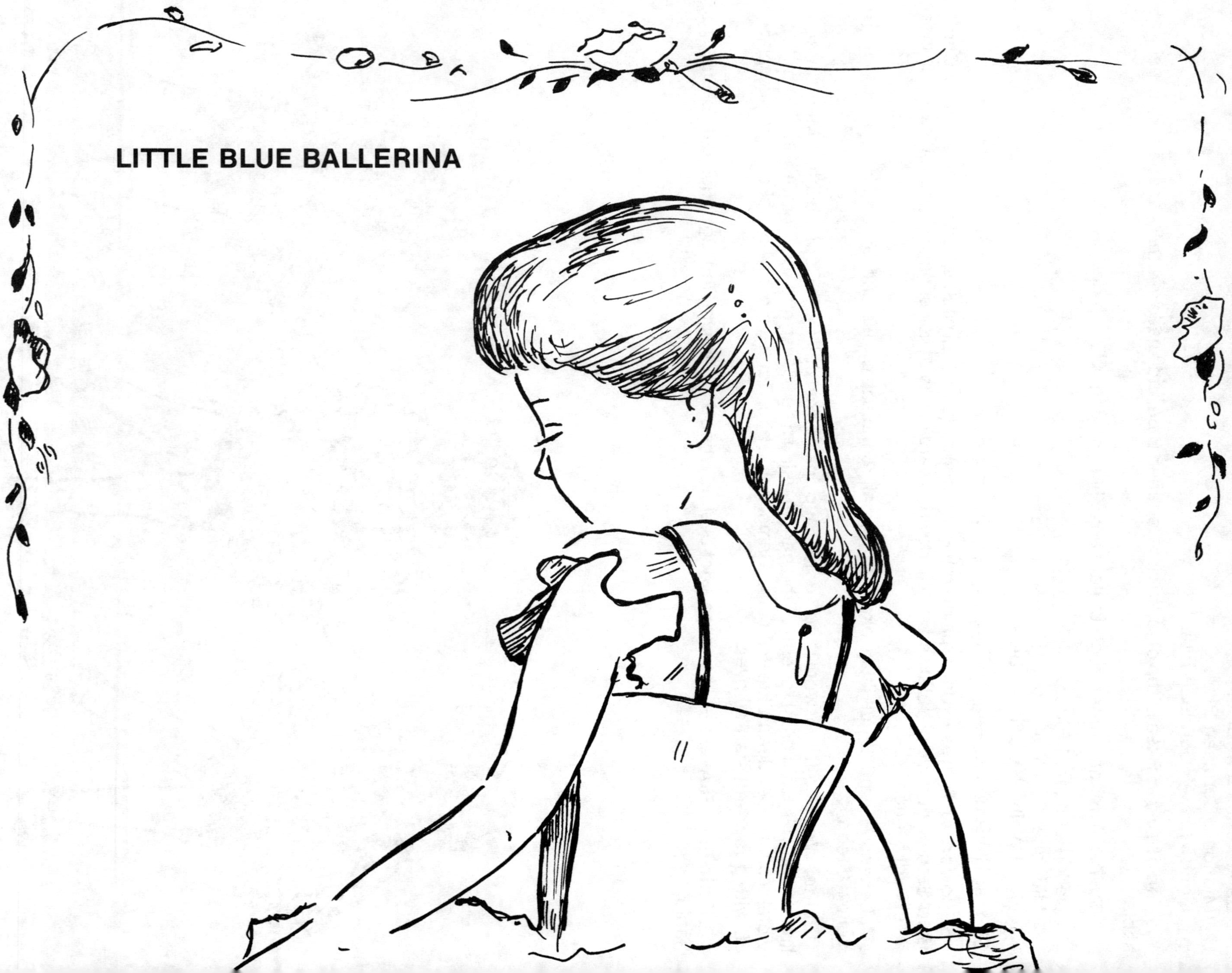

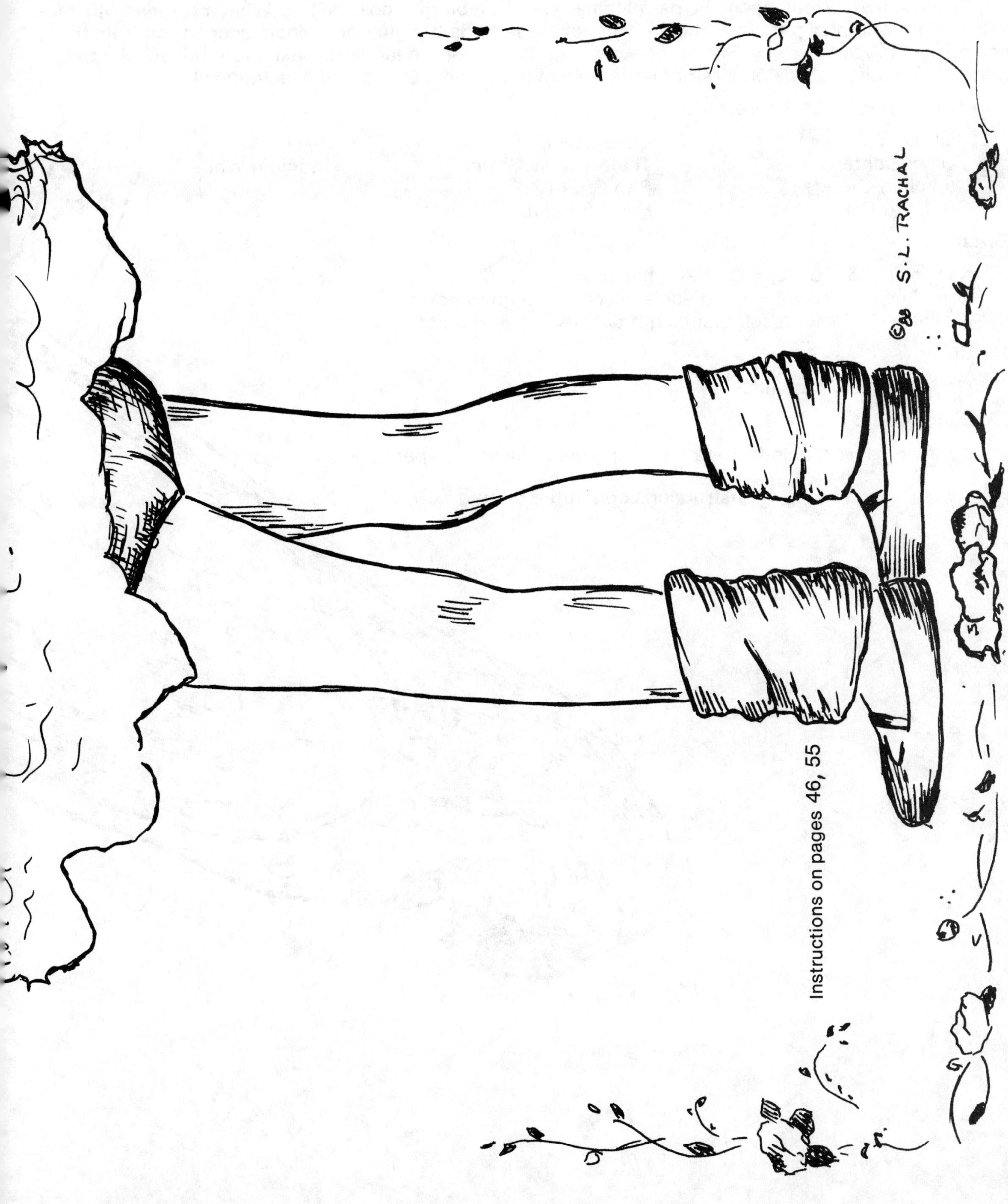

Instructions on pages 46, 55

BLUE AND GOLD MACAW

The Macaw is a member of the parrot family and it is a brightly colored bird. What a surprise when I walked into our local pet store and saw one of these birds hanging on a chain suspended from the ceiling, just jabbering away. He wasn't even caged up. I bet the landlord wasn't too thrilled with this, because the bird had eaten a rather large hole in the ceiling. Course he was friendly!

Palette: Grumbacher Pre-Tested

Cadmium Yellow Light
Yellow Ochre
Cadmium Orange
Cerulean Blue
Cobalt Blue
Thalo Yellow Green
Sap Green
Burnt Sienna
Black
Titanium White

Brushes:

Langnickel 5010 #2, #18, #20 - flat sable
Grumbacher 178 #1 - round sable which has a good point
Peacock 145 #9 - a soft blending brush, feels like rabbit fur

Medium:

Copal Painting Medium.

Miscellaneous:

12 X 16 canvas, palette knife for mixing paint, palette, paper towels or rags.

Instructions continued on page 60, 61

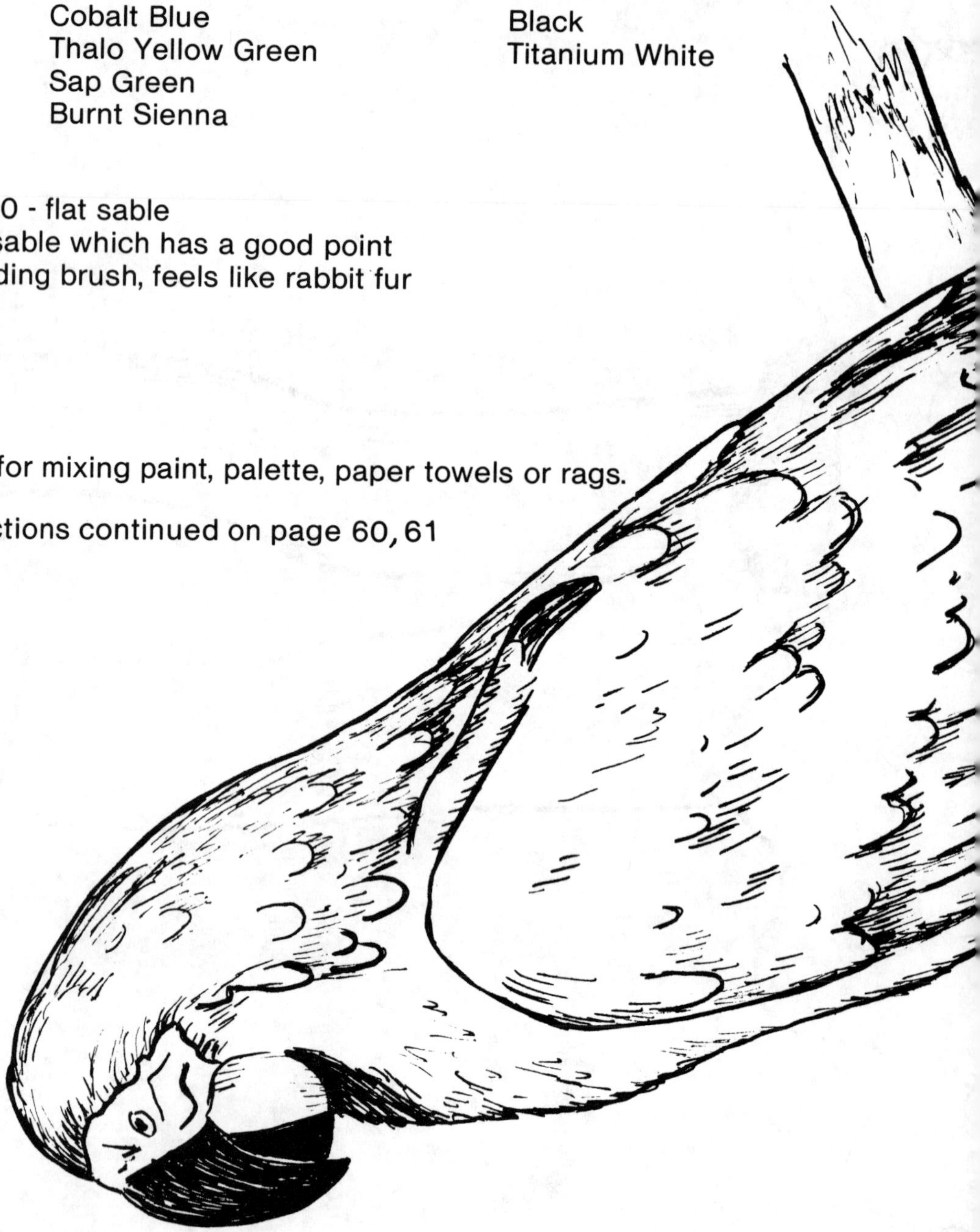

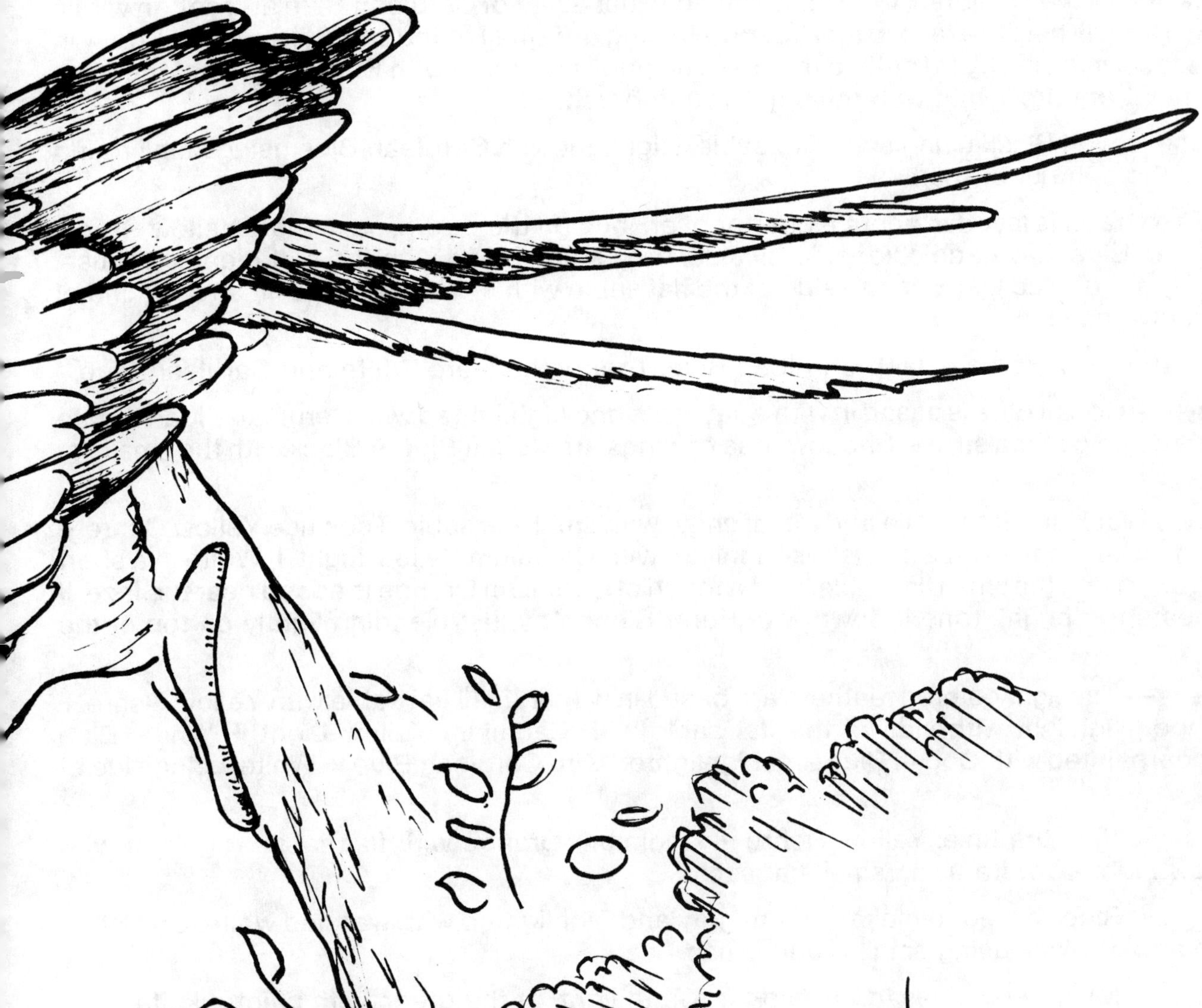
S.L. TRACHAL
©88

BLUE AND GOLD MACAW

DIRECTIONS

1. Trace the Macaw and limb onto a 12 X 16 canvas very carefully.

2. The Macaw will be painted first before the background so that the hand can be rested upon the canvas while doing details without smearing the paint.

Macaw: Mix White with just a hint of Cadmium Orange with the palette knife. The color will be a warmed white, not peachy. Base in face with this warmed white using a small flat sable. Blend and pat just a hint of Black into the chin area, then blend and pat just a hint of Cerulean Blue and soften with a clean dry brush. This will help the face to look round. Holding the small round sable like a pencil, draw in the lines on the face with Black and outline the eye. The pupil is painted with Black. Highlight the pupil with just a pin point of pure White with the small round brush.

3. **Beak** — Base in with Black using small flat sable. Highlight with Cerulean Blue using small round brush, following the contour of the beak.

4. **Crown** — Sap Green is layed in about a quarter of an inch on the crown, next Thalo Yellow Green, and then Cerulean Blue. Lay each color side by side, then softly blend with the soft blending brush. Feathers are only suggested by using the side of the flat sable with a push, pull and lift stroke (kind of like an upside down comma).

5. **Shoulder Wing** — Underpaint with Cerulean Blue. The feathers are White and Cerulean Blue.

6. **Lower Wings** — Cobalt Blue is based in with a flat sable and highlighted with Cerulean Blue + White using the upside down comma stroke. Shadow area of wings are Cobalt Blue + Black with the small flat sable.

7. **Chest** — Base Black under the chin and top of chest with small flat sable. Then use Yellow Ochre + Cadmium Orange with medium size flat sable. Highlight with Cadmium Yellow Light + White in a short over-lapping stroke using the small flat sable. Just a touch of Cadmium Orange is added near the face. If the yellow appears too bright, tone it down with Burnt Sienna by just blending lightly on top of the yellow.

8. **Tail Feathers** — The light colored feathers are based in with a small flat sable with Yellow Ochre + Cadmium Orange. Highlight with side of the flat sable with Cadmium Yellow Light + White. Blue feathers are underpainted with Cobalt Blue and highlighted with Cerulean Blue + White, using side of the flat sable.

9. **Leg** — This is called the tibia. Yellow Ochre + Cadmium Orange with flat sable. Highlight with Cadmium Yellow Light + White using small flat sable.

10. **Feet** — White + Black mixed to make a warm gray and highlighted with warmed white. Underline feet with a thin line of Black using small round brush.

11. **Background** — Mix three values (dark, mid-tone, and light) of the green with palette knife.

Dark value: Sap Green + Burnt Sienna.
Mid-tone: Come off the corner of the dark value and add Yellow Ochre. Do not mix directly into the center of the color.
Light: add Cadmium Yellow Light to the mid-tone mixture.

Make a "U" around the bird for placement of background color. Darkest value will be near lower portion of picture and lighter as it nears the head of the bird. Do not paint a ring around the bird or it will look like a ghost. Using a criss-cross brush stroke, brush away from the bird, then blend with a soft blending brush. Wipe the brush often with a paper towel as you are blending. Criss-cross Cadmium Orange into parts of the upper portion of the background. The orange will mute into the background without being too bright and will add warmth.

12. **Limb** — Burnt Sienna + White with a side stroke using the flat sable. Soften and blend edges with the soft blending brush. Highlight with Cadmium Oarnge + White. On lower portion of limb paint the reflected light with Cerulean Blue + White with small round brush, working on the tip of brush.

13. **Leaves** — Mix Thalo Yellow Green + Cerulean Blue to make a bluish mixture. The leaves are little heart shapes. Draw a line and pull back brush toward the line. Highlight with Cerulean Blue + White usign small flat sable.

14. **Bushes** — Hold flat sable like a pencil, now twist and turn brush in fingers while dabbing against the canvas with Thalo Yellow Green. This will make an irregular shape. Soften with the soft blending brush.

Look at your painting. Do you need to do any more to it? Hold your painting up to a mirror. If something is incorrect, the mirror will show it. I usually paint my pictures and try not to look at them for at least a week. Then when I look at them, I have a new and fresh look. Most beginners make the mistake of over-working their painting. (This means doing too much.) It is better if you just put the brush down when you can't figure out what else you should do.

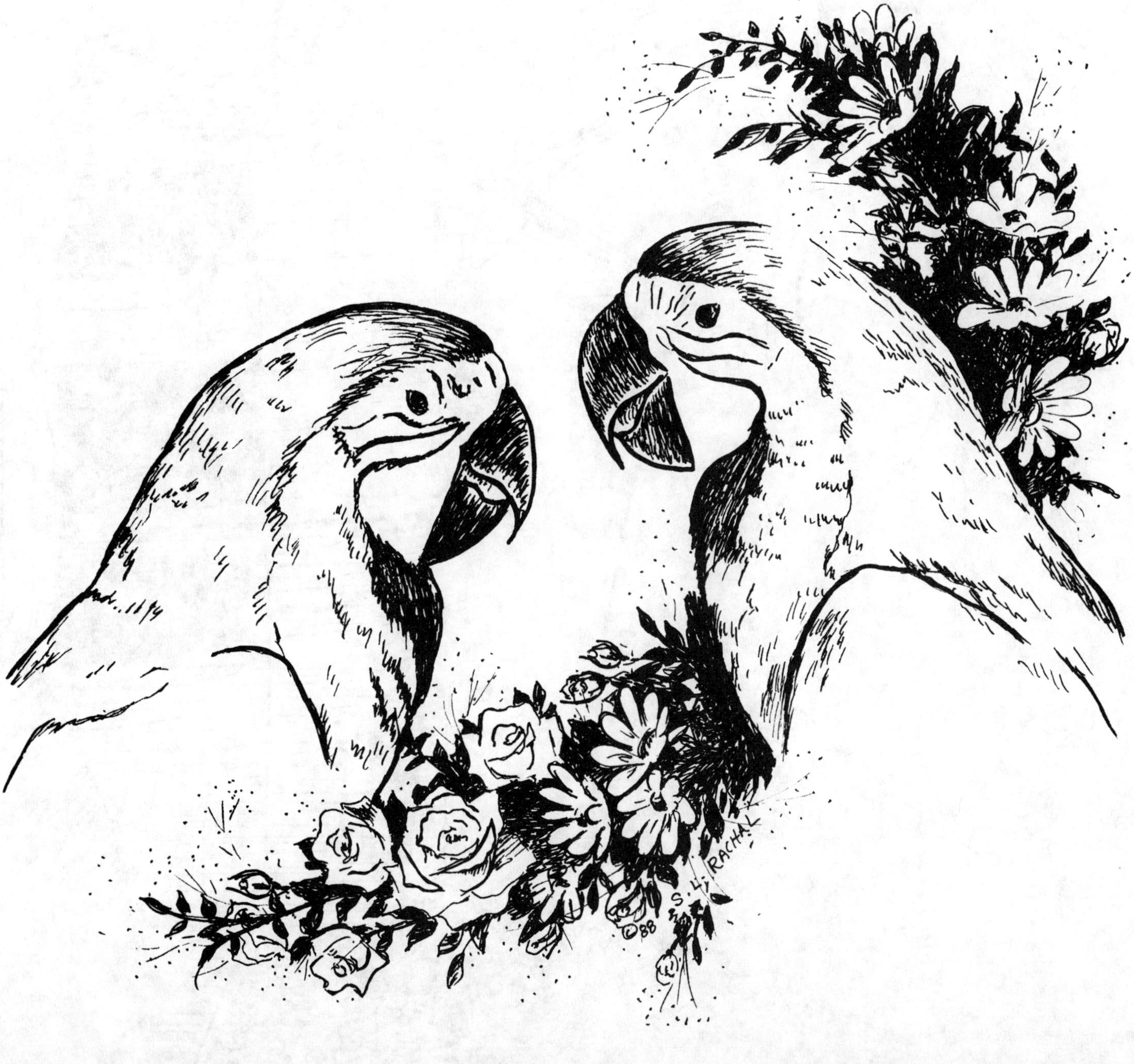

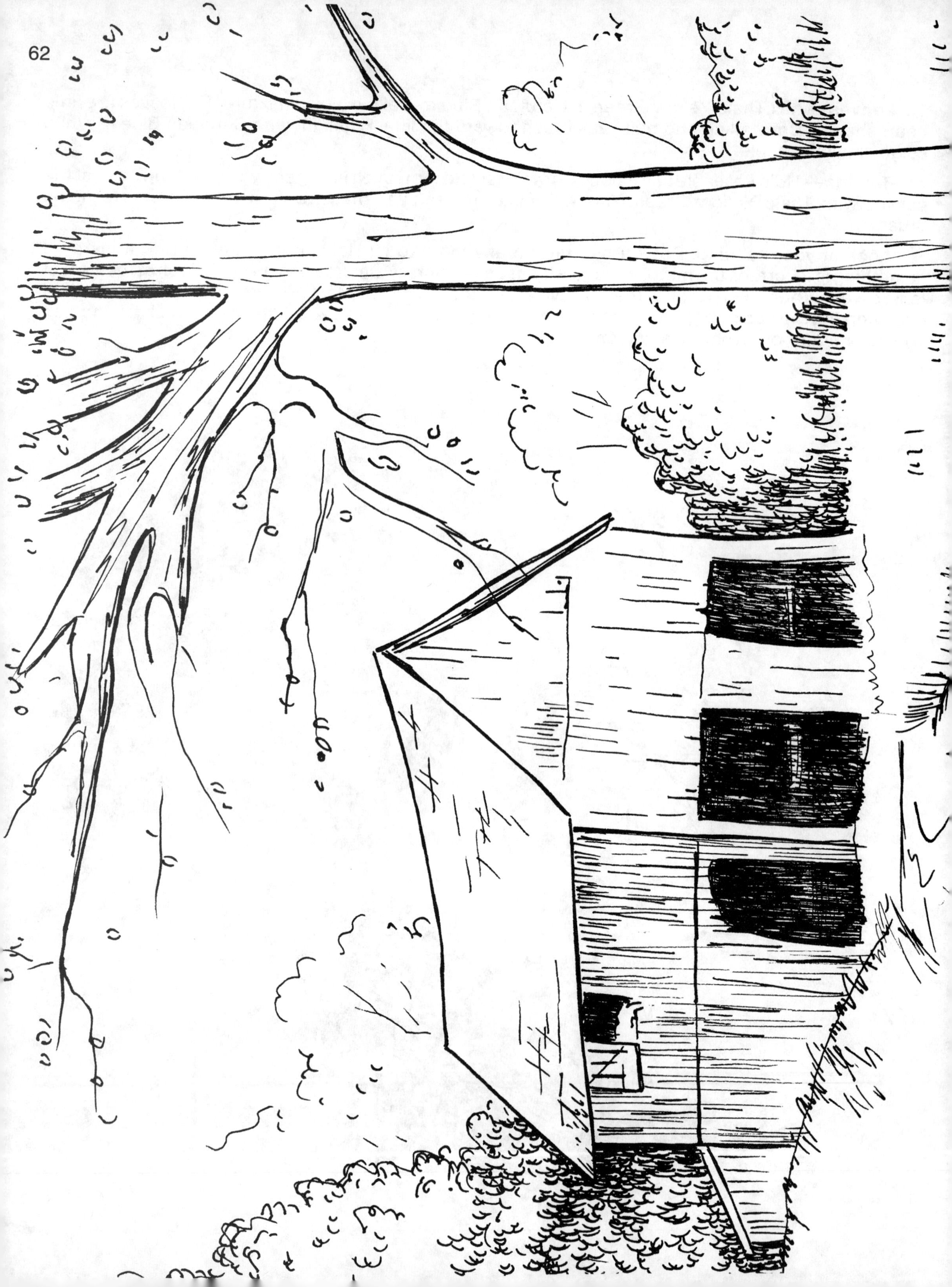

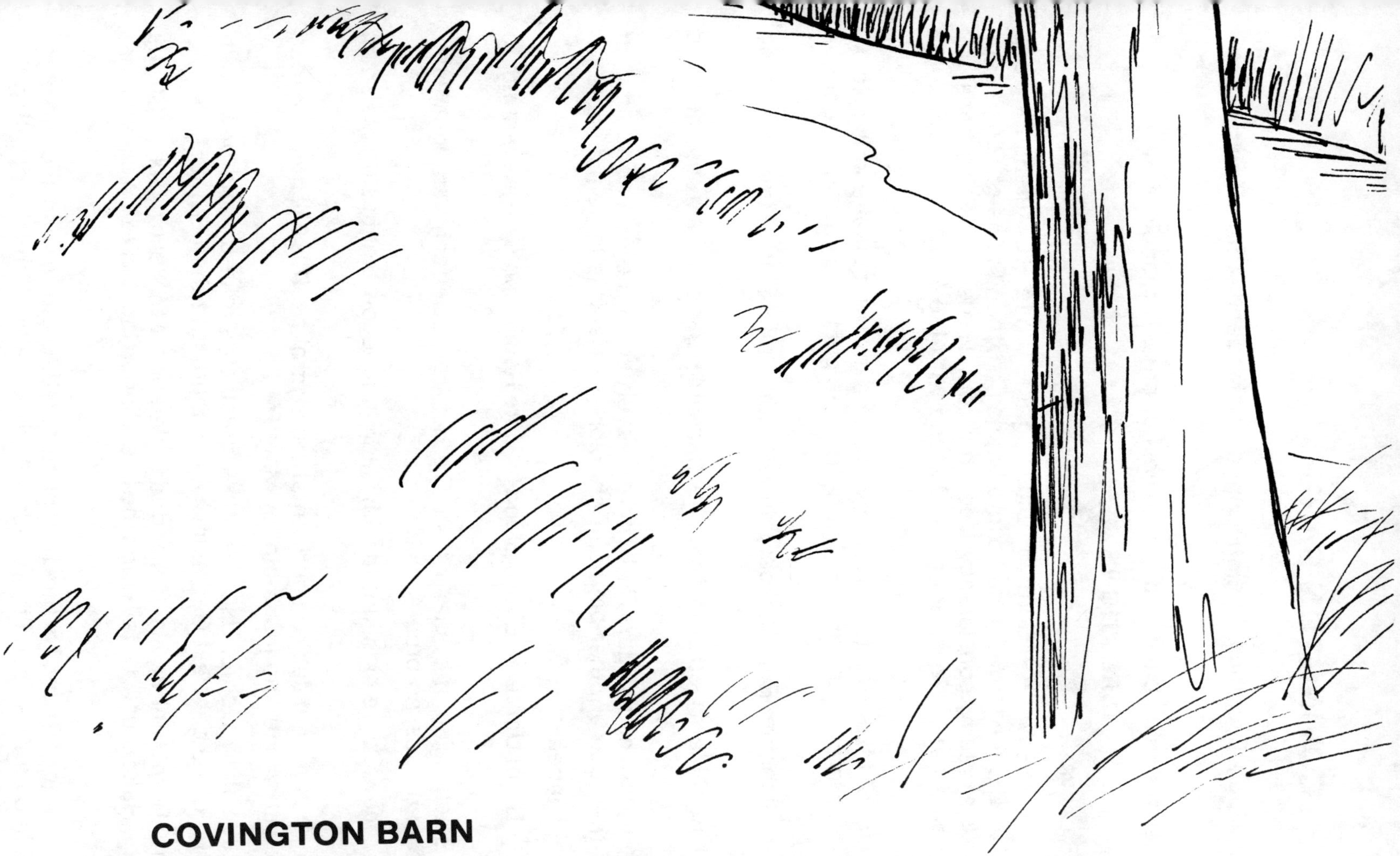

COVINGTON BARN

This barn is painted in a wet into wet technique. This means it was painted all at one sitting. It is lots of fun, try it.

Palette: Grumbacher Pre-Tested

- Cadmium Yellow Light
- Yellow Ochre
- Mars Red
- Sap Green
- Cerulean Blue
- Burnt Sienna
- Black
- Titanium White

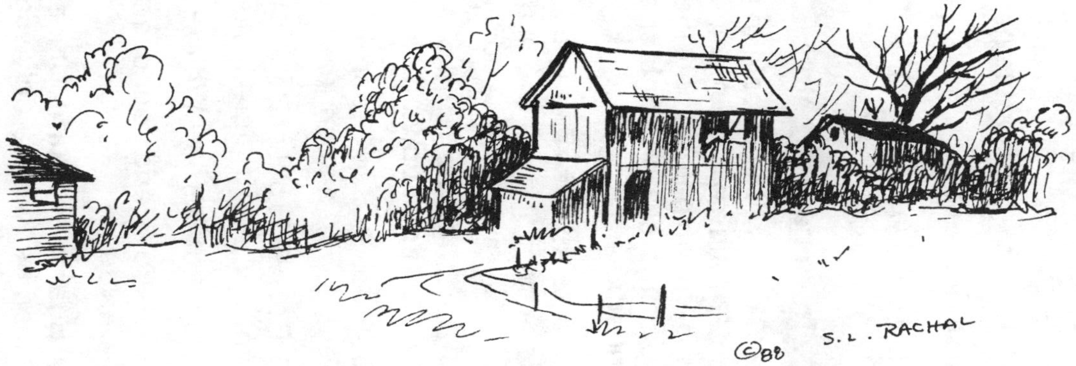

Brushes:

- Langnickel 5010 #8 and #20 - A flat sable
- Grumbacher 7357 #1 - A liner
- Peacock 145 #8 or #9 - A blending brush.
- An old toothbrush

Instructions on page 64

COVINGTON BARN

Medium:

Liquin — A durable non-yellowing alkyd and oil painting medium. It speeds the drying time up.

Miscellaneous:

12 X 16 canvas, a sponge, palette knife, palette, paper towels or rags, Turpenoid.

DIRECTIONS

1. Trace pattern onto a 12 x 16 canvas.

2. **Sky** — Mix with palette knife. Dark — White + Cerulean Blue. Light — White + Cerulean Blue and lighten value by adding more White. Dip the large flat sable into Liquin first, then the paint. Blend back and forth on palette until the paint is a creamy consistency. Use a horizontal brush stroke, darker at the top of the sky and lighter as it nears the horizon. Soften and blend with the Hake brush until it is smooth.

3. **Distant Trees** — Add just a hint of Mars Red to the sky mixture and mix with palette knife. Hold a piece of sponge between thumb and forefinger, squeeze lightly, dip into paint and dab onto tree tops. This will give a light and airy look.

4. **Distant Tree Trunks** — Roll the liner into Burnt Umber thinned with Liquin. Start at the base of the trunk and pull upward and lift up.

5. **Trees** — Sap Green + just a hint of Mars Red mixed with the flat sable. Base in the trees, then dab the tips with a sponge.

6. **Barn** — Front of Barn — White + just a hint of Mars Red. This red is very strong so just use about a pin point of color, if more is needed then add another pin point of color etc. Use the large flat sable.

   Side of Barn — White + Burnt Umber.

   Windows and door openings — Burnt Umber + Black. Blend in Mars Red in spots to give warmth to the inside.

   Boards — Burnt Umber + Black using the liner brush. Do not paint perfectly straight lines. Remember we are only suggesting boards, so break a line.

   Hay — This is inside of barn. Yellow Ochre highlighted with Cadmium Yellow Light using the small flat sable brush.

7. **Road** — White + Burnt Umber using a flat sable in horizontal brush strokes. This will help the road to appear to lay down. Highlight with White and just a hint of Mars Red.

8. **Field** — Underpaint first with Yellow Ochre. Use the Hake brush to stroke up and down with Cerulean Blue + White toward the distance. Next Cadmium Yellow Light and then Burnt Umber.

9. **Grass in Front** — Sap Green + Burnt Umber. Black is added to darker areas. Yellow Ochre. Stroke at a slight angle to the right with the Hake brush. Detail using the liner dipped into White + Yellow Ochre using long sweeping strokes.

10. **Tree** — Underpaint with Burnt Umber. Let dry. Texture is applied with the palette knife. Pick up paint on knife, lay flat on canvas, push into canvas, then lift up. This will create a suction thus creating the texture. Do not thin paint, it should be thick.

    Dark — Burnt Umber + Black
    Mid-Tone — Mars Red
    Light — Yellow Ochre
    Highlight — Yellow Ochre + White
    Reflected Light — Cerulean Blue + White. If color appears to bright just pat with the palette knife and the color will smudge into trunk.

11. **Leaves** — Sap Green + Black. Use the corner edge of the small flat sable and dab on in a push and lift up stroke.

12. Spatter some color on the grass by using an old toothbrush. Dip into White thinned with Turpenoid. Drag thumb across the bristles, toward oneself and the color will splatter out toward the canvas. Cover any area which you don't want splattered with a paper towel.

ELLIE'S PLACE

This is a wet into wet technique. That means it was painted all at once. However, I cheated. After it dryed, I used a ball point marker and drew the lines in on front of the barn. Make sure your marker is a permanent marker..

Palette: Grumbacher Pre-Tested

Cadmium Yellow Light
Yellow Ochre
Cadmium Orange (very little)
White
Cerulean Blue
Olive Green (could use another green like Sap)
Burnt Umber
Burnt Sienna

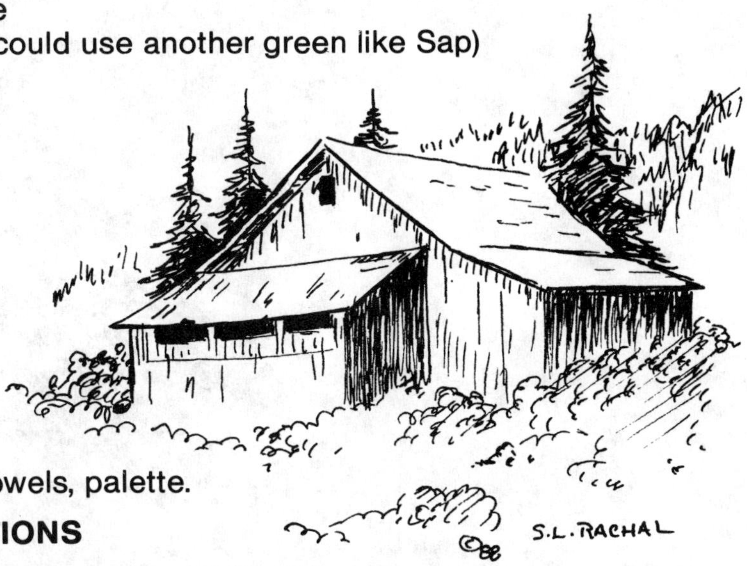

Brushes:

Langnickel 5010 #8 and #20 - A flat sable.
Grumbacher 4229 #6 - A filbert brush.
Peacock 145 #9 - A blending brush.

Medium:

Turpenoid

Miscellaneous:

12 X 16 canvas, sponge, palette knife, paper towels, palette.

DIRECTIONS

1. Trace pattern onto a 12 x 16 canvas.

2. **Sky** — White + Cerulean Blue and just a hint of Burnt Umber. Use long sweeping strokes with the flat sable. The clouds are layed in the same way with White + Cadmium Orange, a peachy hue. Softly diffuse color by blending with the Hake brush in the opposite direction.

3. Distant Trees — Cerulean blue + Burnt Umber and lightened by adding White. Apply in an up and down stroke using the side of the filbert brush.

4. **Pine Trees** — Make a straight line with Olive Green, now make "Z's" across the line — larger ones at the bottom and smaller as they near the top, this is a guide. Work off the corner of the filbert brush, and dab on the Z lines with Olive Green. Highlight with Cadmium Yellow Light.

5. **Barn — Front of Barn** — Make a warm brown hue with White + Burnt Sienna. Stroke up and down with the flat sable, keeping color nice and smooth. After dry, apply highlight with White and the palette knife. When the front is completely dry, then the lines were drawn in with a black permanent marker.

Side of Barn — Burnt Sienna and shaded with Burnt Umber. Windows — Black. Roof — underpaint with Yellow Ochre. Shade Burnt Sienna in with flat sable, working from the edges of roof. Follow angle of roof and paint in shingles with the chisel edge of flat sable with Burnt Umber. Shadow under the roof with Burnt Umber. Highlight roof edge with White + Burnt Sienna.

6. **Ground and Weeds** — First thin Yellow Ochre with Turpenoid and give a wash on the whole ground area, even where the weeds will go. Let dry slightly. Will only take a few minutes using this technique. Wipe with a paper towel. Apply some of the sky color, White + Cerulean Blue + Burnt Umber on side of barn. Refer to painting. Tear several pieces of sponge off and apply from dark to light. DO NOT THIN PAINT.

Dark: Olive Green and Olive Green + Burnt Umber. Mid-tone: Olive Green + Cadmium Orange. Light: Yellow Ochre. Yellow Ochre + White. Cadmium Yellow Light.

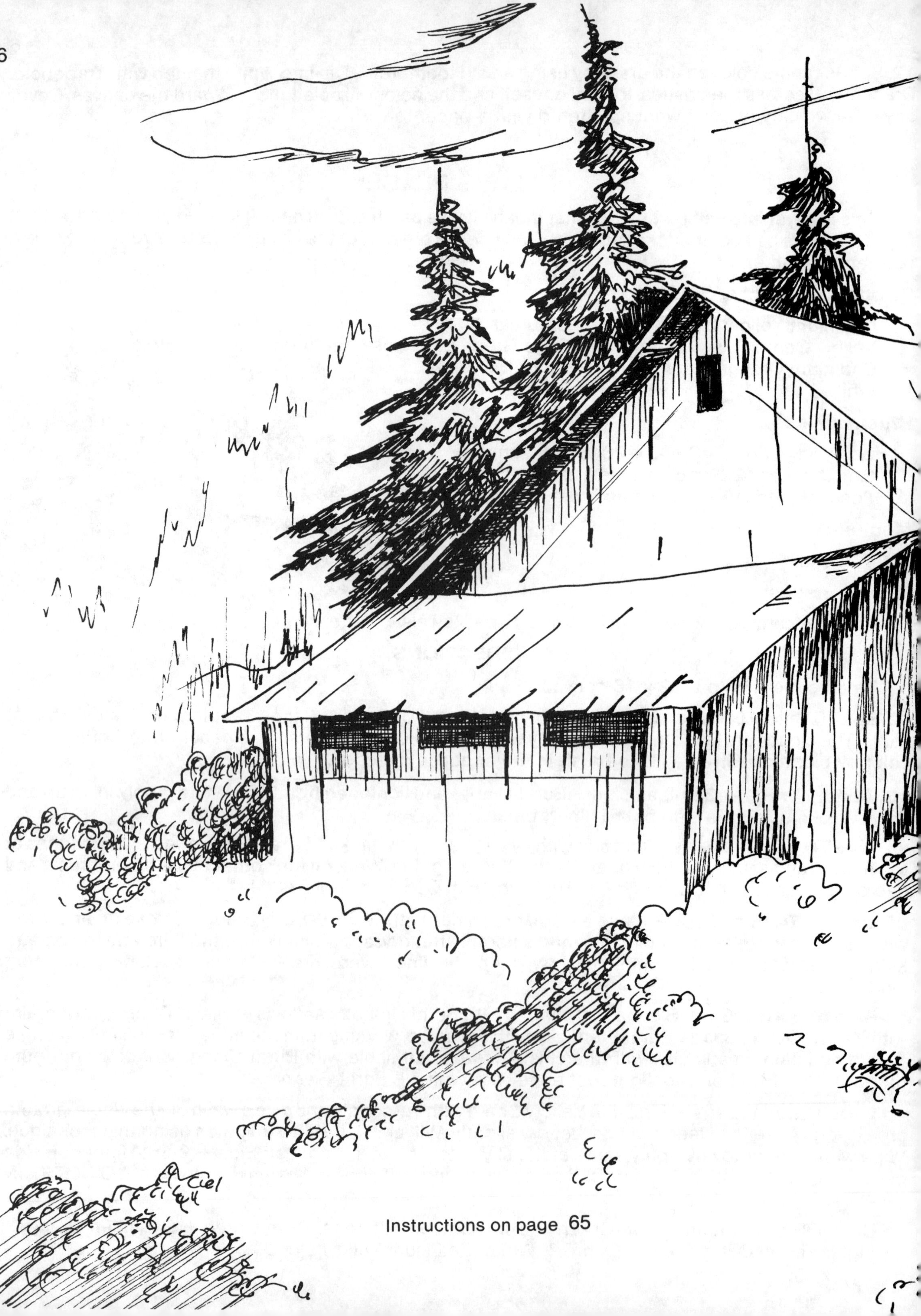

Instructions on page 65

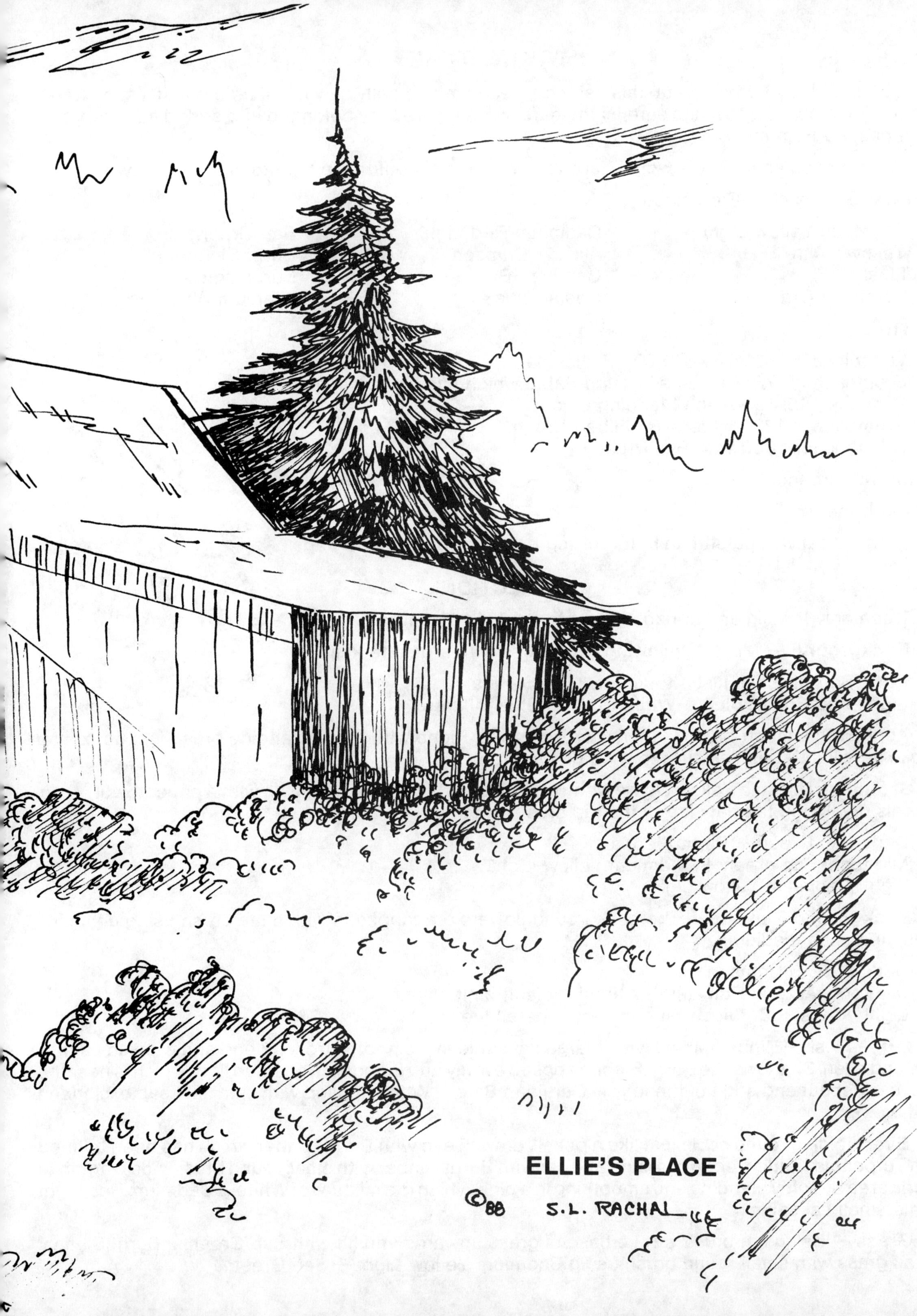

ELLIE'S PLACE

"TAKIN' TIME"

One could say I dreamed up this painting, because I actually saw it in a dream first. I sketched it, checked our local pig to make sure all the parts were where they belonged and added flowers, which were painted from my own garden.

What a happier world we would have if more people would take time to smell the flowers.

Palette: Grumbacher Pre-Tested

Cadmium Yellow Light
Yellow Ochre
Flesh
Cadmium Orange
Cadmium Red Light
Alizarin Crimson
Cerulean Blue
Cobalt Blue
Sap Green
Burnt Sienna
Burnt Umber
Titanium White

Brushes:

Langnickel 5010 #4, #8, #20 - Flat sable.
Grumbacher 178 #1 - Small Round Sable which has a good point.
Peacock 145 #9 - A soft blending brush.
Grumbacher 4229 #6 or #8 - Filbert Brush.
Grumbacher 1060 #3 - Fan Brush.

Medium: Turpenoid

Miscellaneous:

12 X 16 canvas, palette knife for mixing paint, paper towels or rags.

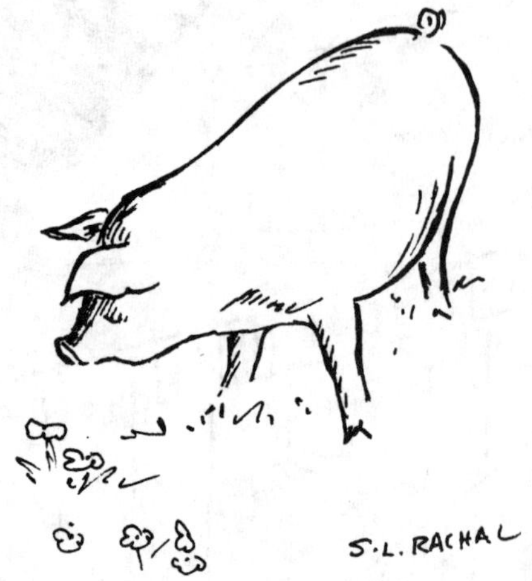

DIRECTIONS

1. Trace only the pig and horizon line onto a 12 X 16 canvas.

2. **Background** — Mix the following two values with a palette knife:

Dark: Sap Green + just a touch of Burnt Sienna.
Light: Add Cobalt Blue + White to dark value mixture.

Apply with a filbert brush in a criss-cross stroke. Blend with a soft blending brush in a horizontal stroke very lightly, making sure to wipe brush often.

3. **Ground** — Use thin Yellow Ochre with Turpenoid and cover by rubbing in with a paper towel or rag. Let this dry. Using the flat side of the fan brush, tap in the following:

Dark: Sap Green + Burnt Sienna.
Mid-tone: Sap green + Cadmium Yellow Light.
Light: Cadmium Yellow Light.

4. **Background Flowers** — The background flowers are tapped in with a fan brush using dry paint. (This means no medium.)

Dark: Alizarin Crimson.
Mid-tone: Alizarin Crimson + White for a soft pink color.
Light: White + Cerulean Blue making a pale blue.

5. **Pig** — Flesh + White applied with a large flat sable in a smooth stroke. Blend and wipe so paint is nice and even. Shadows are Burnt Sienna applied evenly and blended. Reflected light which is near the rear, ears, snout and edge of the legs is Cerulean Blue + White applied with small flat sable, blended softly.

Eye: Holding round sable just like a pencil, draw in eye with Burnt Umber which has been thinned with Turpenoid. Outline edge of mouth and ear with Burnt Umber with small round brush. Add warmth to cheek area by softly blending and smoothing in a pink, which is a mixture of White + Cadmium Red Light with a small flat sable.

6. **Grass** — Using fan brush, stroke base of grass upwards and lift with Sap Green + Burnt Sienna. Detail grass with small round brush using Cadmium Yellow Light + Sap Green.

7. **Flowers** —

Daisies: Stroke from outside of petal toward the center with small round brush using White. Dot centers with Cadmium Orange.

Stock: Dab colors using small round brush in a cone shape. Work from dark to light.

Yellow Stock: First dab in with Yellow Ochre and highlight with a pale yellow which is a mixtrue of White + Cadmium Yellow Light.

Pink Stock: Base in with Alizarin Crimson. Mix White + just a hint of Alizarin Crimson for a soft pink hue. This pink value may be lightened by adding more White or darkened by adding more Alizarin Crimson.

Blue Stock: Base in with Cobalt Blue and highlight with a soft blue which is a mixture of White + Cerulean Blue.

Red Poppies: Base in Cadmium Red Light in a "U" Shape with side of small flat sable. Highlight with Cadmium Orange.

LANDSCAPE WIPE OUT

Here is a fun painting to do. It is called a wipe out and only takes two colors. Try it — you will like it.

Palette: Grumbacher Pre-Tested

Burnt Sienna
Burnt Umber

Acrylics — Liquitex
White

Brushes:

1" Bristle Brush and an old tooth brush
Grumbacher 7357 #1 - liner
Sharpen the end of wood brush handle.

Medium:

Copal Painting Medium.

Miscellaneous:

Canvas, Turpenoid and rags, or 12 X 16 masonite.

DIRECTIONS

This painting can be done on masonite or canvas. The masonite drys faster. That is why I personally like canvas better because I have more time to wipe out colors before they set up and get tacky.

1. A texture is first applied to canvas or masonite with White acrylic paint. Overlap strokes with palette knife, making sure to have a textured surface. This should only take about 15 minutes to dry. However, if drying time needs to be speeded up, one could use a hair dryer, or set outside in the sun.

2. After completely dry, coat entire canvas with Burnt Sienna, thinned with Copal painting medium using 1" brush.

3. Cover index finger with rag and sketch landscape by applying pressure where needed.

4. Wipe out light sky areas, path, and the tree trunks using rag.

5. **Tree Foliage** — Use 1" brush with Burnt Umber, twisting and turning brush as dabbing. Do not thin paint. Sharpen end of old brush handle and scratch in tree trunks.

6. **Fence** — Cover the sharpened end of brush handle with rag, now wipe out. Thin Burnt Umber with Copal painting medium and draw in wire using liner brush.

7. **Tree Trunks** — Outline limbs with Burnt Umber using liner brush. Dab with rag to lift color if too dark.

8. Some texture can be applied to tree trunks and ground by flipping Turpenoid with tooth brush. Dip tooth brush into Turpenoid and pull thumb across brush towards self. Some of the Turpenoid will flip onto canvas. Dab with rag and some of the color will lift off. If too much color is lifted, then just re-apply more Burnt Sienna.

8. **Grass** — Use 1" bristle brush with Burnt Umber. Push brush into canvas then lift up.

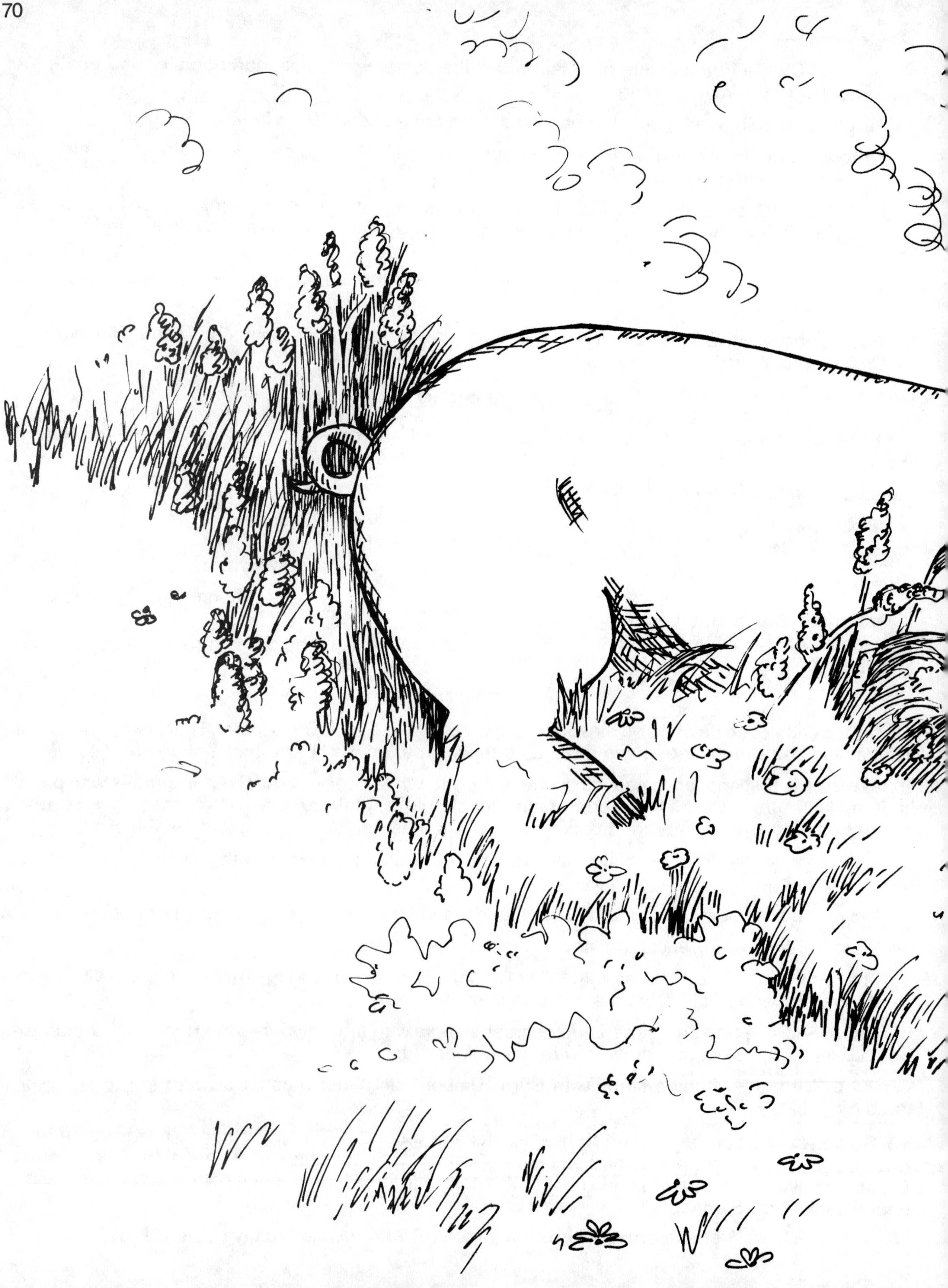

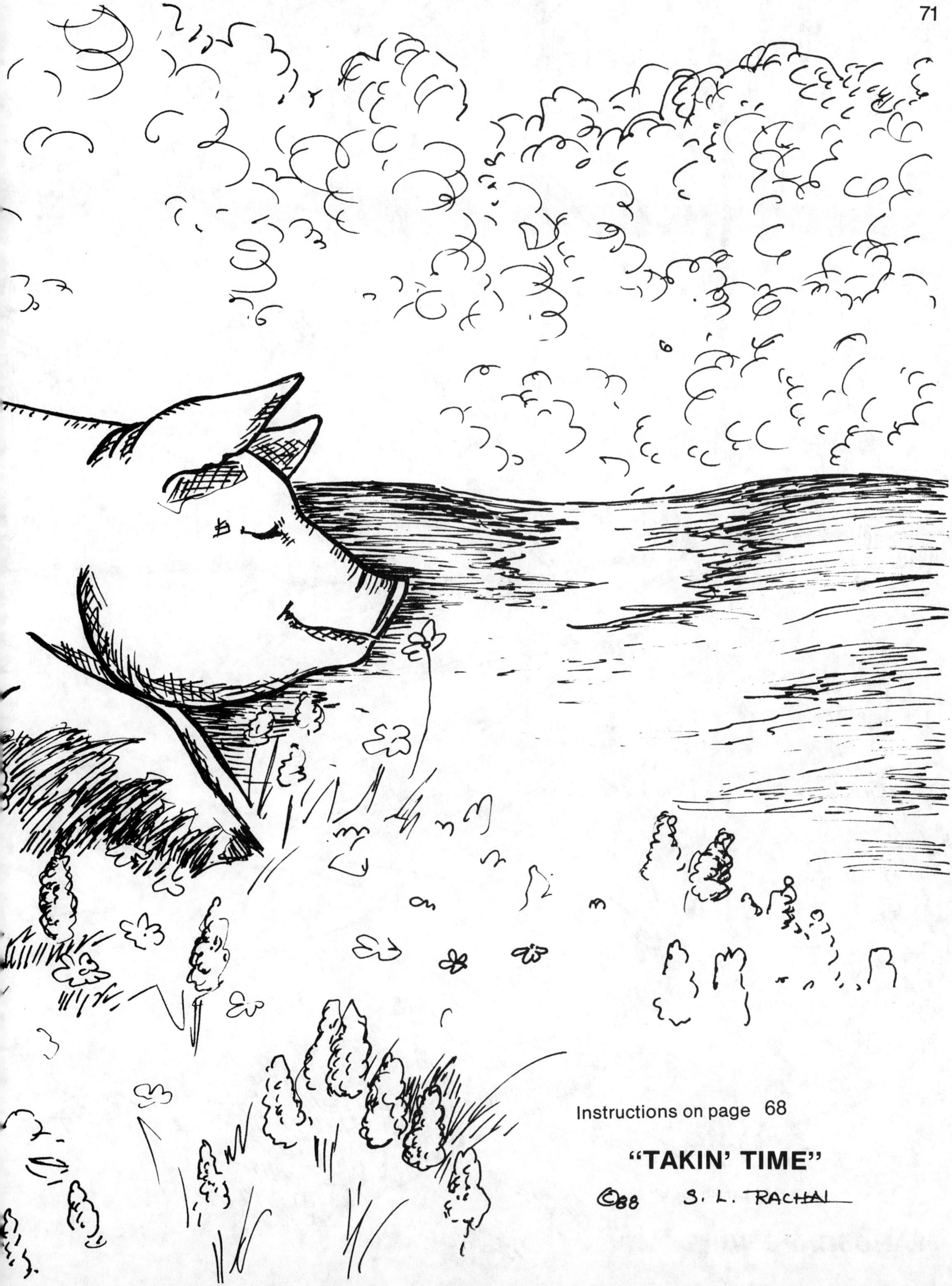

Instructions on page 68

"TAKIN' TIME"

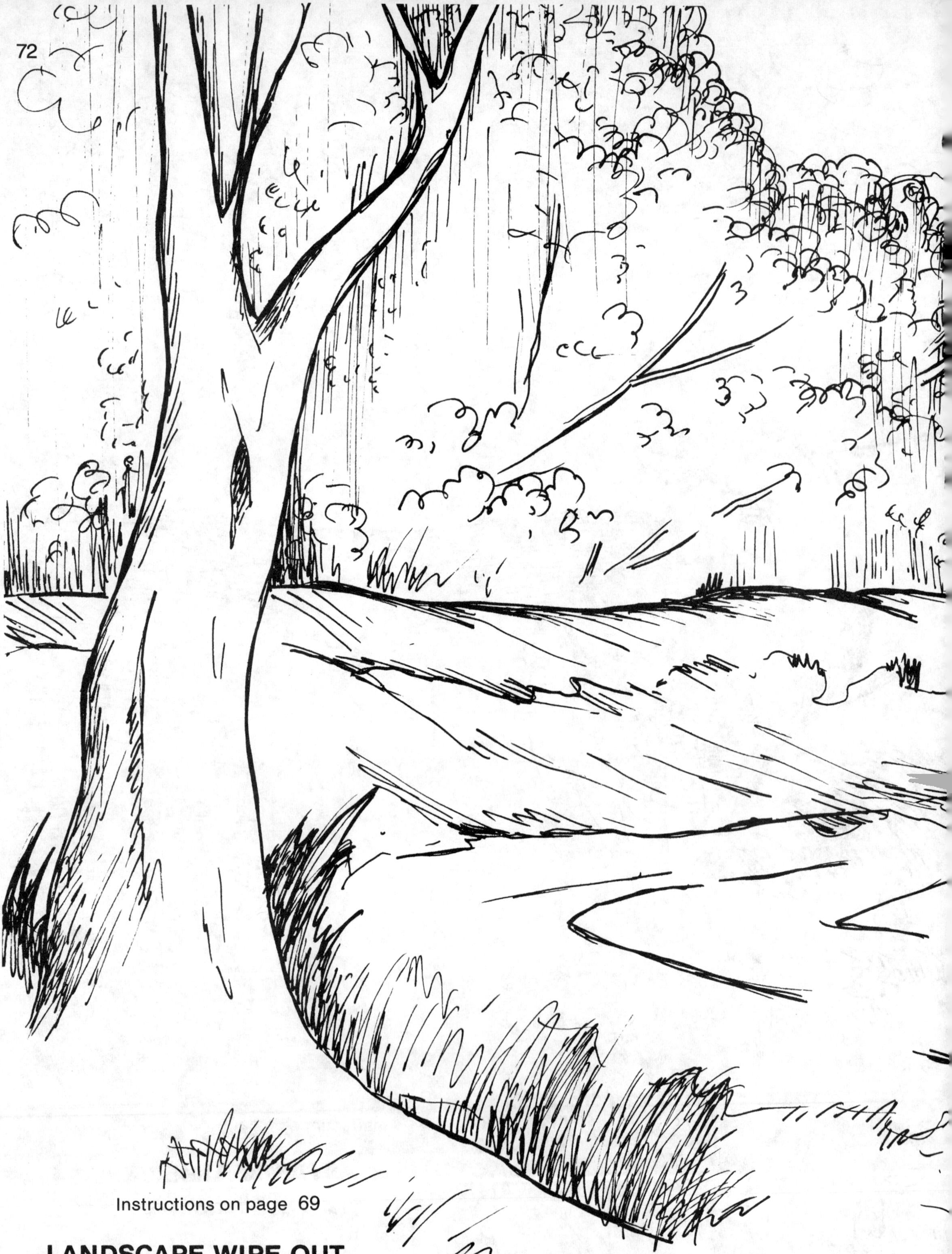

Instructions on page 69

LANDSCAPE WIPE OUT

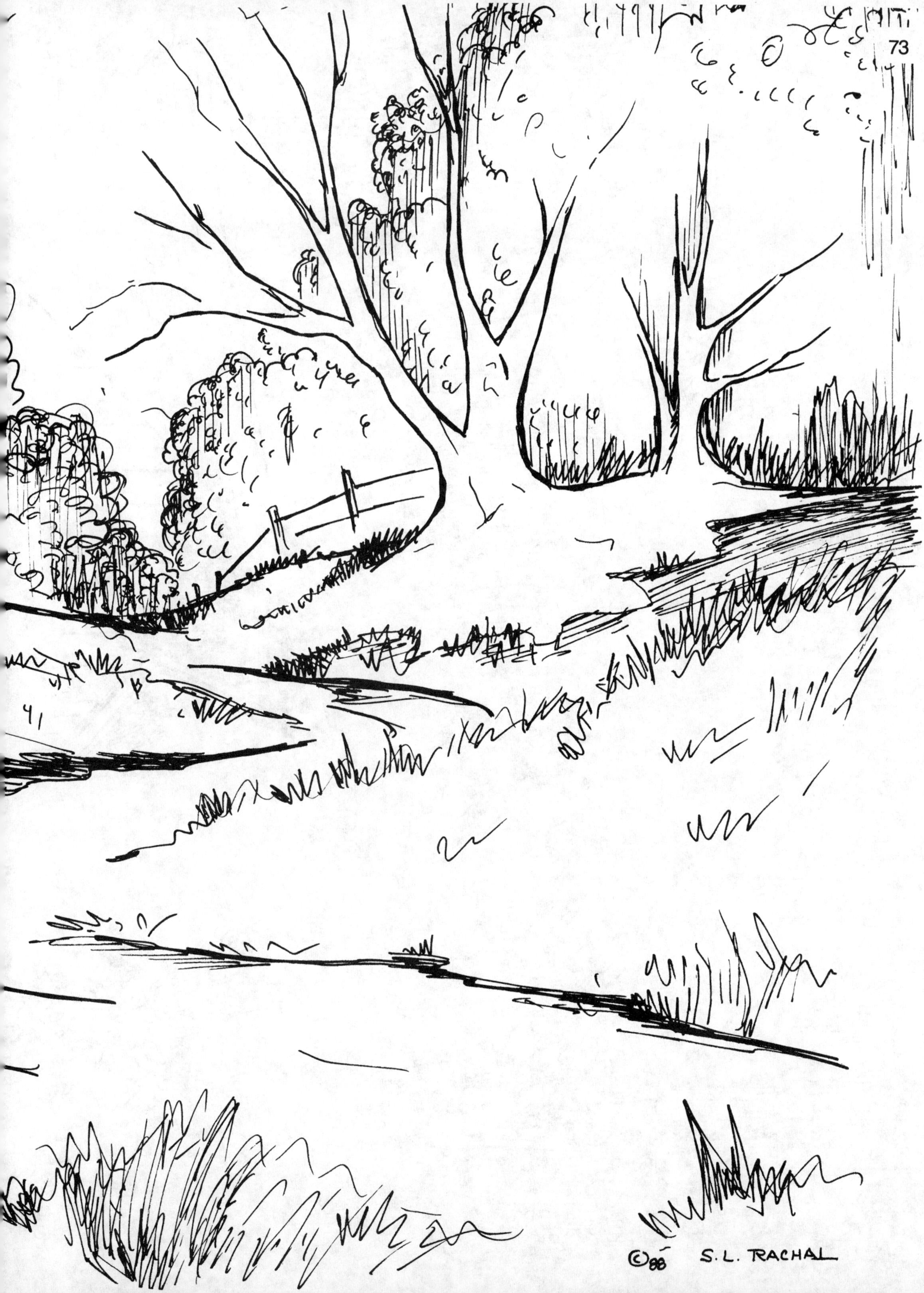
©88 S.L. RACHAL

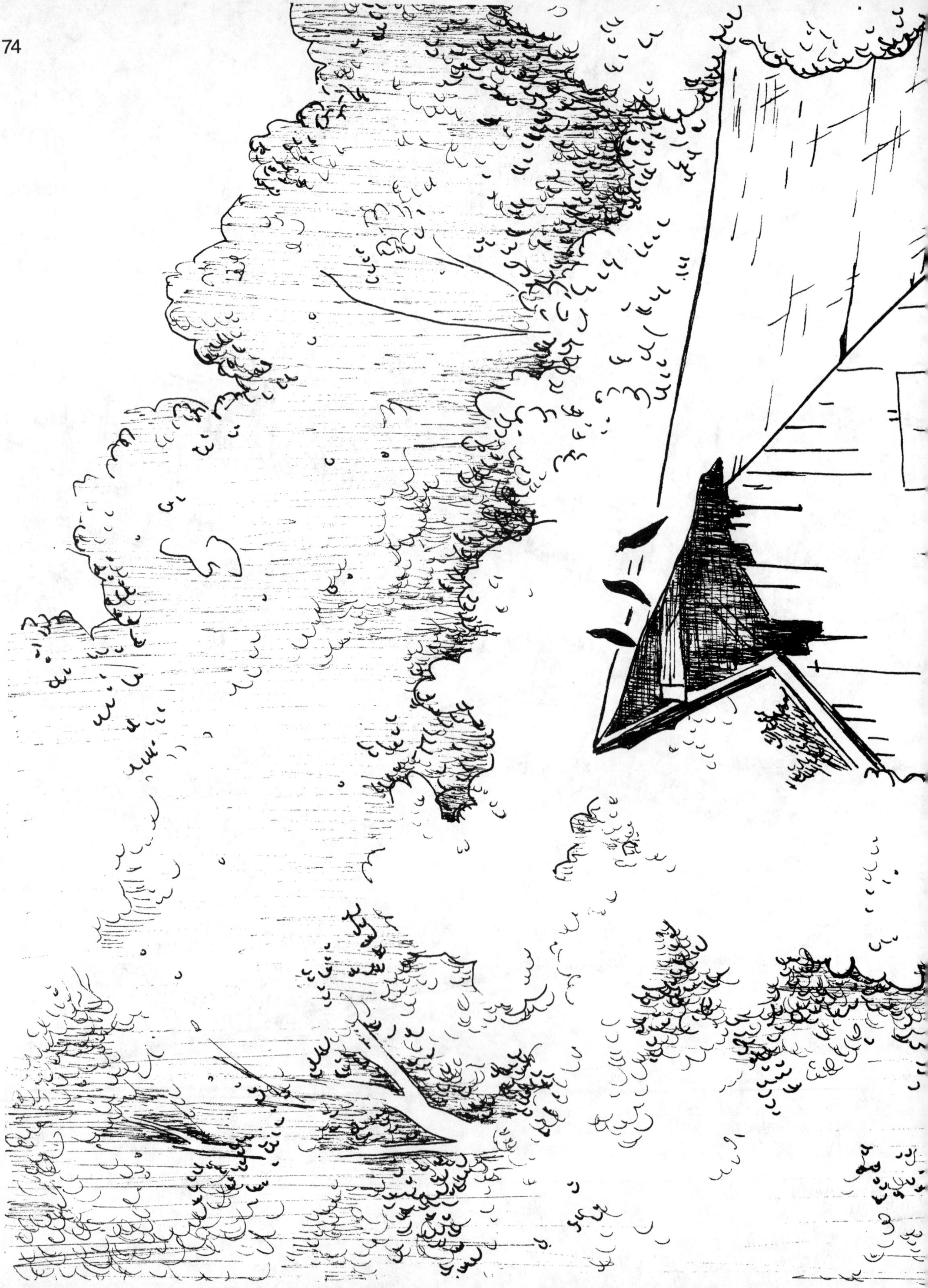

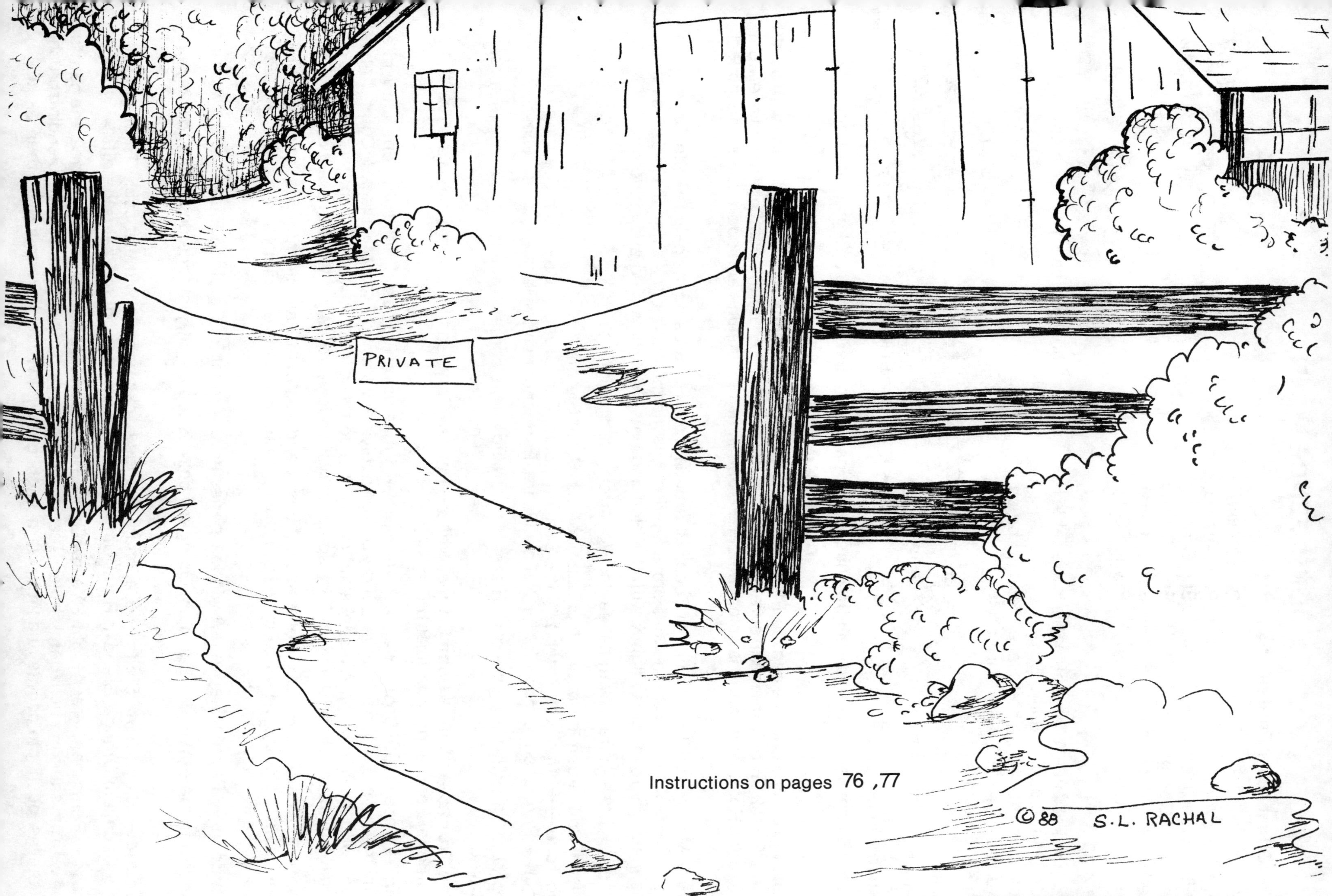

Instructions on pages 76 ,77

DON'T FENCE ME IN

DON'T FENCE ME IN

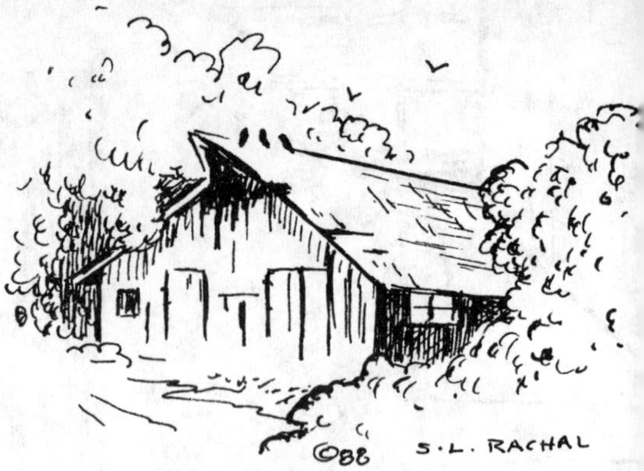

Palette: Grumbacher Pre-Tested

- White
- Zinc Yellow
- Yellow Ochre
- Cadmium Orange
- Red (just a hint of color)
- Cerulean Blue
- Cobalt Blue
- Permanent Green Light
- Sap Green
- Burnt Sienna
- Burnt Umber
- Paynes Gray

Brushes:

Langnickel #20 - A flat sable. (This is the sable I use the most, however you may use many different sizes in the sable family.)
Peacock 145 #8 - A soft Hake blending brush.
Grumbacher 7357 #1 - A liner.
An old toothbrush.

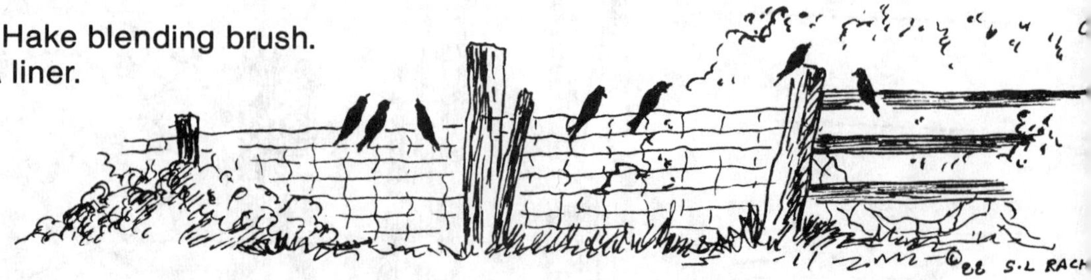

Medium:

Liquin

Miscellaneous:

12 X 16 canvas, Turpenoid, palette knife, paper palette, paper towels and graphite paper.

DIRECTIONS

1. Trace the outline onto the canvas. Place the graphite paper under the tracing and outline with a ball point pen. Check graphite to make sure the correct side is down. Lay out the paint on the palette, from warm to cool. Remember warm is colors that make one think of sunshine and cool makes one think of snow or rain.

2. **Sky** — Mix White with just a hint of Cobalt Blue and Paynes Gray using the palette knife. Criss-cross brush strokes with the flat sable. Criss-cross-flip-flop, this means make big X's and the brush is turned over as making stroke. Blend lightly with the blending brush so sky is nice and smooth.

3. **Trees** — Base in trees with flat sable. Work from dark to light.

Dark — Sap Green + Cobalt Blue. Sap Green + Burnt Sienna.
Mid-Tone — Permanent Green Light + Cerulean Blue. Sap Green + Cadmium Orange.
Light — Permanent Green Light + Yellow Ochre. Permanent Green Light + Zinc Yellow.

Apply the light with the corner of the flat sable, working off the corner, twisting and turning the brush as dabbing.

4. **Tree Trunks** — White + Burnt Sienna. White + Paynes Gray + a hint of Cerulean Blue. Thin paint with Turpenoid and apply with liner brush.

5. **Barn** — Base in with Cobalt Blue + Paynes Gray + White using flat sable. Highlight front with White + Cadmium Orange, a peachy value. Let dry before applying the wood lines. Mix Black + Burnt Umber and apply with the liner brush. After dry, splatter on dark spots. Dip toothbrush into paint, place thumb on the brush, pull thumb toward self and the splatters will go forward. Might want to practice this first.

6. **Roof** — Paynes Gray + Cobalt Blue and lighten by adding White. Paint in short lines to suggest the shingles using the liner brush with Paynes Gray. Blend in some of the tree color. Highlight with a peachy mixture White + Cadmium Orange.

7. **Windows** — Paynes Gray. A few window panes have a touch of Cerulean Blue.

Window frame — White + Cadmium Orange. If color is too bright, just tone down with the Paynes Gray.

8. **Ground** — Blend Burnt Sienna + Cadmium Orange back and forth with flat sable. Highlight with White + Cadmium Orange. Blend in Burnt Umber for the dark areas of road and the ruts.

9. **Grass** — Permanent Green Light + Yellow Ochre. Burnt Sienna + Sap Green. Grass near the barn is stroked with flat sable in a horizontal stroke. Near the fence the grass is applied with the blending brush, touch canvas, push into canvas and lift upward. Highlight with White + Permanent Green Light.

10. **Fence** — Paynes Gray + Burnt Umber using flat sable. Highlight with the gray mixture, Cobalt Blue + Paynes Gray + White and White + Cadmium Orange.

11. **Bushes** — Dark — Sap Green + Cobalt Blue. Mid-tone — Sap Green + Cadmium Orange. Light —Permanent Green Light + Zinc Yellow. Permanent Green Light. Use the corner of the flat sable and dab on.

12. **Rocks** — Base in with the gray mixture, Cobalt Blue + Paynes Gray + White. Highlight with White + Cerulean Blue. Set the rocks down by adding a dark shadow under them using Paynes Gray that has been thinned with Liquin.

13. **Flowers** — Dots of color. Zinc Yellow and Yellow Ochre. Use the tip of the liner and really make little dots of color.

14. **Birds** — Burnt Umber + Paynes Gray using the liner brush.

15. **Chain and Sign on Posts** — Chain is Paynes Gray highlighted with the gray mixture, Cobalt Blue + Paynes Gray + White. Sign is the same gray mixture, and the printing is Burnt Umber.

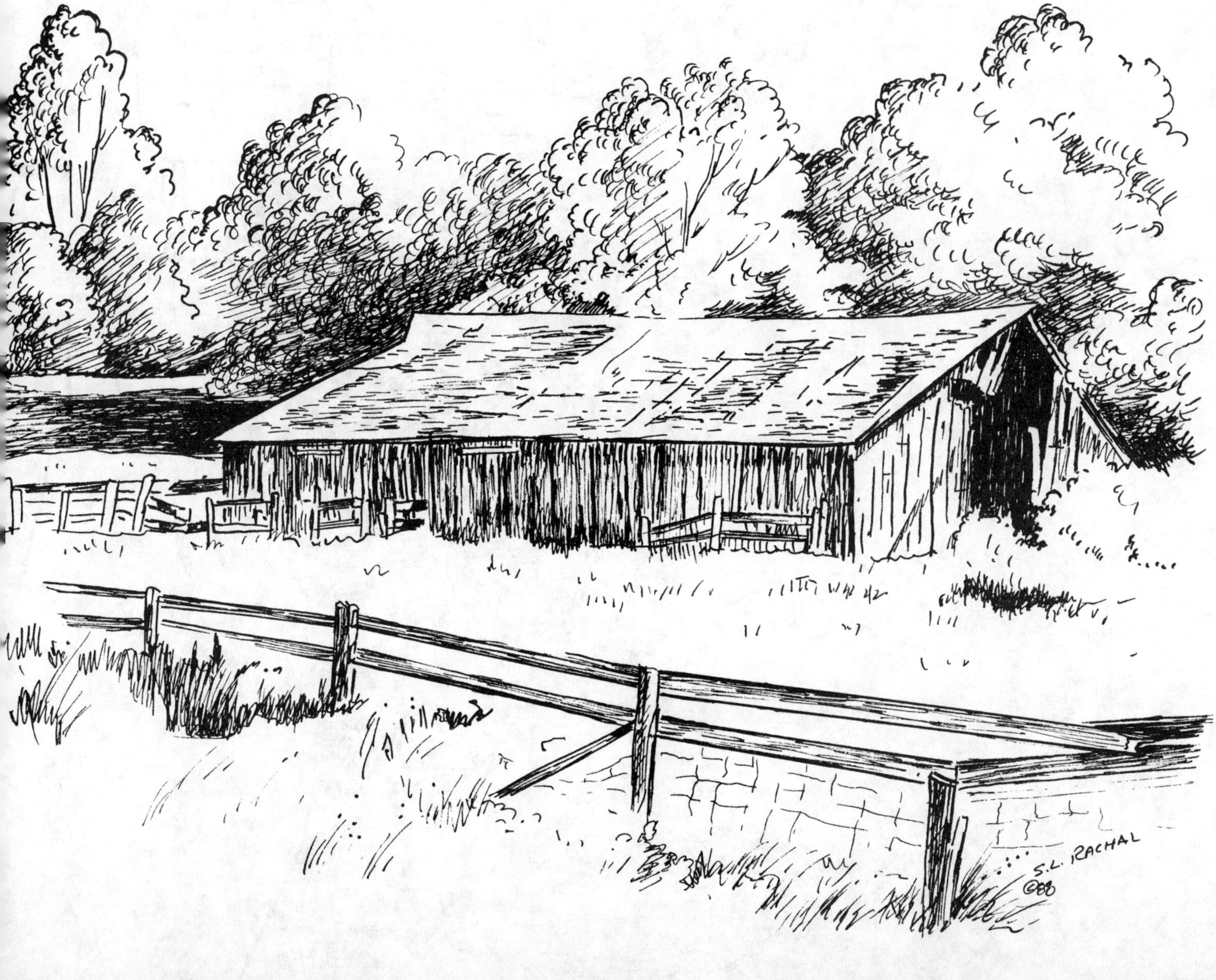

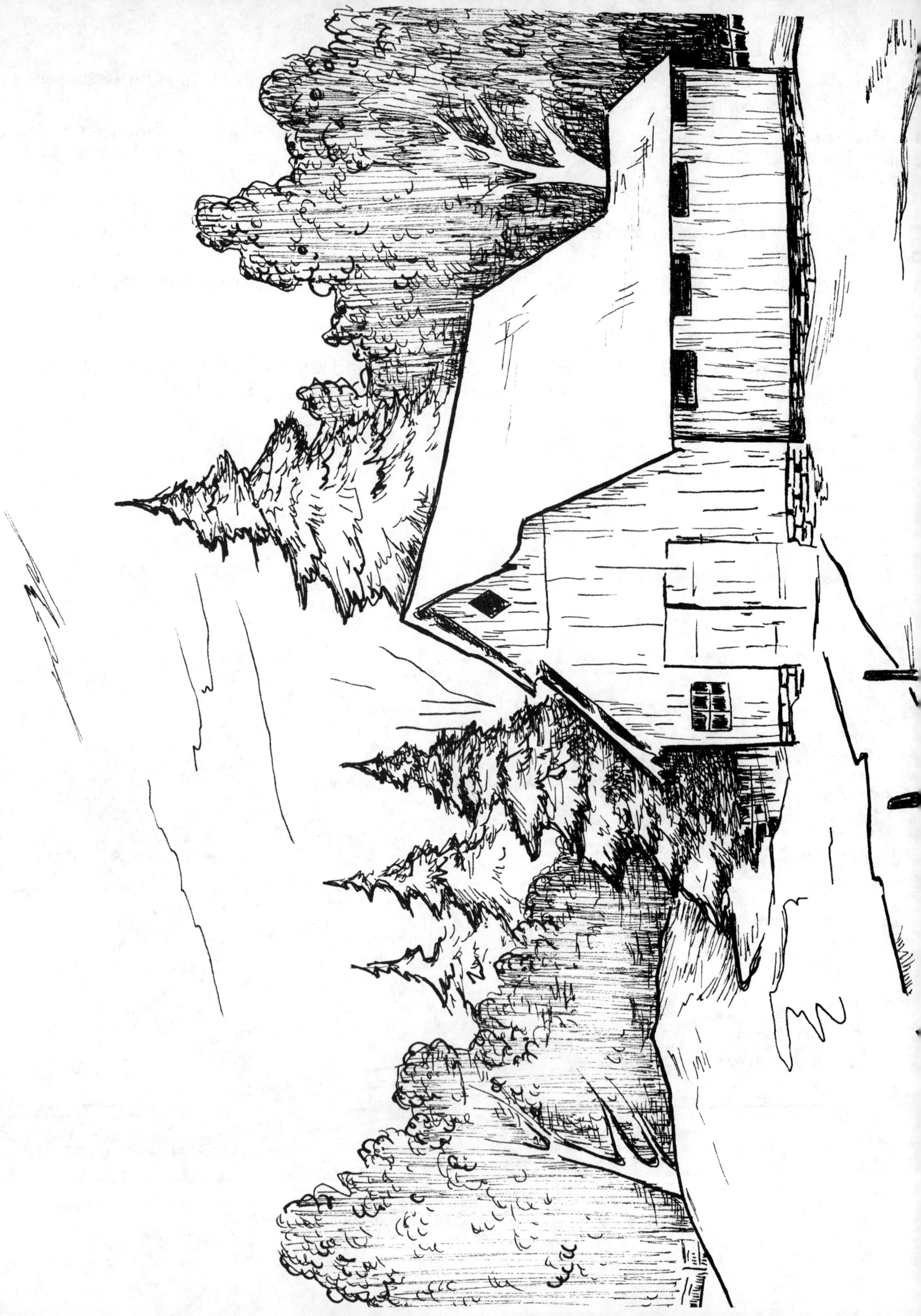

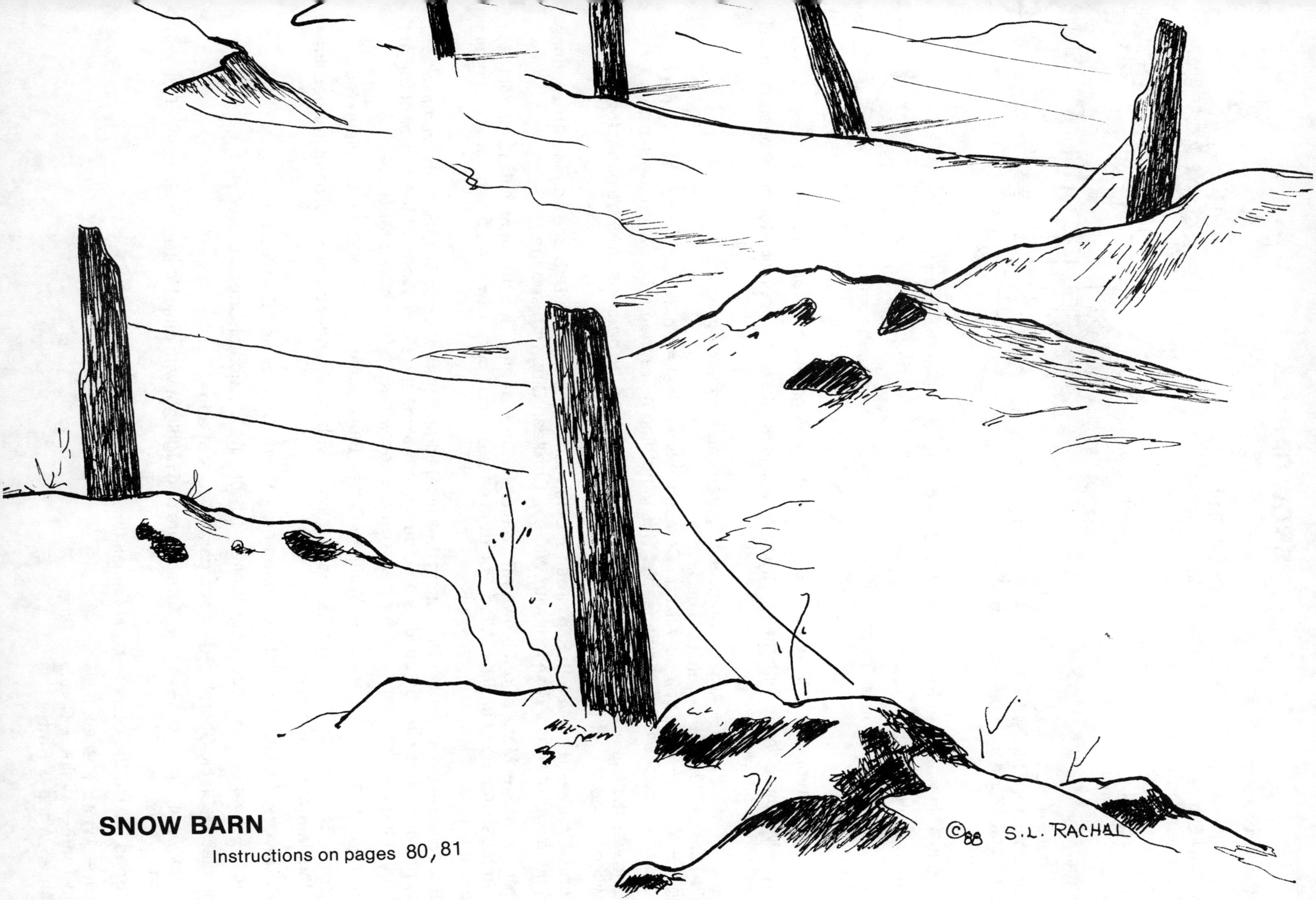

SNOW BARN

Instructions on pages 80, 81

SNOW BARN

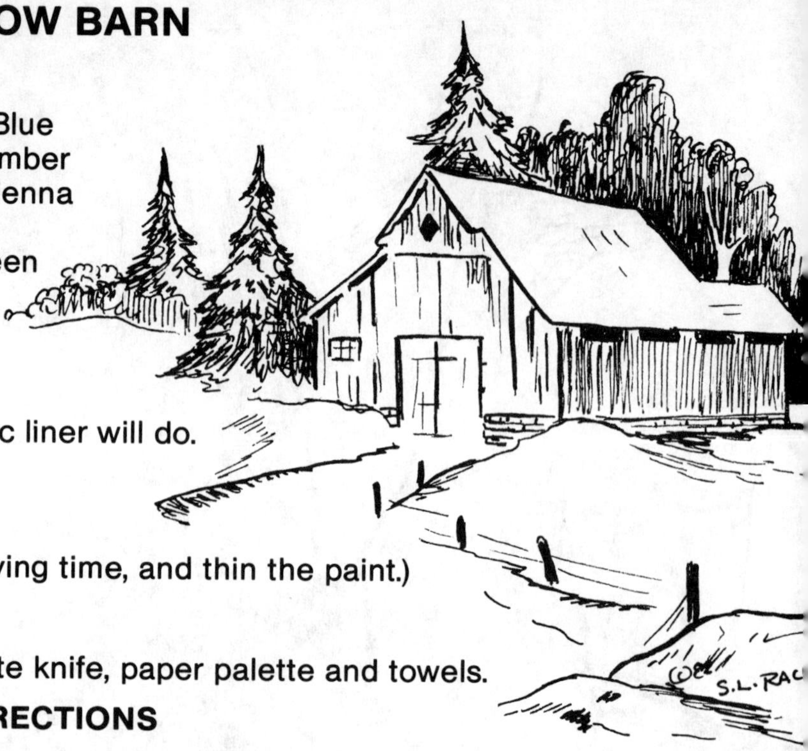

Palette: Grumbacher Pre-Tested

- Titanium White
- Yellow Ochre
- Cadmium Orange
- Red (any bright red will do)
- Cerulean Blue
- Alizarin Crimson
- Cobalt Blue
- Burnt Umber
- Burnt Sienna
- Black
- Sap Green

Brushes:

Langnickel 5010 #20 - A flat sable.
Grumbacher 7357 #1 - A liner. A synthetic liner will do.
Peacock 145 #9 - A blending brush.

Medium:

Liquin (This was used to speed up the drying time, and thin the paint.)

Miscellaneous:

12 X 16 canvas, sponge, Turpenoid, palette knife, paper palette and towels.

DIRECTIONS

1. Trace pattern onto a 12 x 16 canvas. This would look great on a wood piece too.

2. **Sky** — Mix three values with the palette knife. Mix at least a tablespoon of each color because it will be used in the snow too.

   Dark — Cobalt Blue + Alizarin Crimson. Lighten value by adding White.
   Mid-Tone — White + Cerulean Blue.
   Light — White + a pin point of Alizarin Crimson, this will make a pink hue. Apply paint with a criss-cross brush stroke using the flat sable. This is nothing more than a "X" which overlaps.

   Blend with the Hake brush in a diagonal brush stroke. Wipe the brush often with a paper towel or rag so it will not load up with paint.

3. **Scrub Trees** — Base in with Sap Green + Black using the flat sable. Dab tree edges with a sponge to obtain irregular edges. Highlight with White + Cerulean Blue with sponge.

4. **Tree Trunks** — Make a light brown with White + Burnt Sienna. Thin the paint with Turpenoid. Roll the liner brush into paint until it is filled. Pull from base of tree upward, twisting brush between fingers as making trunks.

5. **Pine Trees** — Draw a vertical line using the chisel edge of the flat sable. With Sap Green, make "Z's" across this line. These will be used as a guide when making the trees. Work off the corner of the flat sable following the "Z's" back and forth across the line with Sap Green (NO MEDIUM).

   Snow on trees — Shadow side — White + Cobalt Blue. Sunlit side — White + Cerulean Blue.

6. **Barn** — Base in with Red which has been thinned with Liquin. After paint is dry, paint in wood lines using the liner brush with Black.

7. **Windows** — Black. Highlight with warm gray, White + Black and Cerulean Blue.

8. **Roof** — Base in with a cool gray, White + Black and a touch of Cobalt Blue.

   Shingles — Black. Short broken lines parallel to roof edge.

   Let dry. Apply snow with White + Cobalt Blue and highlight with pink, White + a pin point of Alizarin Crimson.

9. **Stones** — Use the corner edge of small flat sable to make short lines.

   Dark — White + Black
   Mid-Tone — White + Cerulean Blue
   Light — White + Red

0. The colors in the snow are the same as in the sky.

Dark — Cobalt Blue + Alizarin Crimson + White. Shadow side of snow.
Mid-Tone — White + Cerulean Blue. Warm side of snow.
Light — White + a pin-point of Alizarin Crimson. Highlight in snow.

Refer to the painting as applying the color with the flat sable. Soften and diffuse color with the Hake rush.

1. **Road** — Base in Yellow Ochre which has been thinned with Liquin. Blend in Burnt Sienna near the arn with flat sable. Paint in lines with Burnt Umber using the liner brush. Let dry. Apply snow with White · Cerulean Blue in a back and forth brush stroke.

2. **Fence Posts** — Dark — Burnt Sienna + Black. Mid-Tone — Yellow Ochre. Shadow side — Cerulean lue + White. Make a texture on post by using the side of the palette knife. Thin Black with Turpenoid nd paint in wire using the liner brush.

3. **Weeds** — Black thinned with Turpenoid and stroked in with the liner brush. Start stroke at base of ne weed and pull upward.

4. **Rocks** — Base in Black + Cobalt Blue. Let dry then apply the snow on the rocks with the palette nife. Wipe knife off before applying each color.

Dark — Cobalt Blue + Alizarin Crimson + White.
Mid-Tone — White + Cerulean Blue.
Light — White + a pin point of Alizarin Crimson.

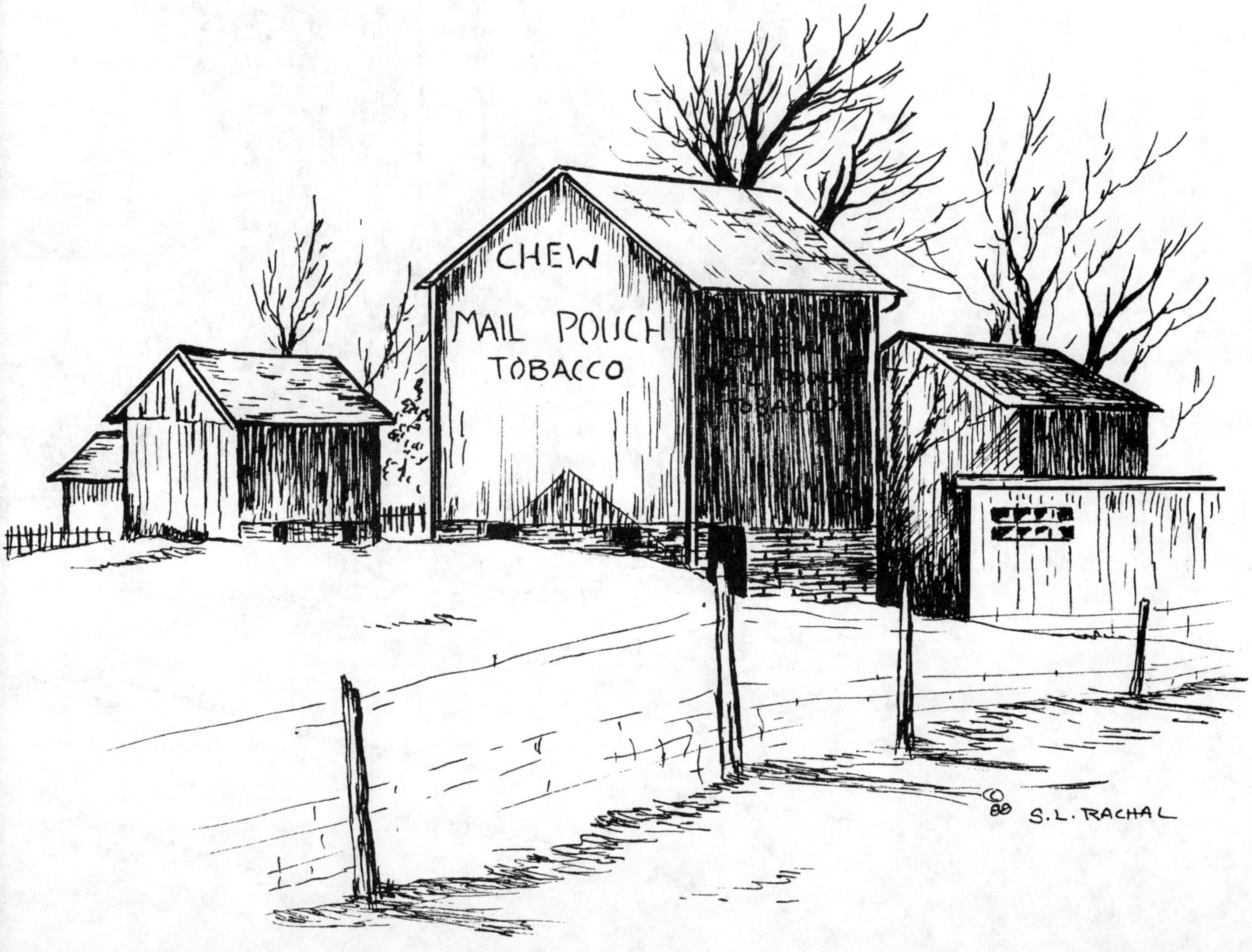

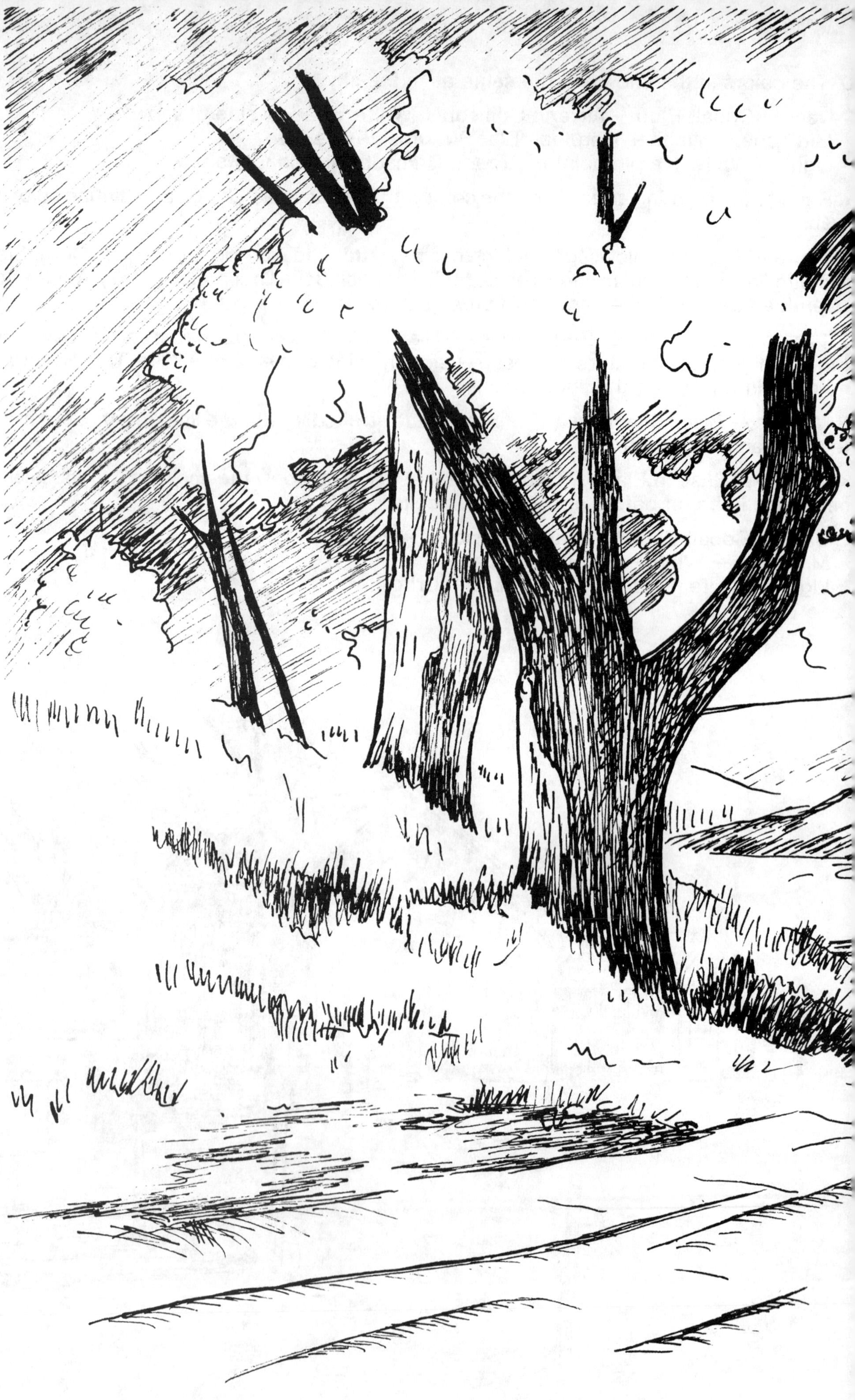

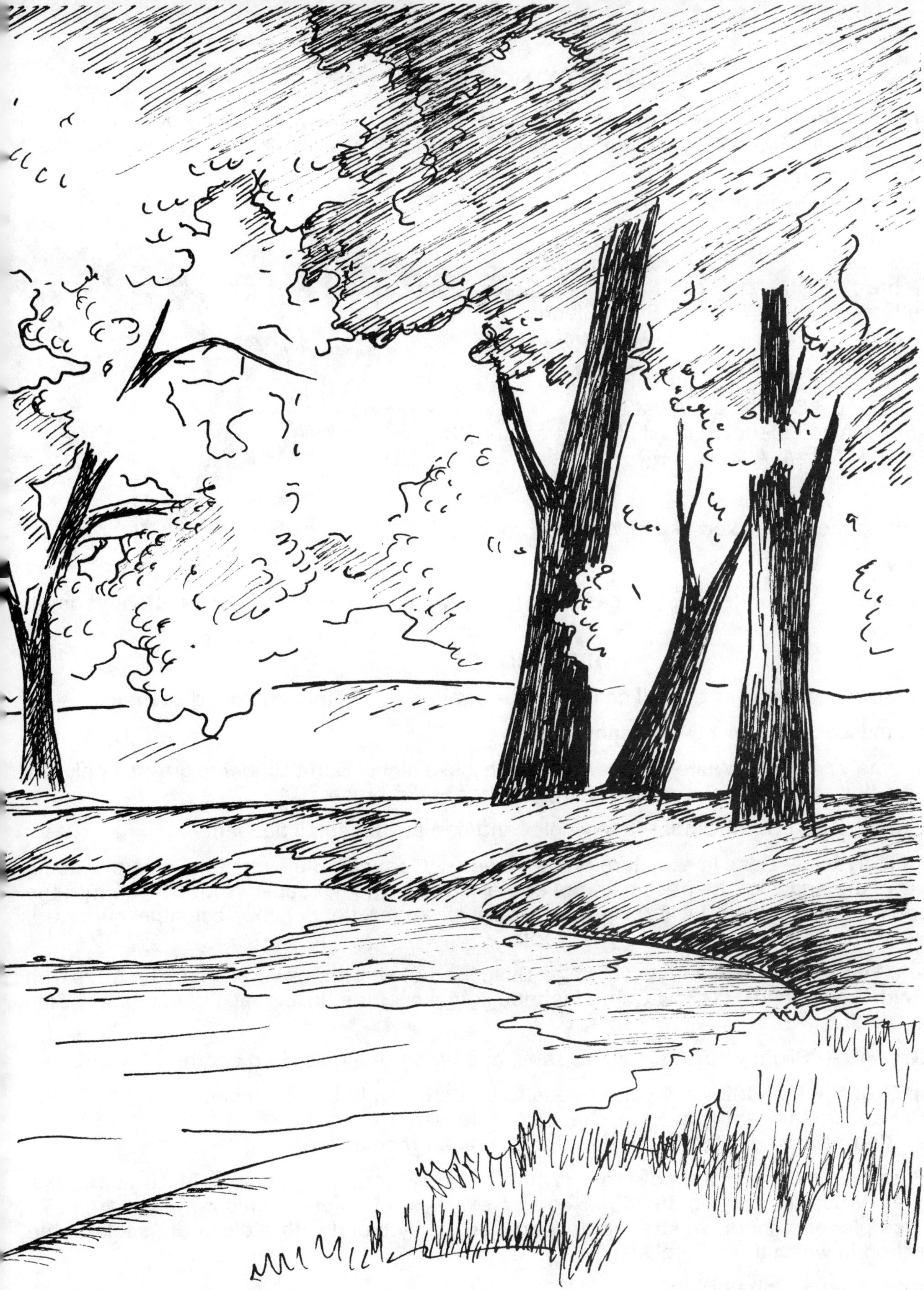

Instructions on pages 84 85

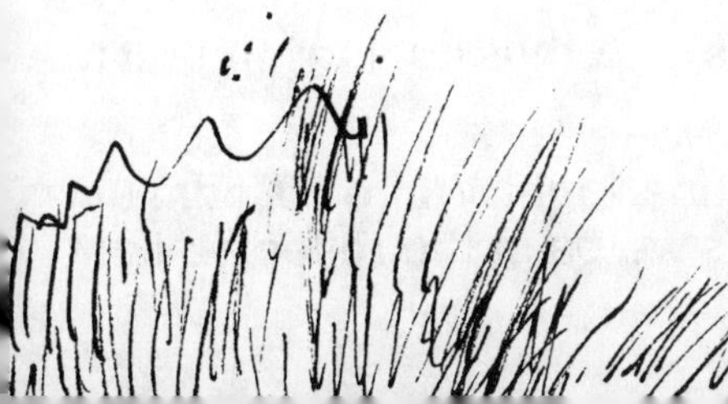

COUNTY ROAD #2

COUNTY ROAD #2

This scene is only a few minutes from my home. However, the trees were more brown and since I had just returned from a trip where everything was so green, it was only natural that I would paint something "green".

Palette: Grumbacher Pre-Tested

Titanium White
Zinc Yellow
Yellow Ochre
Cadmium Orange
Cerulean Blue
Cobalt Blue
Sap Green
Permanent Green Light
Burnt Sienna
Burnt Umber

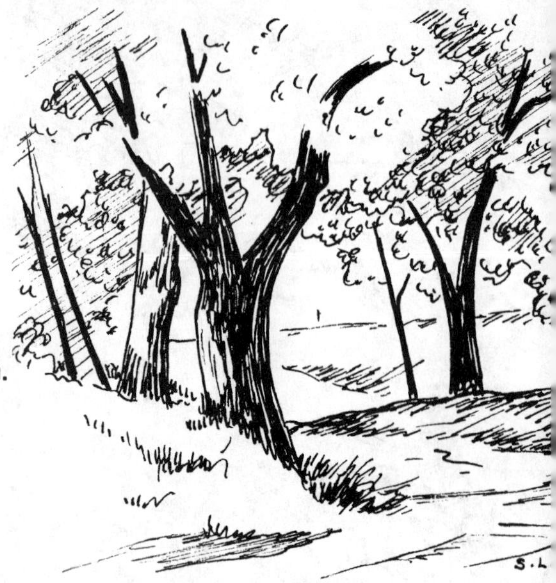

Brushes:

Langnickel 5010 #8 and #20. A flat sable.
Hake 145 #9. A soft blending brush, I call it a bunny brush.
Grumbacher 7357 #1. A liner.

Medium:

Copal painting medium mixed ½ and ½ with Turpenoid.

Miscellaneous:

11 X 14 canvas or masonite. If using masonite, give it several coats of Gesso. Palette and paper towels.

DIRECTIONS

The secret to this painting is that all colors have Copal painting medium added to them.

1. Trace the landscape onto a 11 X 14 canvas.

2. **Sky** — Extremely pale blue, White + Cobalt Blue with just a hint of Burnt Umber to gray it. Apply in a circular stroke using small flat sable. Blend softly with the Hake brush.

3. **Distant Trees** — Add Burnt Umber to sky color and dab in with small flat sable.

4. **Background Trees** — Base in a mixture of Sap Green + Cerulean Blue. Lighten value by adding some White. Dab the edges of the trees with the corner edge of the flat sable. Notice if you turn the brush back and forth as dabbing, it will cause some irregular edges. Let dry, then scumble in White + Cerulean Blue at the base of the trees to give depth.

5. **Hill** — Dark: Yellow Ochre + Cadmium Orange. Base in whole hill area, even behind the trees with this mixture. Mid-Tone: White + Yellow Ochre blended lightly over the base coat. Light: White + Zinc Yellow on top of hill.

6. **Middle Ground** — Slightly curve small flat sable and blend one color into another.

   Dark: Sap Green + Cobalt Blue. If color needs to be darker, add Burnt Umber.
   Mid-Tone: Sap Green + a hint of Burnt Sienna to add warmth.
   Light: Lay Zinc Yellow over the top of the other colors in the sunlit area.

7. **Road** — Base in whole road in a sandy brown, White + Burnt Sienna, using a horizontal brush stroke. Let dry completely before applying any other color. Next layer of colors should be transparent. To achieve this use plenty of medium. After color is applied, softly blend with a clean dry sable in the opposite direction in which it was applied.

   Dark: Burnt Umber + Cobalt Blue.
   Mid-Tone: Burnt Sienna. White + Cadmium Orange.
   Light: White + Zinc Yellow. This is where the sun hits the road and lights it up, thus adding interest to the painting.

8. **Tree Trunks** — Dark: Cobalt Blue + Burnt Umber. Mid-Tone: Burnt Sienna. Light: White + Cadmium Orange, a peachy hue. White + a hint of Zinc Yellow. In the shadow areas we paint the reflected light — White + Cerulean Blue.

9. **Foliage** — Darks: Sap Green + Cobalt Blue. Sap Green + Burnt Sienna. Mid-Tone: Sap Green + 'ellow Ochre. Permanent Green Light. Light: Permanent Green Light + White.

Leaves can be suggested by using the corner edge of the small flat sable or the tip of the small ound sable. Try each brush, you will know in a minute which brush works best for you.

0. **Grass** — I used an old sable brush to achieve this grassy look. The hairs were all split, then I hit the rush with a hammer a few times to make it better. Stroke from the base of the grass upward.

Dark: Sap Green + Burnt Sienna. Sap Green + Cobalt Blue.
Mid-Tone: Permanent Green Light + Yellow Ochre.
Light: White + Permanent Green Light.

Use the liner brush to indicate a few thin blades of grass here and there.

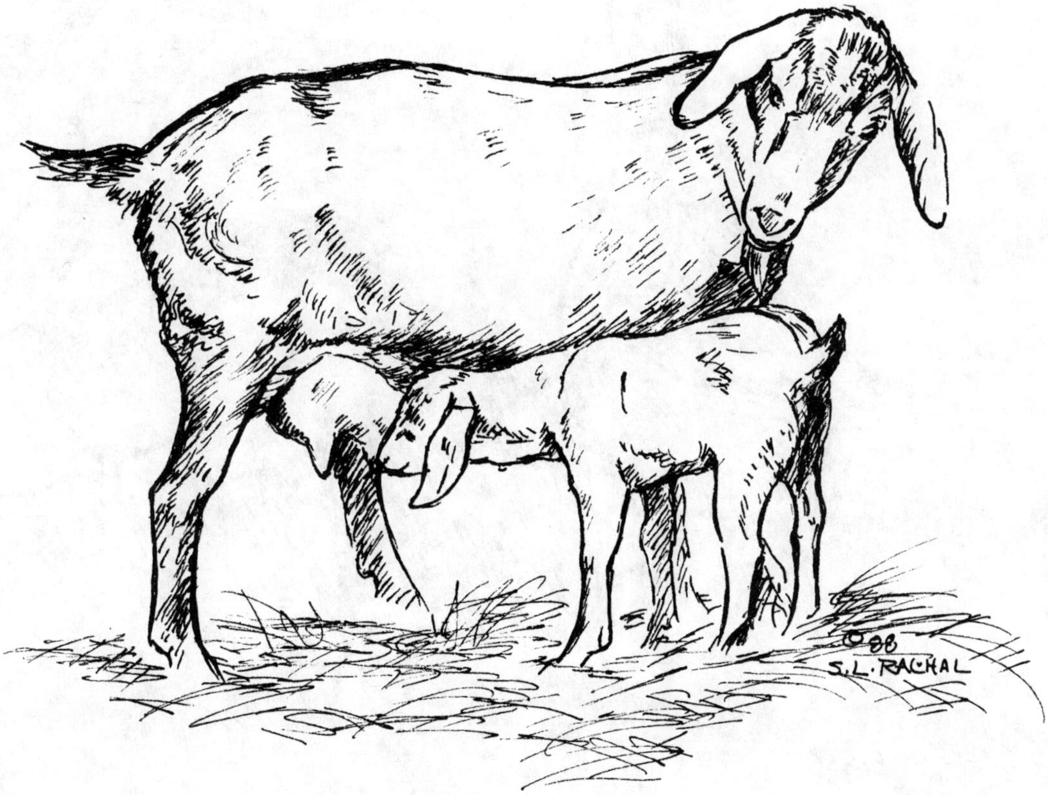

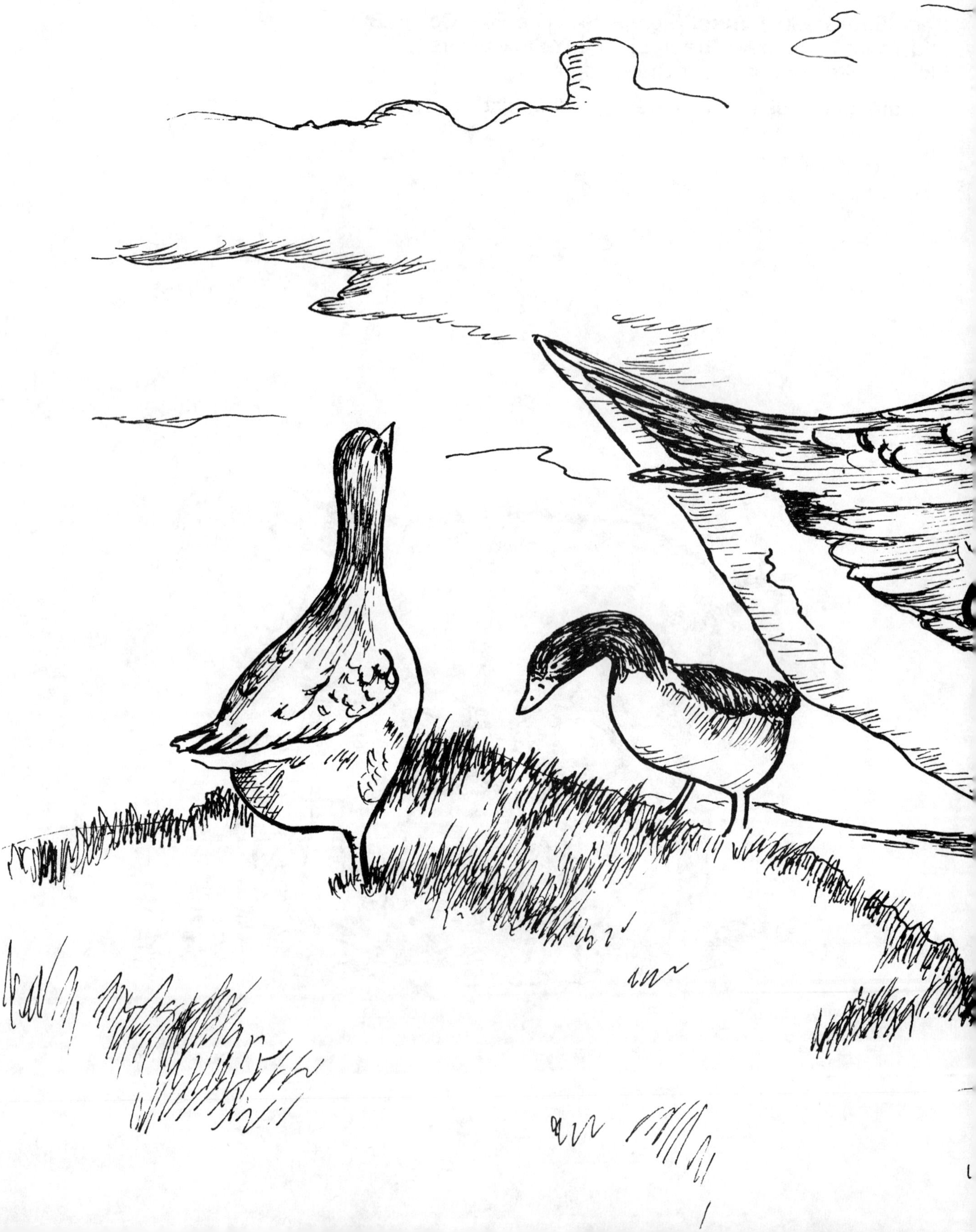

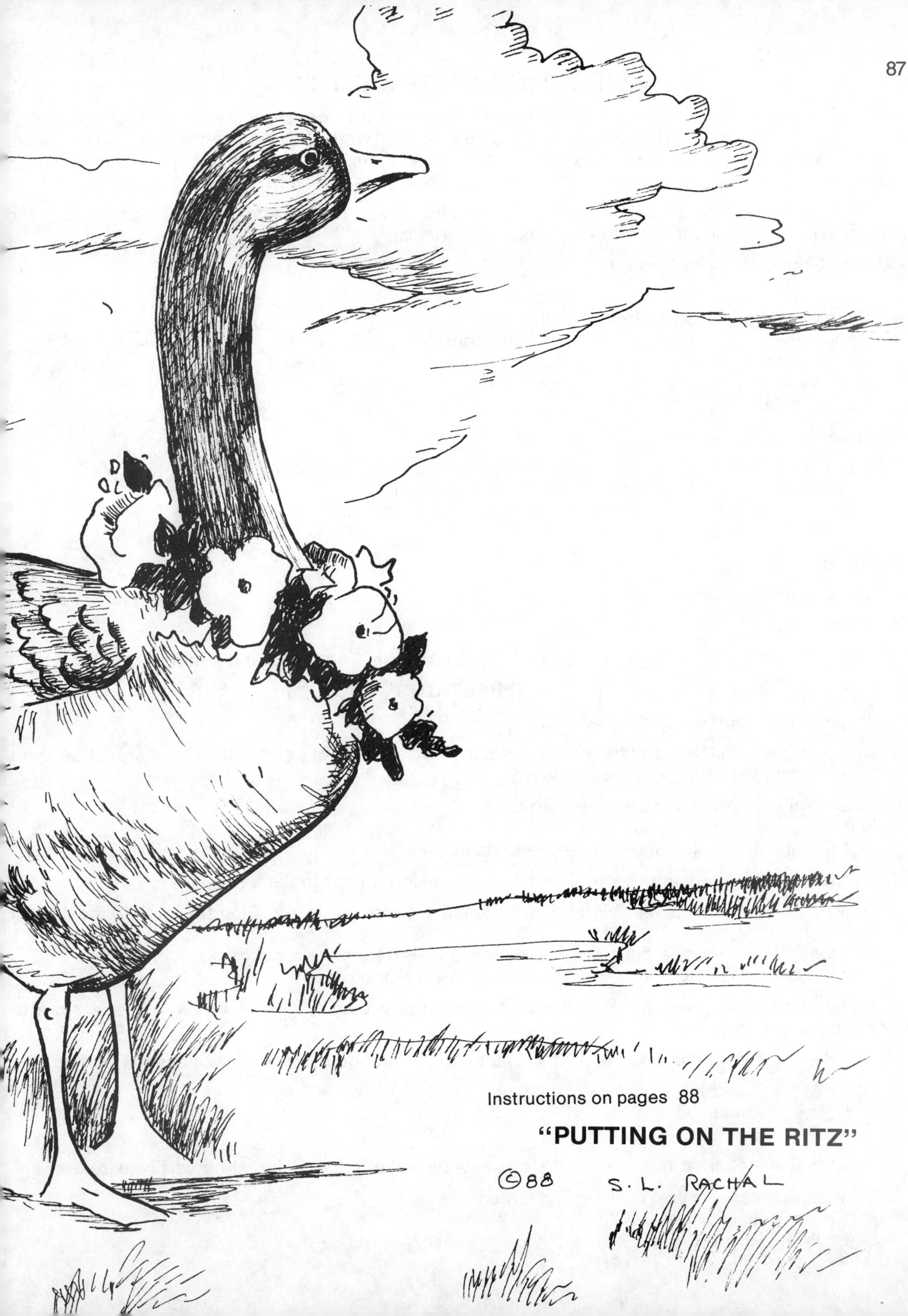

Instructions on pages 88

"PUTTING ON THE RITZ"

"PUTTING ON THE RITZ"

Two friends of mine were trying to feed a few ducks and geese some bread crumbs, while I attempted to photograph them. Before I could take what I felt would be a great shot, I noticed they were running for the car with the ducks and geese right behind them. They had run out of food and the birds didn't like that one bit, so they were biting at my friends' legs. It was really funny.

This painting is from a combination of several photographs taken that day. The regal pose of the main bird gave me the idea for flowers around her neck.

Palette: Grumbacher Pre-Tested

Titanium White
Zinc Yellow or Lemon Yellow
Cadmium Orange
Grumbacher Red
Mars Violet
Cerulean Blue
Cobalt Blue
Sap Green
Viridian Green
Burnt Sienna
Burnt Umber

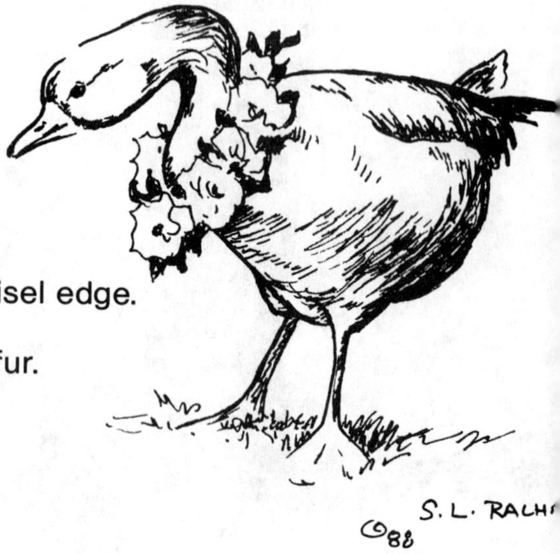

Brushes:

Langnickel 5010 #10 & #20 - A flat sable with a good chisel edge.
Grumbacher 178 #1 - A small round sable with a point.
Peacock 145 #9 - A soft blending brush, feels like rabbit fur.
Any small fan brush.

Medium:

Copal painting medium.

Miscellaneous:

12 X 16 canvas, trowel type palette knife, paper palette, Turpenoid and paper towels.

DIRECTIONS

1. Trace pattern onto a 12 x 16 canvas.

2. **Sky** — Work from the top of the sky towards the bottom. Do not paint in the cloud area. Use short overlapping strokes with the large flat sable.

Dark: White + Cobalt Blue + Cerulean Blue.
Mid-Tone: White + Cerulean Blue.
Light: White + Viridian Green, near the horizon.

3. **Clouds** — Apply with a criss-cross brush stroke using the large flat sable.

Dark: Mix Cobalt Blue + Mars Violet + White to make a soft purple hue. Blend in lightly at the base of the cloud.
Mid-tone: White + just a pin point of Grumbacher Red to make a soft pink.
Light: A hint of Yellow Ochre + White, this will be a warm white.

Softly blend in with the Hake brush in a 45 degree angle wiping the brush often with a paper towel to keep it clean and dry.

4. **Road** — To create this texture, lay the palette knife flat against the canvas, push in - lift up.

Dark: Burnt Sienna.
Mid-Tone: Cadmium Orange.
Light: Burnt Sienna.

5. **Grass** — Start at the base of the grass with the fan brush using short vertical strokes.

Dark: Sap Green + Burnt Umber. Sap Green.
Mid-Tone: Yellow Ochre.
Light: White + Sap Green.

6. **Geese** — Even though each goose is in a different pose, their colors are all the same. Refer to the picture when you are applying the colors, it will help you to understand. Use the small flat sable for the small areas and the large flat sable for the large areas. The round sable is used for the fine details in the birds. Copal painting medium is mixed into all colors used.

Head and Neck — Dark: Cobalt Blue + Mars Violet, a black mixture. Mid-Tone: White + Cobalt Blue. Light: White + Mars Violet, a pinkish hue.

Eye — Cobalt Blue + Mars Violet. Outline with White + Cadmium Orange.

Chest — White + Mars Violet. Shadow: White + Cobalt Blue.

Back and Wings — Dark: Mars Violet + Cobalt Blue. Mid-Tone: Mars Violet. Light: Mars Violet + White. White + Cobalt Blue.

Bottom — This area looks so soft and fluffy. White + Mars Violet, real pale pink. Shadow with purple made by mixing Cobalt Blue + Mars Violet and White.

Beak and Feet — Base in Cadmium Orange. Shadow with Burnt Sienna. Highlight with White + Cadmium Orange.

7. **Flowers** — Use the small flat sable and base in with Grumbacher Red. Centers are a mixture of Cobalt Blue + Mars Violet in small dots. Highlight flowers with Cadmium Orange. Outline edges of flowers with Zinc Yellow using small round sable. Back flower is shadowed with Mars Violet.

8. **Leaves** — Base in with Sap Green using small round sable. Highlight with Zinc Yellow.

Want to change this painting? Trace the main bird, turn tracing over and reverse it, place the two birds looking at each other. Gives almost a heart appearance when they are facing each other.

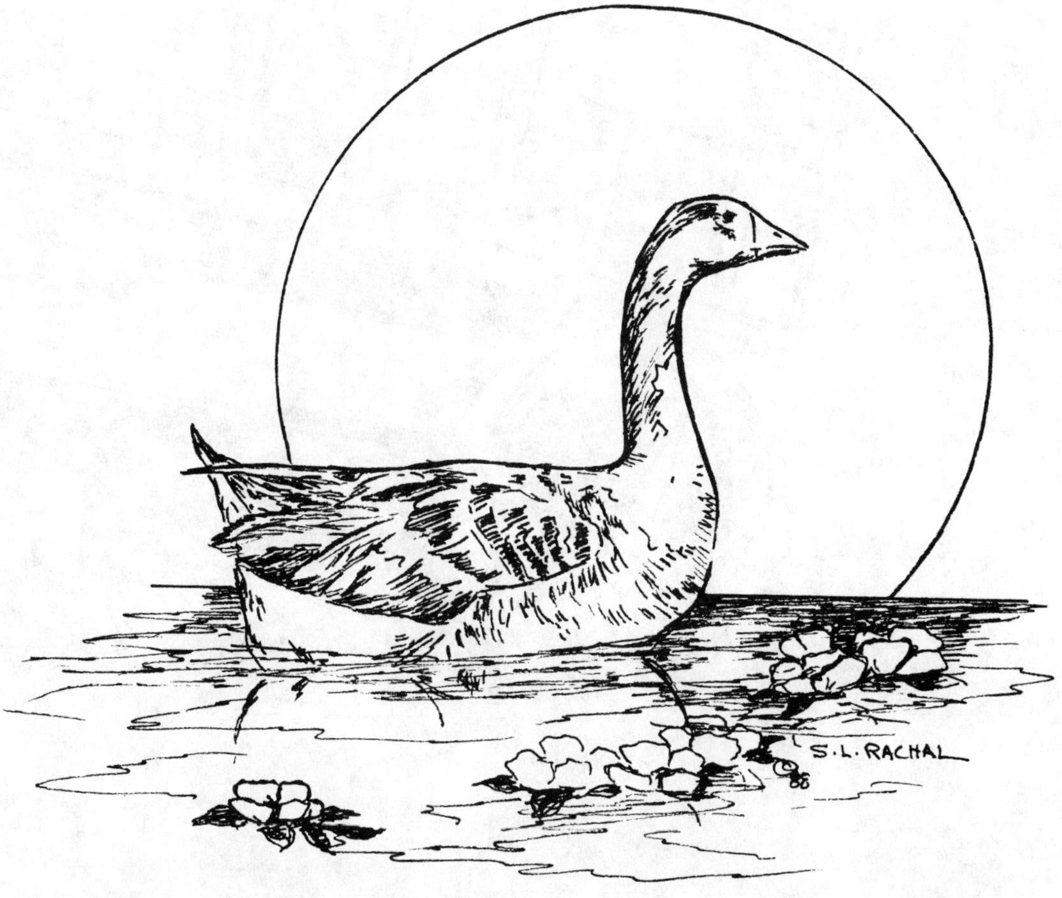

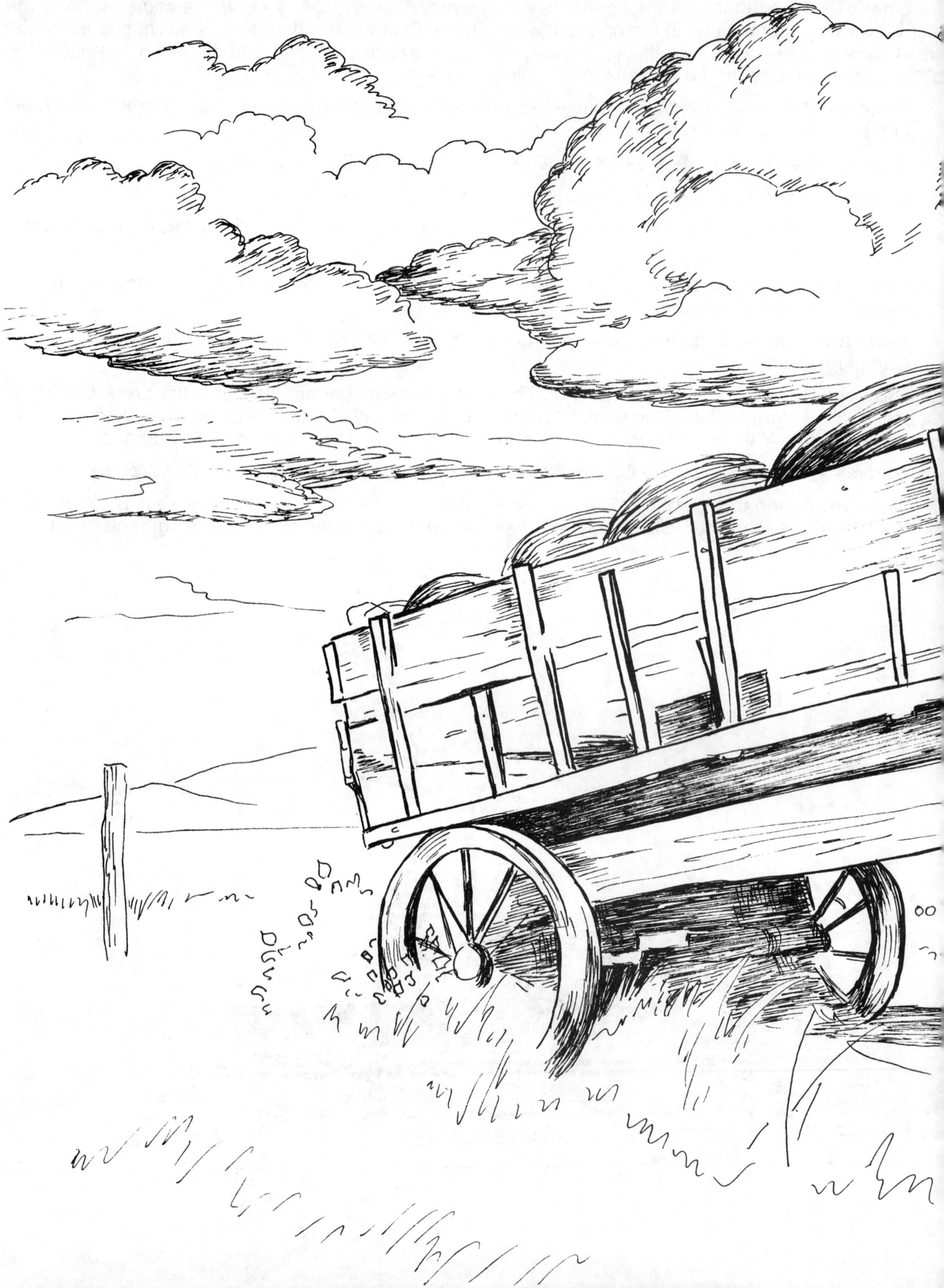

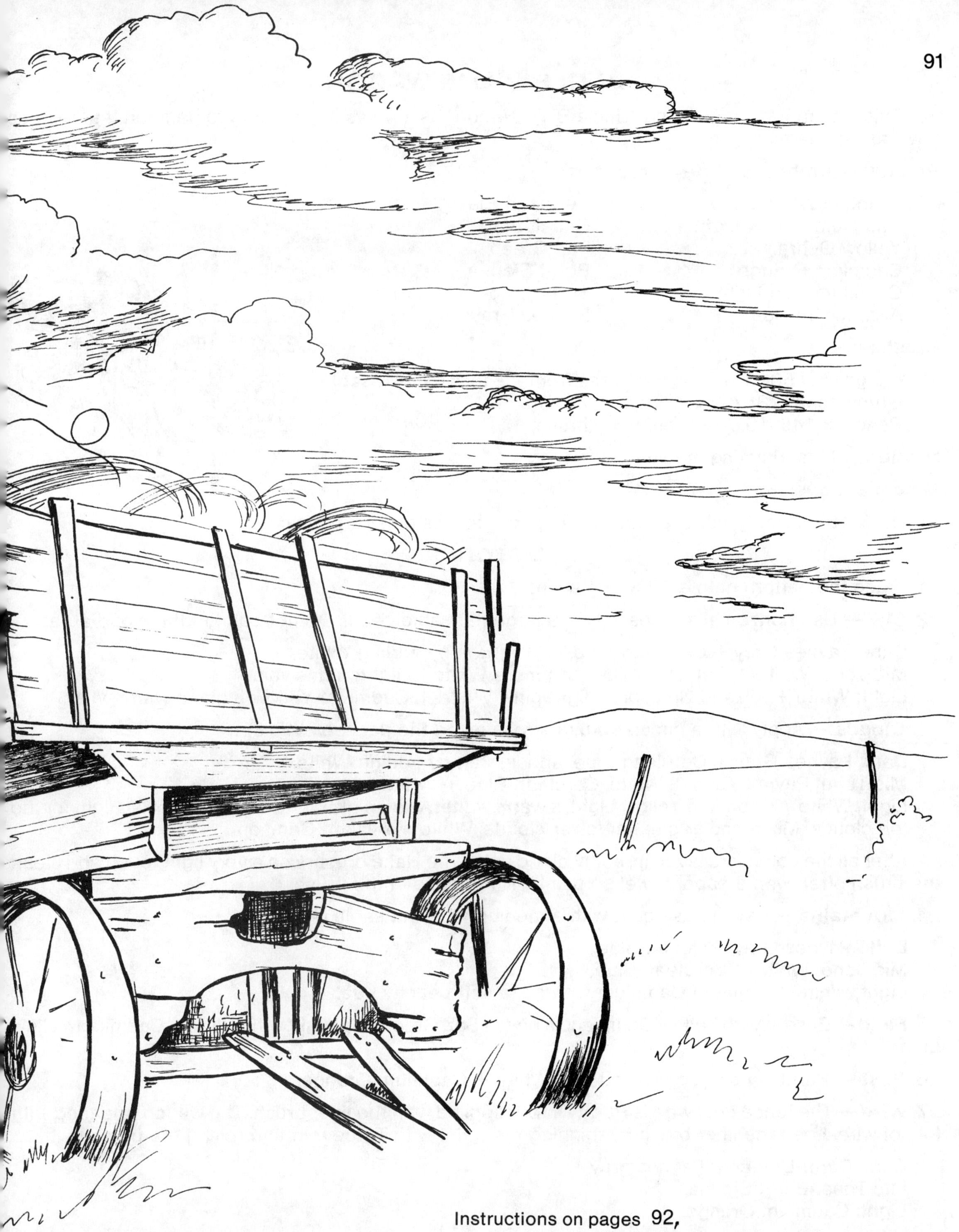

Instructions on pages 92,

UNCLE BILL'S WAGON

UNCLE BILL'S WAGON

This wagon has been called "Uncle Bill's Wagon" as long as anyone can remember. It sure does have rustic charm.

Palette: Grumbacher Pre-Tested

Titanium White
Cadmium Yellow Light
Yellow Ochre
Cadmium Orange
Cadmium Red Light
Alizarin Crimson
Cerulean Blue
Cobalt Blue
Sap Green
Burnt Sienna
Burnt Umber
Paynes Gray

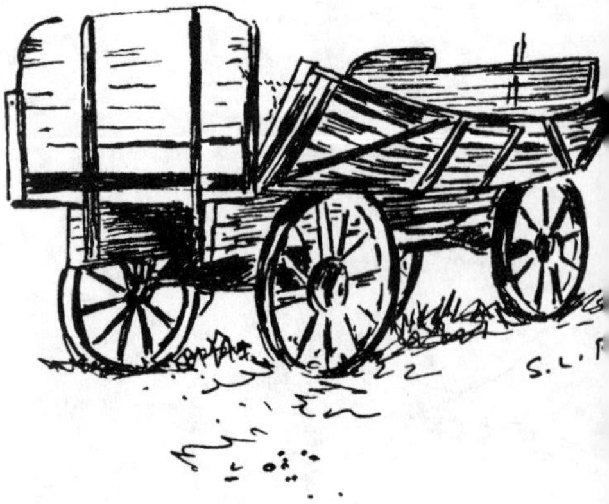

Brushes:

Langnickel 5010, a variety of sizes from #2 to #10. Flat sable.
Grumbacher 7357 #1. A liner.
Peacock 145 #9. A soft blending brush.

Medium: Copal painting medium.

Miscellaneous:

12 X 16 canvas, palette, palette knife, paper towels and Turpenoid.

DIRECTIONS

1. Trace the pattern onto a 12 X 16 canvas.

2. **Sky** — Use horizontal strokes with the large flat sable (#20). Do not paint in the cloud area.

   Dark: Paynes Gray + Cerulean Blue, and lighten by adding White.
   Mid-Tone: White + Cerulean Blue. Add more White to lighten this value.
   Light: White + Alizarin Crimson, a light pink. White + Cadmium Yellow Light, a warm white.

3. **Clouds** — Apply with a circular brush stroke using the flat sable (#16).

   Dark: Paynes Gray + Cerulean Blue, and lighten by adding White.
   Mid-Tone: Paynes Gray + White. Cerulean Blue + White.
   Light: White + Cadmium Yellow Light, a warm white. A soft pink, White + Cadmium Red light for the top clouds. Mix a cooler pink for lower clouds, White + Alizarin Crimson.

   After all the colors are layed in, softly blend using the Hake brush. Use a very light touch and clean the brush often with a paper towel so paint will not cake in the brush.

4. **Mountains** — Lay in base coat with a medium size flat sable (#14).

   Dark: Paynes Gray + Cobalt Blue.
   Mid-Tone: White + Cerulean Blue.
   Light: White + a hint of Cadmium Orange, a soft peachy hue.

5. **Field** — Base in with Yellow Ochre and a hint of Sap Green. Highlight with White + Cadmium Yellow Light.

6. **Post** — Burnt Umber highlighted with White + Cadmium Orange.

7. **Wire** — The fence post wire is Burnt Umber applied with the liner brush. The wagon is loaded with lots of wire. Load the liner brush by thinning the paint with Turpenoid and rolling the brush in it.

   Dark: Burnt Umber + Paynes gray.
   Mid-Tone: Burnt Sienna.
   Light: Cadmium Orange.

8. **Wagon - Front of wagon** — Dark: Burnt Umber + Paynes Gray. Use small flat sable.
   Mid-Tone: Burnt Sienna. Cadmium Red Light. Cadmium Orange.
   Light: White + Cadmium Orange. White + Cadmium Yellow Light.

Side of wagon — The shadow side. Base in whole side with Burnt Umber thinned with Turpenoid sing large flat sable (#20). Let set up and dry. Overpaint with White + Cerulean Blue. This will give an ld wood look. Use the liner brush for painting in the dark lines, using Paynes Gray. Highlight with White - Cadmium Orange.

Wheels — Shadow areas are Burnt Umber + Paynes Gray. Use small flat sable.

Front wheels — Mix Cadmium Orange + Burnt Sienna. Add a touch of Cadmium Red Light. Highlight with White + Cadmium Orange.

9. **Grass** — Use the Hake brush to lay the grass in.

Darks: Sap Green + Cobalt Blue. Sap Green + Burnt Sienna.
Mid-Tone: Sap Green + Yellow Ochre.
Light: Sap Green + Cadmium Yellow Light.

Use the liner brush to detail the grass. Thin paint with Turpenoid. Roll brush into various colors on palette and stroke on canvas.

Darks: Sap Green + Burnt Umber.
Mid-Tone: White + Cadmium Orange. White + Cerulean Blue.
Light: White + Cadmium Yellow Light. White + Sap Green.

10. **Bushes** — Mix Sap Green + Cobalt Blue and dab in using small flat sable. Work off the corner of the brush. Highlight with White + Cadmium Orange in the sunlit areas.

11. **Flowers** — Dip Hake brush into paint (no medium), and tap lightly onto canvas. Use Cadmium Yellow Light + White. White + Cobalt Blue. Cerulean Blue.

Extra pattern

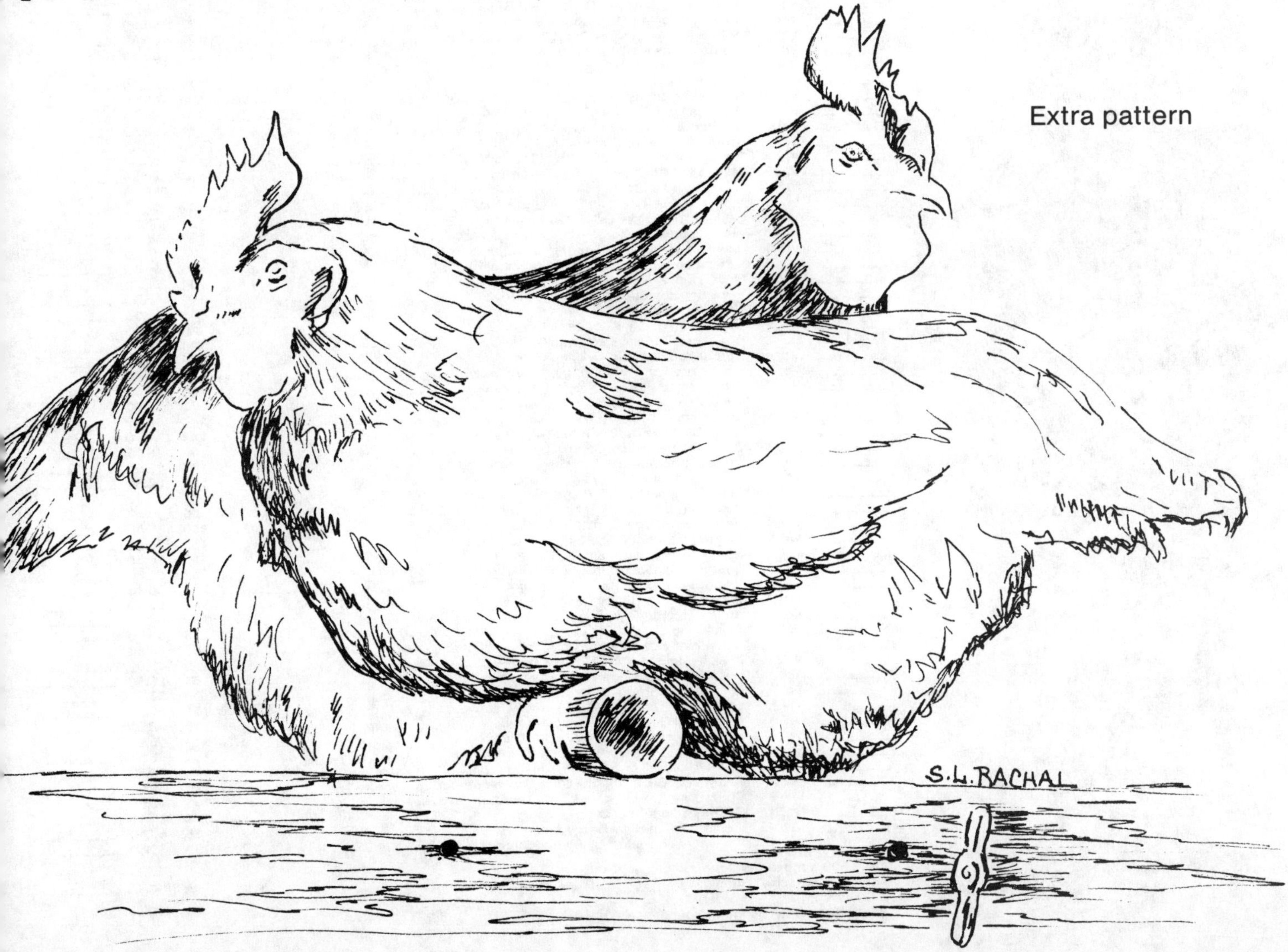

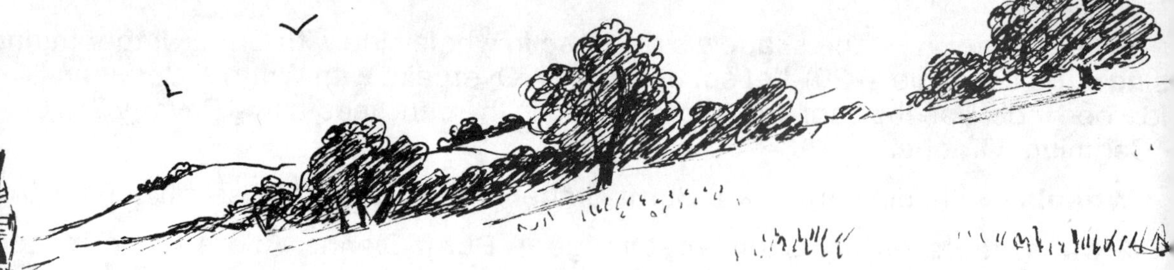

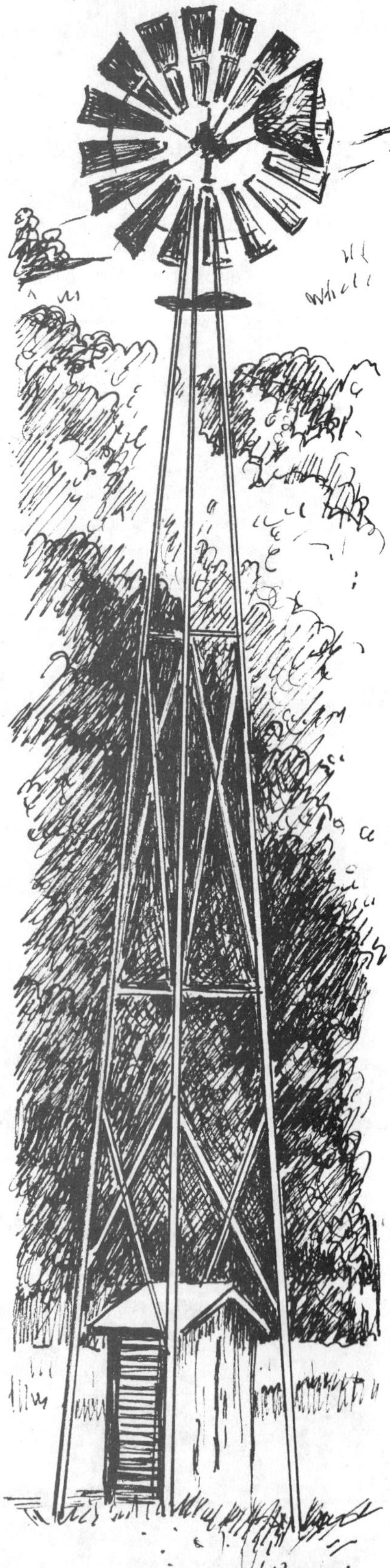

BOOK LIST

______	Vol. 1	"His and Hers" by Susan Scheewe	101	$6.50	______
______	Vol. 5	"So Dear To My Heart" by Susan Scheewe	105	$5.50	______
______	Vol. 6	"Brushed With Elegance" by Susan Scheewe	106	$5.50	______
______	Vol. 7	"Paint 'n Patch" by Susan Scheewe	107	$5.50	______
______	Vol. 8	"Painting Patterns" by Susan Scheewe	108	$6.50	______
______	Vol. 9	"Painting Happy Critters" by Susan Scheewe	109	$6.50	______
______	Vol. 10	"Painting Landscapes" by Susan Scheewe	110	$6.50	______
______	Vol. 11	"I Love To Paint" by Susan Scheewe	111	$6.50	______
______	Vol. 12	"Christmas With Love" by Susan Scheewe	112	$6.50	______
______	Vol. 13	"Nature's Wonderland" by Susan Scheewe	113	$6.50	______
______	Vol. 14	"Enjoy Painting Animals" by Susan Scheewe	114	$6.50	______
______	Vol. 15	"Landscapes Made Easy" by Susan Scheewe	115	$6.50	______
______	Vol. 16	"Landscapes For Everyone" by Susan Scheewe	116	$6.50	______
______	Vol. 17	"Countryside Reflections" by Susan Scheewe	161	$6.50	______
______	Vol. 1	"Keepsake Sampler" by Scheewe/Stempel	162	$6.50	______
______	Vol. 2	"Keepsake Sampler" by Scheewe/Stempel	167	$6.50	______
______	Vol. 3	"Keepsake Sampler" by Camille and Susan Scheewe	173	$6.50	______
______	Vol. 1	"Anyone Can Watercolor" by Ken Johnston	117	$6.50	______
______	Vol. 2	"Anyone Can Watercolor" by Ken Johnston	118	$6.50	______
______	Vol. 3	"Anyone Can Watercolor" by Ken Johnston	119	$6.50	______
______	Vol. 1	"The Way I Started" by Gary Hawk	120	$6.00	______
______	Vol. 1	"Stepping Stones" by Judy Nutter	121	$6.50	______
______	Vol. 2	"Stepping Stones" by Judy Nutter	122	$6.50	______
______	Vol. 1	"Fantasy Folk" by Don Weed	123	$6.50	______
______	Vol. 2	"Painting The Clowns" by Don Weed	124	$6.50	______
______	Vol. 3	"Carnival Holidays" by Don Weed	168	$6.50	______
______	Vol. 1	"Effective Methods In Oil" by Dale Gehrman	125	$6.50	______
______	Vol. 2	"Effective Methods In Oil" by Dale Gehrman	126	$6.50	______
______	Vol. 1	"Fantasy Flowers" by Georgia Bartlett	127	$6.50	______
______	Vol. 2	"Petals and Places" by Georgia Bartlett	128	$6.50	______
______	Vol. 3	"Fantasy Flowers 2" by Georgia Bartlett	129	$6.50	______
______	Vol. 4	"Beautiful Blossoms" by Georgia Bartlett	156	$6.50	______
______	Vol. 5	"Soft Petals" by Georgia Bartlett	171	$6.50	______
______	Vol. 1	"Rustic Memories" by Ellie Cook	130	$6.50	______
______	Vol. 2	"Echoes From The Past" by Ellie Cook	131	$6.50	______
______	Vol. 3	"I'm Partial To Flowers" by Ellie Cook	157	$6.50	______
______	Vol. 1	"Creative Quill" by Claudia Nice	133	$6.50	______
______	Vol. 2	"Barnyards and Billygoats" by Claudia Nice	134	$6.50	______
______	Vol. 3	"Wings and Wildflowers" by Claudia Nice	135	$6.50	______
______	Vol. 4	"Wings Over Water" by Claudia Nice	136	$6.50	______
______	Vol. 5	"Pen and Brush Animals" by Claudia Nice	137	$6.50	______
______	Vol. 6	"Journey of Memories" by Claudia Nice	166	$6.50	______
______	Vol. 7	"Scenes from Seasons Past" by Claudia Nice	183	$6.50	______
______	Vol. 1	"Landscapes For All Seasons" by Carol Binford	138	$6.50	______
______	Vol. 2	"Landscapes For All Seasons" by Carol Binford	139	$6.50	______
______	Vol. 3	"A Different Kind of Magic" by Carol Binford	184	$6.50	______
______	Vol. 1	"New Beginnings" by Norma Hudson	141	$6.50	______
______	Vol. 1	"The Sky's The Limit" by Jean Green	142	$6.50	______
______	Vol. 2	"The Sky's The Limit" by Jean Green	143	$6.50	______
______	Vol. 3	"The Sky's The Limit" by Jean Green	144	$6.50	______
______	Vol. 4	"The Sky's The Limit" by Jean Green	165	$6.50	______
______	Vol. 1	"Roses Are For Everyone" by Bill Huffaker	145	$7.50	______
______	Vol. 2	"Baskets and Blossoms" by Bill Huffaker	146	$6.50	______
______	Vol. 3	"Nature's Beauty" by Bill Huffaker	177	$6.50	______
______	Vol. 1	"Old Friends" by Gene Waggoner	147	$6.50	______
______	Vol. 2	"More Old Friends" by Gene Waggoner	148	$6.50	______
______	Vol. 3	"Seaside Friends" by Gene Waggoner	149	$6.50	______
______	Vol. 4	"Friends We've Known" by Gene Waggoner	187	$6.50	______
______	Vol. 1	"Mini Mini More" by Terri and Nancy Brown	150	$6.50	______
______	Vol. 2	"Mini Mini More" by Terri and Nancy Brown	151	$6.50	______
______	Vol. 3	"Yesterday's Trails" by Terri and Nancy Brown	160	$6.50	______
______	Vol. 4	"Heritage Trail" by Terri and Nancy Brown	169	$6.50	______
______	Vol. 1	"Painting Flowers With Augie" by Augie Reis	152	$6.50	______
______	Vol. 1	"Southern Exposure" by Sue Sickel	153	$6.50	______
______	Vol. 2	"Southern Exposure" by Sue Sickel	182	$6.50	______
______	Vol. 1	"Expressions In Oil" by Delores Egger	154	$6.50	______
______	Vol. 2	"Expressions In Oil" by Delores Egger	164	$6.50	______
______	Vol. 1	"Art Is Living" by Tello/Huff	155	$6.50	______
______	Vol. 1	"Something Special For Everyone" by Mildred Yeiser	158	$6.50	______
______	Vol. 2	"Something Special For Everyone" by Mildred Yeiser	178	$6.50	______
______	Vol. 1	"In All Its Splendor" by Melonie Bradley	159	$6.50	______
______	Vol. 1	"Sunshine and Rainbows" by Donna Kephart	163	$6.50	______
______	Vol. 1	"Love Lives Here" by Mary Lynn Lewis	170	$6.50	______
______	Vol. 2	"Love Lives Here" by Mary Lynn Lewis	185	$6.50	______
______	Vol. 1	"Ducks and Geese" by Jean Lyles	172	$6.50	______
______	Vol. 1	"Windows of My World" by Jackie Claflin	174	$6.50	______
______	Vol. 2	"Windows of My World" by Jackie Claflin	181	$6.50	______
______	Vol. 1	"Rustic Charms" by Sharon Rachal	175	$6.50	______
______	Vol. 1	"Count Your Blessings" by Chris Thornton	176	$6.50	______
______	Vol. 2	"Count Your Blessings" by Chris Thornton	180	$6.50	______
______	Vol. 1	"Country's Edge" by Shirley Koenig	179	$6.50	______
______	Vol. 1	"Western Images" by Becky Anthony	186	$6.50	______
______	Vol. 1	"Forever In My Heart" by Diane Richards	188	$6.50	______

Add $1.25 for first book for packaging and shipping
Add 75¢ per each additional book.
U.S. Currency
Prices Subject to change without notice

SHIPPING ______

TOTAL ______

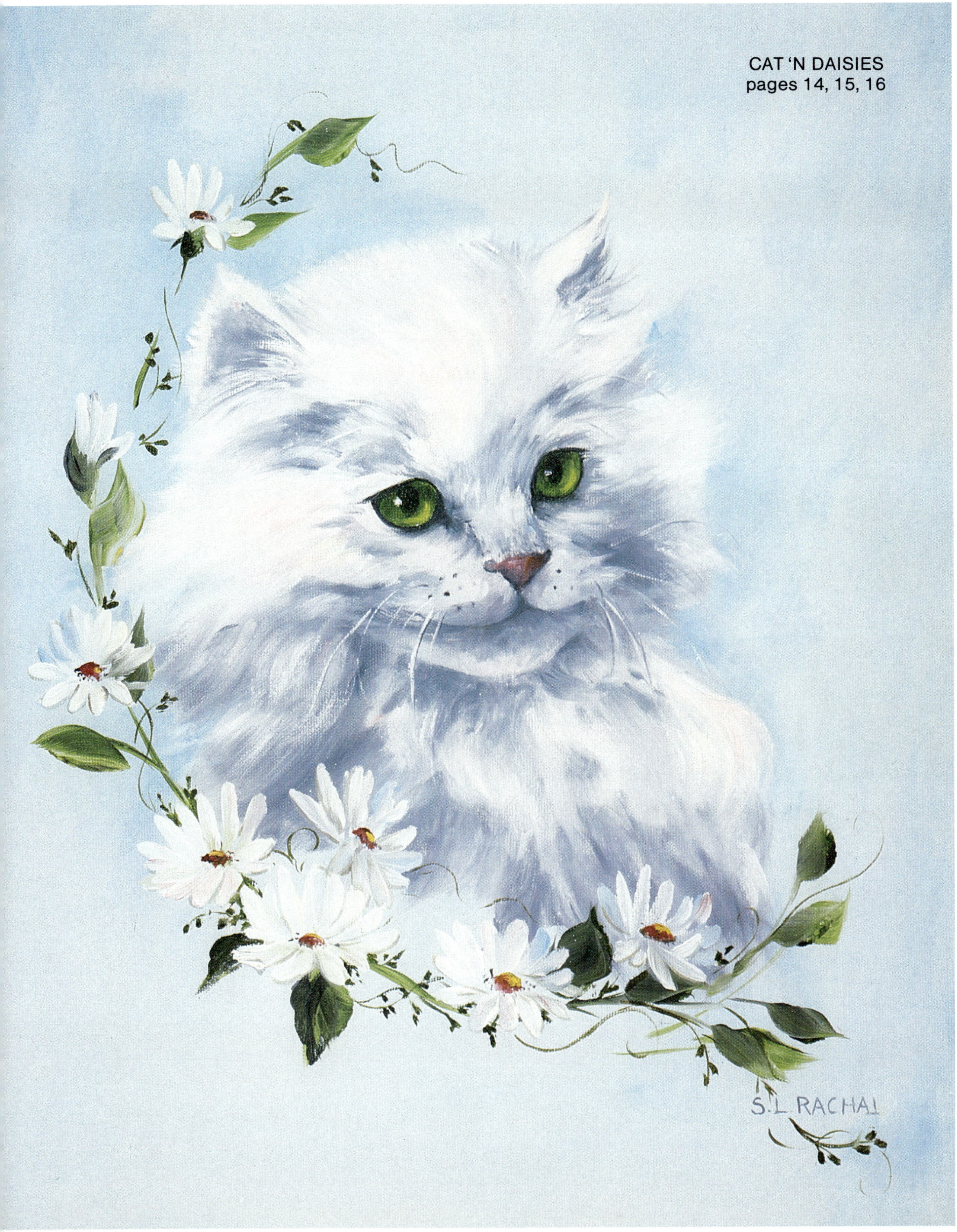

CAT 'N DAISIES
pages 14, 15, 16

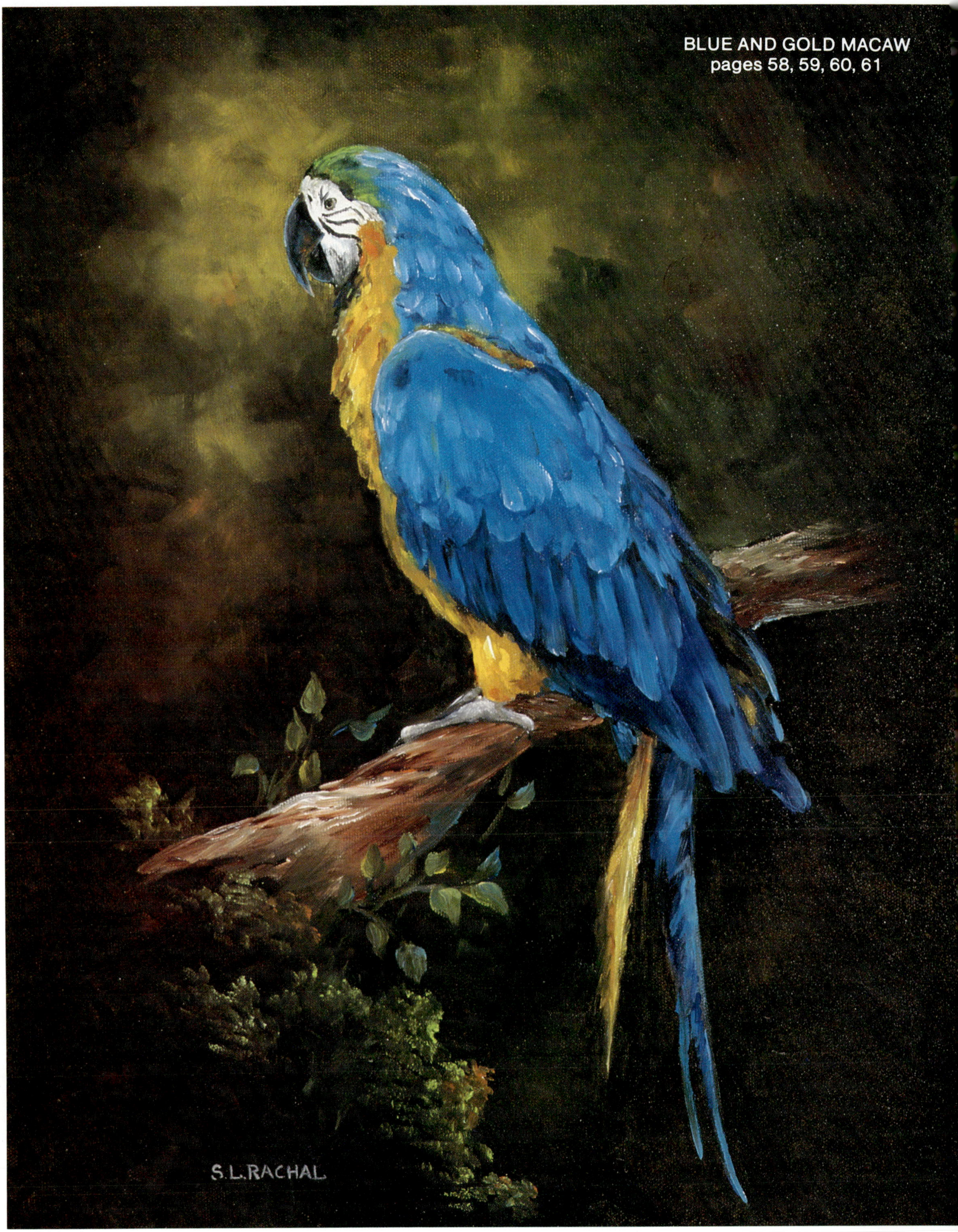

BLUE AND GOLD MACAW
pages 58, 59, 60, 61

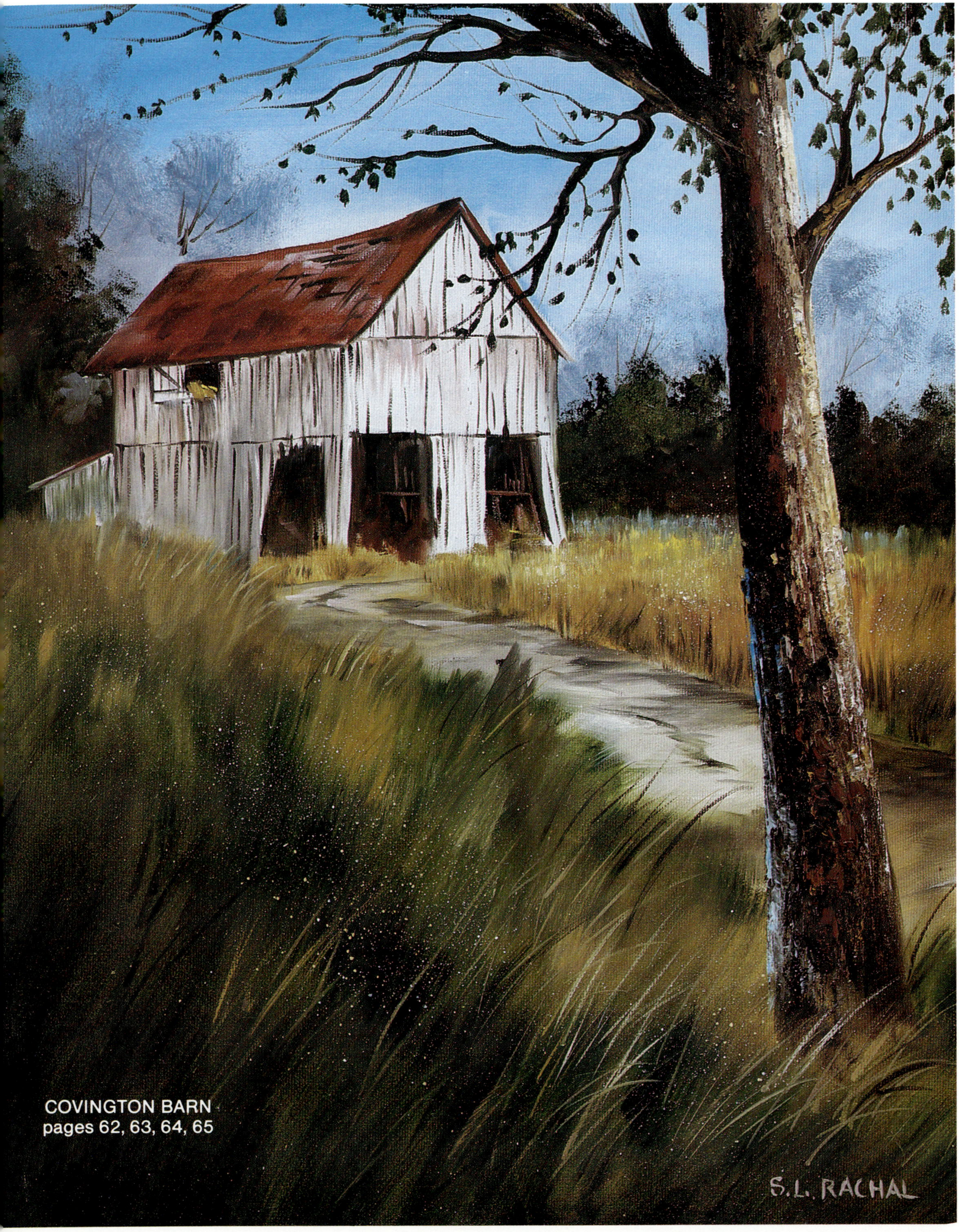

COVINGTON BARN
pages 62, 63, 64, 65

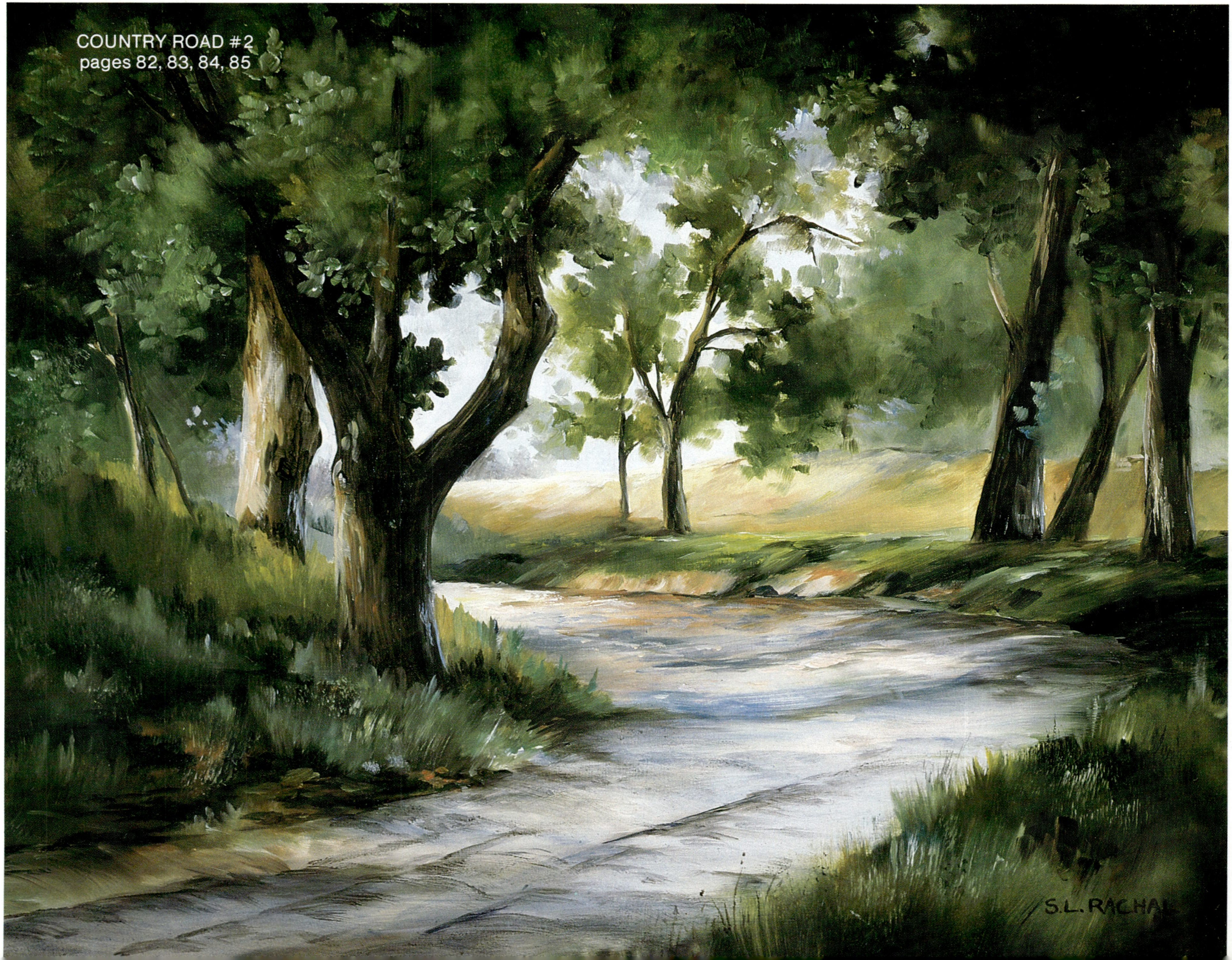

COUNTRY ROAD #2
pages 82, 83, 84, 85